Persistent Oligarchs

PERSISTENT

OLIGARCHS

Elites and Politics in

Chihuahua, Mexico

1910–1940

Mark Wasserman

DUKE UNIVERSITY PRESS

Durham and London 1993

© 1993 Duke University Press
All rights reserved
Printed in the United States of America
on acid-free paper ∞
Designed by Cherie Holma Westmoreland
Typeset in Bembo by Yankee Typesetters, Inc.
Library of Congress Cataloging-in-Publication
Data appear on the last printed page
of this book.

This book is dedicated with great love to two generations: to my mother and father, Deborah S. and Herbert B. Wasserman, and to my children, Aaron and Danielle

Contents

Acknowledgments

A project of over a decade's duration incurs large debts. I should first thank the universities and foundations that have supported my work over these years. The Tinker Foundation awarded me a postdoctoral fellowship in 1976–77. The American Council of Learned Societies–Social Science Research Council Joint Committee on Latin American Studies provided me a fellowship for 1985–86. The American Philosophical Society (1980) and the Research Councils of Rutgers University (1980, 1981–91), and Northern Illinois University (1976) furnished funds for summer research.

Paul Kleppner showed me how to write a grant proposal and, although the project did not turn out quite the way it was planned, I thank him for his guidance. Peter H. Smith also gave me early encouragement. At Rutgers, Samuel L. Baily has been unwavering in his support and friendship. His constructive critiques have always served to focus my writing. Friedrich Katz has given me helpful research leads and used his name to open many doors for me. Although I have not always followed his advice, it has always been sound. His work remains a standard for all of us. Tom Slaughter and Sam Baily read the manuscript in different stages and offered valuable comments. Enrique Florescano allowed me to work under his auspices for a year.

Pamela and Marc Scheinman hosted me in one long stay in Mexico City and provided great company during another. David Oshinsky put me up and showed me the sights in Austin. Cheryl and Charles Martin did the same in El Paso.

In Mexico, the staff of the Archivo General de la Nación was extraordinarily helpful. Jesús Vargas, in Ciudad Chihuahua, provided me with access to his excellent research. Norma Mireles de Ogarrio and the staff of the Archivos Plutarco Elías Calles y Fernando Torreblanca allowed me to use those invaluable papers. Thanks, too, to Eduardo Creel, who furnished me with his son's biography of Enrique Creel. Margarita Terrazas, whom I never met, sent me an unexpurgated version of her biography of her father, Silvestre. María Luisa Muller de Prieto provided me with her mother's history of the Terrazas family.

Thanks, too, to staff of the State Department section of the United States National Archives in Washington, the staff of the Almada Collection at the University of Texas at El Paso, and the Nettie Lee Benson Collection at the University of Texas at Austin.

My most important thanks go to my family: to Danielle for her good cheer, smart-aleck remarks, and dancing; to Aaron for sharing the tribulations of the Highland Park Board of Education; to Marlie, to whom I owe the most for her encouragement and love.

Persistent Oligarchs

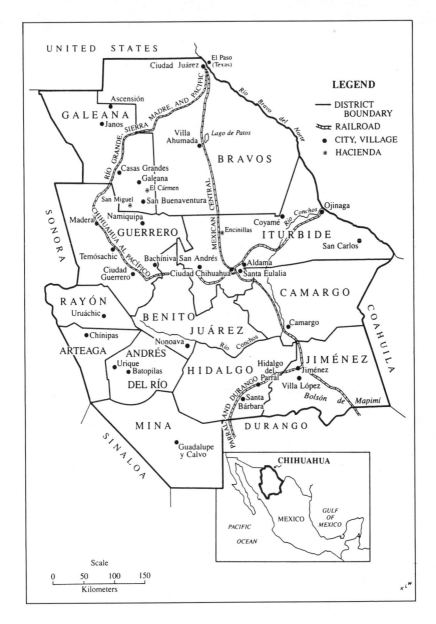

Chihuahua, Mexico, 1910. Reprinted, by permission of the publisher, from *Capitalists, Caciques, and Revolution: The Native Elite and Foreign Enterprise in Chihuahua, Mexico, 1854–1911*, by Mark Wasserman. Copyright © 1984 by the University of North Carolina Press.

1 Introduction

The three watersheds of Mexican history are the Conquest (1519–21), the Hidalgo revolt (1810), and the Revolution (1910–20). None of the three was a clearly definable event or set of events in terms of either chronology or effect. One could argue that the Conquest lasted a hundred years. The wars for independence begun and symbolized by Hidalgo's uprising dragged on for more than a decade (and the chaos they created lasted considerably longer). When, exactly, the Revolution ended is still much debated. The most violent civil wars concluded in 1917, but the overthrow of Venustiano Carranza in 1920 and the end of the presidency of Lázaro Cárdenas in 1940 are other benchmarks often used. In the case of each of the three watersheds, their outcomes are the source of long-standing, ongoing, historical controversies. In all three instances, the core of the debate over their impact revolves around the concepts of continuity and change.

Revolutions must be measured by the transformations they wreak. But it is not enough to prove that change resulted, because some change will take place over time regardless of cataclysmic events. Simply put, we must separate the changes that would have or might have taken place without revolution from those brought about by the revolution. This is not an easy assessment to make. The whole concept of revolutionary transformations is, moreover, often greatly exaggerated. The possibilities for extensive alterations in society and economy are at best limited; the likelihood of immediate, earth-shattering change is even less. In sum, most aspects of social and economic life remain the same or change very slowly regardless of larger events. The concept of revolutionary change therefore applies to only a few, though crucial, aspects of politics and economy.

Defining change requires making a series of value judgments and imprecise measurements. The extent of change that can be defined as revolutionary is subject to continuing discussion. In the case of the Mexican Revolution, historians have divided into traditional and revisionist camps over these judgments. Three central questions have emerged: (1) to what extent did the Revolution destroy the ruling class (elite) of the old regime? (2) to what extent has the new ruling class (if there is one) or the state or regime changed its methods? and (3) to what extent was there popular participation in the Revolution?[1]

The traditionalists maintain that the Revolution brought about profound political and economic change: the old elite was destroyed—or at least rendered noncompetitive; there was a substantial redistribution of wealth, especially from the old, landed elite to the peasantry; and a new, democratic political system replaced the dictatorship. Furthermore, armed peasants and workers played a preeminent role in causing these transformations. Revisionists counter that the Revolution retained the major characteristics of the old regime: centralization, cooptation, and corruption. They argue that, although the popular classes were to some extent the soldiers of the upheaval, they had no lasting effect on its outcome.

Persistent Oligarchs explores these questions of change by studying the survival of the elite of the old regime, the rise of a new revolutionary elite, and the relations between the two in the postrevolutionary era in the northern state of Chihuahua from 1920 to 1940. The interaction of old and new elites shaped Mexican and Chihuahuan political and economic development, and thus the outcome of the Revolution.

In order to provide the necessary context for the study, I will first present a brief overview and interpretation of the causes and course of the Revolution; then a short summary of national and state politics in the postrevolutionary era, followed by a sketch of the role of the elite; and, finally, an outline of my themes.

The Mexican Revolution: An Overview

Mexico entered the twentieth century on the tide of its first economic "miracle." The wave of United States and European investment since the 1880s had created an extensive railroad network, a large mineral export industry, and an export agriculture boom. The nation's government and politics seemed to be secure in the hands of the president-dictator Porfirio Díaz and his military and bureaucratic henchmen. But dictatorship and export-led economic development, while in the short term consolidating the hold of the alliance of landowners, military, and bureaucrats (then known as *científicos* and more recently as *técnicos*), in the long run undermined the political and social order.

During his thirty-four years in power (1877–1911), Díaz constructed a pragmatic network of alliances with regional political bosses that employed the technique of reward and punishment (*pan o palo,* or "bread or the club"). After his first decade and a half of rule, he rarely had to resort to harsh measures: a lucrative concession or tax exemption usually sufficed to win over the uncooperative. The system required steady, if not spectacular, economic growth to operate smoothly. In both 1902 and 1907, downturns, caused by declines in export commodity prices, eroded the cement that held together the carefully crafted mosaic of the Porfirian regime. Competition for suddenly scarce resources (credit and water were the most bitterly contested) reminded those who had "sold out" to Díaz just how crucial regional and local political power was to their economic interests. The Díaz government made a series of decisions between 1907 and 1910 that adversely affected the economic holdings of a number of regional elite families, once competitors for political power in their home states, who had lost out to Porfirista factions during the 1880s and 1890s, but who had remained generally quiescent (except in the early 1890s) in return for access to wealth. Revolutionaries like José María Maytorena and Francisco I. Madero came from these families.

At the same time, particularly in the north, the economic boom created a new, entrepreneurial middle class. As in the case of the regional elites, they did not raise widespread objections to an inherently unfair system so long as the economy continued to expand. When the depression of 1907 crushed their dreams, they, too, learned the lesson of economics and politics: they could never obtain equal opportunity until they had influence in the political process. Joining forces with the dissident elites described above, the middle class proved a powerful force in overthrowing the Díaz dictatorship in 1911.

But even together, the regional elites and the entrepreneurial middle class could not have defeated the Díaz regime; they needed soldiers to fight their battles. The disruptions caused by the formation of the export agricultural sector furnished armies of rural dwellers (campesinos, or country people) comprised of villagers and smallholders, robbed of their ancestral lands by large landholders and politicians who sought to increase commercial crop production. Added to their numbers were industrial workers (most importantly, miners) left unemployed by the depression of 1907.

The contradictions inherent in this multiclass alliance are easily apparent. The dissident elites and middle class sought, at the very least, reform of the political system to include them so that they would have equal opportunity and, at the most, control of the system to use it for their own advantage. Peasants and workers, on the other hand, often sought profound changes in the distrubution of property and income. They, too, realized that political control was crucial, but in the case of the campesinos or peasants, they saw the importance only of local or, at most, regional political power.

The multiclass alliance of 1910–11 was victorious because its internal differences were subsumed in the face of a common enemy and because the dictatorship fell victim to a fatal internal crisis (in the form of a dual failure of elite will and coercive power). The triumph was relatively quick because of the recognition by the Porfirian elite of the possibility that the predominant aims of the rebels were not revolutionary. If forced to do so by the deterioration of their coercive power, this elite was willing to share with a new group. And had the matter ended with the ascendance of Francisco I. Madero as president in 1911, there would have been no revolution, merely a transfer of hegemony from one faction of the elite to another and, perhaps, the opening of ranks to some new blood from the middle class. Porfirio Díaz knew better, for as he left (albeit an apocryphal tale), he warned his country of having "unleashed a tiger." There were, as it turned out, two tigers: regionalism and the popular classes.

Madero became a man in the middle. On one side he faced a Porfirian elite (many of whom were his relatives) not entirely willing to place full confidence in him and not unwilling to combat his regional agents. The prerevolutionary regional elites, in particular, saw an opportunity to reassert their long-lost autonomy. On the other side, he confronted the popular classes—the most dangerous being the campesinos—who were not satisfied with temporizing land reform. Not surprisingly, Madero, who had little control over either the regions or the popular classes, did not last long. His replacement and murderer, Victoriano Huerta, took the reins in 1913, enduring for little more than a year. Huerta represented the resurgence of the Porfirian elite. He, too, failed to meet the challenge of the two tigers, regionalism and the popular classes.

By 1914 the military and political situation had greatly fragmented. For the next three years, there was, in effect, no Mexican state (national government). At the state and local levels conditions were little better. The civil war among the groups which had defeated Huerta, led by Francisco Villa, Emiliano Zapata, and Venustiano Carranza, raged for three years. The centrifugal force of regionalism pulled the country apart. Carranza had won by 1917, though Zapata (until 1919) and Villa (until 1920) remained in the field. The victor represented a coalition of former dissident elites (of whom Carranza was one) and the entrepreneurial (predominantly northern) middle class. The losers were the popular class movements.

The triumphant alliance endured only until 1920, when the entrepreneurial middle class, led by Carranza's best general, Alvaro Obregón, and his Sonoran cohorts, threw out Carranza. The ouster of the so-called First Chief represented an important realignment, for the Sonorans, though unwilling to enter into an equal partnership, recognized the need to satisfy some of the demands of rural people and workers. They had shown this inclination earlier, when they concurred in the radical Constitution of 1917. Carranza had adamantly refused. He had, instead, sought allies among the ranks of the Porfirian elite.

The balance of political power was quite uncertain in 1920. The Sonorans, or middle class, stood uneasily among the popular classes, twenty or so regional factions, powerful revolutionary generals (out for their own good), Porfirian oligarchs, and local bosses. None alone could challenge them, so they had to satisfy the demands of each group enough to keep it from allying with one or more of the others. Obregón (1920–24) and his successor, Plutarco Elías Calles (1924–28), proved adept at maintaining the equilibrium sufficiently to withstand the challenges of three major revolts—de la Huerta (1923–24), Cristero (1926–29), and Escobar (1929). Even when one of the contending groups rebelled, Obregón and Calles managed to prevent the others from joining. Many of the generals joined Adolfo de la Huerta, but the popular classes stayed loyal to the regime. Western peasants became Cristeros, but the other groups were quiet. As the threat lessened, so did the responsiveness of the Sonorans. Two other crucial considerations affected the regime after 1920. Most important, it had to begin repairing the enormous material and economic damage done by the civil wars. It was an effort just to feed the population. The needs of recovery often would be set off against the needs of the popular classes. The demand for agrarian reform, for example, contradicted the need to increase agricultural production. In addition, the Sonorans confronted the hostility of the United States. Any major reforms encountered vociferous objections from the U.S. government.

Over the course of the 1920s, the entrepreneurial middle class concluded that the Sonoran dynasty of Obregón and Calles, however capable, was not the long-range solution to the dilemma of conflicting interests and demands. The assassination of the recently reelected Obregón in 1928 proved that the nation required permanent structures, not personalism. For the next six years, with Calles running the government from behind the scenes as *jefe máximo,* through a series of three presidents, Emilio Portes Gil (1929–30), Pascual Ortiz Rubio (1930–32), and Abelardo Rodríguez (1932–34), the middle-class winners sought the formula that would satisfy or defeat the competing groups and institutionalize their own rule.

The establishment of the Partido Nacional Revolucionario (PNR) in 1929 was the first step. This constituted a two-part method of dealing with the two tigers, regionalism and the popular classes, which Díaz had correctly predicted would torment Mexico. The PNR, under Calles's prompting, initially attempted to bring the regional bosses and factions into the national context. The effort succeeded to the extent that the party was able to reach accord on the nomination of Lázaro Cárdenas for the presidency in 1934, to weather the rupture between Calles and Cárdenas that led to the latter's exile in 1936, and to crush the rebellion of Saturnino Cedillo in 1938. The second part of the strategy involved the popular classes. They had been the pillar of the Sonoran regime in that they had rallied to defend it during each of the major rebellions. They had also formed the bases of regional bosses like Cedillo, Adalberto Tejeda of Veracruz, and Emilio Portes Gil of Tamaulipas. In times of dire threat, the regime had repaid their loyalty with land and better wages. But as long as the popular classes were allied to the regime through regional bosses, they were always a potential danger. Thus, if the national party could obtain their direct loyalty it would capture, or at least defang, the two tigers. Cárdenas's agrarian and labor reforms were the price paid by the regime; the peasants and workers paid with the restriction of their independence, losing their organizations to the PNR and its successors. The regional elites, which had no popular base because they could no longer provide patronage and services, could not maintain their autonomy.

The Mexican one-party state, as it existed from 1940 to 1984, resulted from the strategy begun by the Sonorans in 1920 and perfected by Cárdenas. The revolutionary regime constructed a strong centralized state by employing the popular classes, first to defeat rebellious factions within, and then by using popular class organizations to counter regional elites. It was an arduous process, however. Elites in the regions, both old and new, fiercely resisted centralization. Their opposition moderated the course of the Revolution.

The ascendance of three consecutive conservative governments after 1940—those of Manuel Ávila Camacho (1940–46), Miguel Alemán Valdés (1946–52), and Adolfo Ruiz Cortines (1952–58)—clearly indicates that the entrepreneurial middle class, by now a political elite and an industrial bourgeoisie, often in alliance with the surviving remnants of the old oligarchy, had emerged irreversibly triumphant.

Postrevolutionary Politics

Mexican and Chihuahuan politics consisted of a series of intertwined conflicts and accommodations. The oldest was the struggle among elites at different levels, national, regional (in this case, the state of Chihuahua), and local (municipal). The first two sought to extend their control over the level below. The latter two sought to maintain their autonomy from the level immediately above. Just as important was the struggle of the lower classes for economic justice. Elites could not confine their disagreements and accommodations to themselves, for in order to further their own interests they needed the support of the workers and agriculturalists. Another important factor was the desperate need for economic recovery from the ruin of a decade of war. Maintaining a workable balance among the demands of these elements—elite conflict, clamor for reform, and necessity for economic reconstruction—comprised Chihuahua's political economy from 1920 to 1940.

The Revolution stymied and to some extent reversed two of the major trends of the dictatorship of Porfirio Díaz (1877–1911): political centralization and economic development through foreign investment and export of raw materials. The civil wars between 1911 and 1917 destroyed the national regime so painstakingly built during the Porfiriato. They also devastated the Mexican economy. The toll in human and physical destruction was enormous. A generation of leaders perished. Farms, factories, mines, and railroads were ruined. It took the better part of the next twenty years to regain the levels of 1910.

The clock was not turned all the way back, however. Chihuahua was not isolated to the extent it had been during the Apache wars of the mid-nineteenth century. What went on in Mexico City was and would be of incontrovertible importance to its politics and economy. Moreover, the state's ecomony could never separate itself from the workings of the world market.

During the 1920s the national government was relatively weak. The Sonorans, who had wrested control of the revolutionary regime from Venustiano Carranza in 1920, were unsteadily in power. President Alvaro Obregón faced not only the problem of consolidating his control over recalcitrant generals and regional bosses, but the daunting tasks of fostering recovery from economic ruin and of winning diplomatic recognition of his government from the United States. He established his rule and gained U.S. recognition through compromise. Obregón walked a tightrope between the demands of reconstruction and reform. His record of land reform, for example, directly reflected the armed challenges to his government.[2] Plutarco Elías Calles, who followed him as president, employed the same overall strategy of not interfering with the generals and bosses and of employing land reform as a political instrument. More secure after the defeat of the rebellion of Adolfo de la Huerta in early 1924, Calles took advantage of opportunities to extend his regime's influence into state politics.[3] The assassination of Obregón in 1928, and the brief ascension of Emilio Portes Gil, set back the outreach of national control. The turn of the decade brought a retrogression to political instability, with yet another armed rebellion (José Gonzalo Escobar in 1929) and a quick succession of three presidents. All of this affected Chihuahuan politics. Not surprisingly, not one of the major figures in state politics in the 1920s maintained his influence into the new decade.

The founding of the national revolutionary party, the PNR, by Calles in 1929 accelerated the process of centralization. The 1930s produced the change from personalism to party politics. Nationally it took a great, charismatic leader, Lázaro Cárdenas, to accomplish the transformation. He melded the conflict among elites to the demands of the lower classes for economic justice by harnessing labor unions and peasant leagues to the national party.[4] The alliance of PNR and popular class organizations was strong enough to rein in most (though not all) of the regional satrapies.

The Elites

The literature on elites is enormous and I present only a cursory summary of it here. It derives primarily from the classical elite theorists Pareto and Mosca, and from Marx. The classical theorists divide society into two classes, the rulers, or elite, and the ruled. For Marx the ruling class consisted of those who controlled the means of production.[5] Neither approach is particularly satisfactory in the Mexican case, because politics and economics (for much of the period under study) were so closely linked and because class identification was so fluid. For my previous book, *Capitalists, Caciques, and Revolution,* the problem of definition was simpler, for the elite consisted of the Terrazas-Creel extended family and a small number of allies, who together dominated both politics and economy. In *Persistent Oligarchs* this family again plays an important role in the analysis; for it, for the most part, defines the sector of the elite I label the old, or Porfirian, elite. But the Revolution in Chihuahua permitted considerable upward mobility and expansion of the elite. Over time (though I will argue that it did to a lesser degree than has been thought), the development of the revolutionary party separated political and economic elites. The new elite consisted of the generals, governors, and other political officeholders who ruled Chihuahua and the most important landholders, bankers, merchants, and industrialists.

The emergence of a new elite and the fate of the elite of the ancien régime after the violent stages of revolution are relatively unexplored, especially given the enormous literature on the causes and courses of revolutions. Comparatively little is known about the processes through which new elites construct themselves and old elites survive. This gap is especially evident for Mexico. This is the first study to focus on pre- and postrevolutionary elites in Mexico.

Perhaps no better illustration of the convergence of old elite, new elite, regional politics, and popular pressures exists than the gala wedding of Jesús Antonio Almeida, governor of Chihuahua, and Susanna Nesbitt Becerra, on October 6, 1925, and the subsequent history of the Almeida family. The marriage shows us how a new elite emerged from the Revolution, how the old elite survived it and made a place in the new order, and how the two elites reached accommodation. The subsequent fate of the Almeidas, moreover, demonstrates both the political pressures exerted by the popular classes and the political conflict between regional elites and the national regime. The Almeida brothers—politicians, ranchers, lumbermen, and merchants—represented the middle class that emerged from the years of chaos to reach for economic opportunity and political power. The Becerras had ruled Urique, a mining center in western Chihuahua, for a century and had been pillars of the old regime. Strikingly, the guest list for the wedding included the most prominent families of the old order: Terrazas, Creel, Luján, Falomir, and Prieto.[6] Thus, less than a decade after the bloodiest battles of the Revolution and only five years after Pancho Villa had laid down his arms, revolutionary generals ate, drank, and danced with the scions of the dictatorship they had overthrown. But the Revolution was not a sham. While the newlyweds were on their honeymoon, the acting governor, Jorge M. Cárdenas, expropriated 3,168 hectares from the bride's family as part of the state's program of land reform.[7] Two years later, a coup backed by Calles ousted Governor Almeida. The family nevertheless prospered and formed one of Mexico's leading entrepreneurial groups.

The new postrevolutionary elite had a diverse class base that narrowed increasingly over time and varied considerably according to region. The civil wars that lasted from 1911 until 1917 offered the greatest opportunities for upward mobility. From 1913 to 1916, soldiers of modest and lower-class origins dominated the Revolution. Over time, certainly by the mid-1930s, the more educated middle class, often possessing technical skills, assumed a more important role, pushing aside the rougher soldiers. The revolutionaries in states like Sonora and Coahuila—the two most notable examples—arose from so-called dissident elites or those notables excluded from political power by Porfirio Díaz and his henchmen, while they enjoyed substantial economic favor. (The Maytorena and Madero families were the most prominent examples.) In Chihuahua and Morelos, these dissident elites were either not present or scarce. By the 1930s, however, even the extreme examples had come together in the experience of elite formation.

The victorious Constitutionalists and the Sonorans who succeeded them, many of whom arose from middle- and lower-middle-class ranks and from disaffected sectors of the old elite, set about to acquire the spoils of victory and to establish themselves as the new ruling elite. Ideologically they were more compatible with the old elite than with the agrarians or workers. For the most part, they were capitalists with a firm belief in private property. They had participated in the Revolution in order to obtain their fair share of the spoils of economic development and politics. New and old elite would prove useful allies in preserving and protecting their respective property and privilege.

The cooperation between old and new elites occurred primarily at the regional level, which during this period was synonymous with the state level. (It may have been strongest at the municipal level.) The alliance of old and new elites that emerged during the 1920s in the regions, by the mid-1930s threatened the hegemony of the national revolutionary regime. The national revolutionary government, most effectively under Lázaro Cárdenas, then used popular support, channeled through agrarian and labor organizations into the official party, to consolidate power. Cárdenas used this support against the alliances of old and new elites at the state level. Thus, from 1934 to 1938, agrarian reform took an enormous toll on the landowning class. New (and some old) regional elites learned their lesson and quickly incorporated themselves into the party. Agrarian reform then ended. In the struggles between center and region the prerevolutionary elite played a crucial role, for without its support the new revolutionary regional groups would not have resisted the central government as long and won as great concessions.

Chihuahua and the Revolution

Chihuahua was extraordinarily important in the history of the Mexican Revolution: the Revolution began in Chihuahua and its first victories, which led to the overthrow of Porfirio Díaz, were won there. Moreover, the prerevolutionary elite of the state was one of the strongest in Mexico. The 1910 revolution in Chihuahua had a broad popular base, the main aim of which was to oust precisely this powerful oligarchy. Pancho Villa, the most important revolutionary leader in Chihuahua, led the most broadly based popular movement in the north and carried out the most radical actions against the old guard. Chihuahua can be a benchmark against which we measure the Revolution.

This book is not meant to be a chronicle of the war years between 1910 and 1920. Nonetheless, it begins with a brief overview of the political and economic history of the state during the years of the violent revolution to lay the groundwork for what followed in the succeeding two decades. Endemic violence and disorder prevented the emergence of a new elite at the state level during this period. The Revolution, moreover, did not destroy the old elite, though it was badly damaged.

The next focus is on the political economy of Chihuahua during the 1920s and 1930s. The 1920s were an era of transition, when the central government did not exercise effective control over Chihuahua. It could and did "veto" the ascension of groups or leaders, but could not impose its will. The following decade brought the evolution from personalist to party rule in Chihuahua. The national government finally established control over the state, but only at the cost of compromise with entrenched local elites, old and new.

A careful delineation and analysis (some of the latter of which is somewhat speculative) of Chihuahua's political and economic (though not business) history from 1920 to 1940 is much needed: first, because existing works furnish only erratic description and no discussion of the hows and whys of state politics and economics; and, second, because such a study can provide the critical context for the evolution of the Chihuahuan elite. The discussion of the interplay of the three levels of politics—national, state, and local—is crucial in laying the groundwork to explain how and why a new elite emerged and how it operated; how the old elite survived and flourished; and how the two elites cooperated and conflicted. The fractionalization of state politics and the weakness of the national regime, described in chapters 3 and 4, created the political space for the old elite to emerge as a valuable ally for the new elite and to assure its own survival. The chronology divides by decades because the years 1929 to 1931 demarcated the stages of the struggle for Chihuahuan autonomy.

The Chihuahuan elite is the subject of the next two chapters, which examine the survival of the old elite and the emergence of a new elite at the state level, respectively. Another chapter analyzes the development of political power at the local level. The emphasis is, first, on determining which elite groups survived the revolution and transition, why they survived, and to what effect. The central example is the most powerful prerevolutionary elite family, the Terrazas. The investigation then records the rise of the new political and economic elites, like the Almeidas (1920s), Quevedos (1930s), Bermúdez (1930s), and Vallinas (from the 1920s on), and examines the relation between political and economic power. The last chapter of this section looks at old and new elites at the local level. Ciudad Juárez is the primary example.

The final chapter is an essay on comparative history, encompassing the different regions in Mexico in the revolutionary and post revolutionary era in order to construct a framework for the study of elites in Mexico. It includes a comparison of the fates of the elite in the Mexican and French revolutions.

The core of the book resides in the three chapters on the elite. In Chihuahua the old elite survived the Revolution and prospered in its aftermath. As a group it lost much of its land, but not all. Members of the Terrazas family, for example, emerged again as important cattle ranchers. The old elite retained crucial influence in industry and finance as well. Although its members never regained direct political power, they exerted strong, indirect influence through intermarriage with the new elite and through economic power. The old elite joined with an important sector of the new elite that had common interests in private property and economic development. It persisted and, in doing so, helped shape the course of Mexican history in the postrevolutionary era.

A final word about what this book is not is in order. As in the case of its preceding volume, *Capitalists, Caciques, and Revolution*, it is a study from the top down. As such, it does not extensively discuss the popular classes and their organizations other than in the context of how they affected elite politics. Nowadays some consider elite studies to be outmoded. But it seems to me that it is important for us to know the oppressors at least as well as the oppressed. Moreover, *Persistent Oligarchs* is less of an economic history than its precursor study: first, because the role of elites was not as clear as it was during the Porfiriato and thus required a fuller exploration; and, second, because sources for economic history were not as readily available as they were for the earlier era.

2 The Age
of the
Centaur

The politics and economy of Chihuahua during the years 1910 to 1920 reflected the nature of its homegrown revolution and the impact of war. The most important political figures of the era, Abraham González, Francisco Villa, and Ignacio C. Enríquez, represented the major phases of the revolution in the state: the first tried to implement the moderate political reforms advocated by Francisco I. Madero; the second attempted to transform the region in order to meet the needs of the popular classes and the armed struggle; the third sought to restore peace and implement the moderate politics of the victorious Constitutionalists. Hidden beneath the combat of the civil wars lay three other important struggles: the Porfirian oligarchy battled to survive; municipalities strove to maintain their independence; and a new, revolutionary elite sought to form and establish itself. Subsumed in the war, too, was the century-long conflict between the national regime(s) and the state(s) for political hegemony. Each successive regime grappled with the contradictory demands of warfare, economic reconstruction, political conciliation, and reform.

The enormous destruction and disruptions of a decade of war severely dislocated Chihuahuan politics and economy. At the state level, no governor lasted longer than nineteen months. The state legislature did not meet from 1913 until 1920. There were no municipal elections from 1912 until 1916. Two Maderistas, Abraham González and Aureliano González, and two Huertistas, Antonio Rábago and Salvador R. Mercado, faced constant rebellion. The Villista regime, which included governors Pancho Villa, Manuel Chao, Fidel Avila, and Silvestre Terrazas, brought a measure of stability between December 1913 and May 1916, but on a constant wartime footing. Seven Constitucionalista governors, most notably

Ignacio C. Enríquez, Arnulfo González, and Andrés Ortiz, furnished continuity of policy but confronted the insistent menace of Pancho Villa.

Politics in Revolution

The month after Maderista rebels, under the command of Pascual Orozco, Jr., took Ciudad Juárez in May 1911, the Chihuahuan legislature named Abraham González the first revolutionary governor. A member of a prominent family from the western part of the state that had lost out to the Terrazas in a contest for power during the 1890s, the new chief executive had joined the antireelectionist opposition to Porfirio Díaz in 1908. He subsequently supported Madero and acted as his agent in procuring military supplies. Like Madero, González advocated moderate reform aimed at opening up politics and creating an environment of equal economic opportunity.[1] He confronted hostile opposition not only from each side of the political spectrum, but from among the ranks of the rebels themselves. On the right an entrenched, powerful Terracista old guard resisted. Until the fall 1911 elections, it controlled the state legislature. On the left, the Partido Liberal Mexicano, dissatisfied with the speed and scope of reforms, staged a number of unsuccessful uprisings. Most important, González encountered a disgruntled group of Chihuahuan revolutionaries led by Pascual Orozco, Jr. In 1912, financed by the Porfirian oligarchy, Orozco rebelled against the Madero-González regime.[2]

In keeping with his stated goals, González as governor took steps to open the political system and equalize economic opportunities. He replaced the old bureaucracy in state government and raised salaries for state offices to make them available to men of modest means.[3] He realigned the state's tax system in order to shift its burden to the upper classes (big merchants and large landowners). The governor also abolished the hated office of the *jefe político* and reorganized municipal government.[4]

Shortly after winning election to a full term, González left Chihuahua to take the post of *secretario de gobernación* in Madero's cabinet. It proved to be a fatal mistake. He had to return in February

1912 to deal with the growing unrest. In early March, Pascual Orozco revolted, and in only a few days controlled the state. When González fled, the state legislature joined the Orozquistas, demanded Madero's resignation, and named a new governor, Felipe R. Gutiérrez.[5] González resumed his post in July after General Victoriano Huerta defeated the Orozquistas. He came into sharp disagreement with President Madero over the latter's efforts to conciliate his opposition.[6] Days after the coup in Mexico City by which Victoriano Huerta overthrew Madero, on February 22, 1913, the rebels ousted González and two weeks later executed him.

Two Huertista generals, Antonio Rábago and Salvador R. Mercado, ruled from February to November 1913. They concentrated their efforts on fighting the Constitutionalists, governing through extraordinary powers granted by the legislature.[7] At this they were unsuccessful, for their regime lasted barely ten months. Evidently, the Huertistas controlled little more than the major cities.[8]

The victorious Constitutionalist general Pancho Villa marched into Ciudad Chihuahua on December 8, 1913, and took over the governorship until he left office in early January 1914 to pursue the military campaign against Huerta. His henchmen—Chao, Terrazas, and Avila—governed until Villista rule ended in December 1915.

The Constitutionalists scattered but did not completely defeat the Villistas. For the next four years Villa kept the region in turmoil. This made the Carrancistas's task of rebuilding the economy extremely difficult. Ignacio C. Enríquez was the first Constitutionalist governor of Chihuahua. His father had been *jefe político* of the Iturbide District, which included the capital, during the Terrazas regime. He had joined the revolution in 1913 after the coup against Madero, rising rapidly through the ranks. He served first from December 1915 to May 1916 and returned from July to November 1918. Of all the political figures of the revolutionary war era, Enríquez was one of only two who were to play a major role in Chihuahuan politics during the 1920s.[9] After his second period as chief executive, Enríquez took command of the irregular forces in the state, the *defensas sociales.* He used this as a popular base from which to run in, and win, the 1920 election for governor.[10]

The Carrancistas supervised the gradual return to order. Francisco L. Treviño, governor from May to December 1916, oversaw the first municipal elections in four years. His successor, Arnulfo González (December 1916–July 1918), revamped the civil code and the law of public education. Andrés Ortiz took over as chief executive from November 1918 until February 1920.[11]

Although defeated soundly by Alvaro Obregón, the military commander of the Carrancistas, in a series of battles in the center of the country in the spring of 1915, Pancho Villa remained a potent force in Chihuahua until he retired in 1920 after Obregón ousted Carranza in the Plan de Agua Prieta revolt. Villa was particularly dangerous in late 1918 and 1919. By mid-1919 the federal government had ten thousand troops in Chihuahua.[12] In late November 1919, Villa wiped out a regiment of *federales,* killing 674. He gave up his arms in May 1920.[13] However, the general's presence just across the border in Durango at the Hacienda de Canutillo was a constant threat to the revolutionary regime until his assassination in 1923.

Economy in Revolution

The Chihuahuan mining economy was strong through 1913. Until then the heaviest damage and costliest disruptions took place on the railroads, caused by intermittent guerrilla activities.[14] In 1913 the big smelters closed because they could not obtain fuel.[15] This closed down the mines, which had nowhere to ship their ores. Unemployment rose. Disruption to transportation sent staple prices soaring. For the first time, in June there were reports of hunger in Parral.[16]

The nadir came in 1914 and 1915. Transportation broke down entirely. There was virtually no rolling stock and roadbeds were seriously damaged. Mines were looted.[17] The following year began with hope, with resurgent activity in Parral and Santa Eulalia and Santa Bárbara almost restored to normal, only to disintegrate by midyear in the face of Villista guerrillas.[18] Mining operations were hampered in 1916 and 1917 because of the Pershing expedition.

With the end of the U.S. intervention and the heaviest fighting, recovery began in 1918. The *El Paso Morning Times* reported that 1918 was the best year for mining since 1912. Forty producing properties were led by the El Potosi Mining Company (Santa Eulalia), Cusi Mining Company (Cusihuiriachic), the American Smelting and Refining Company, ASARCO (Santa Eulalia), and Alvarado Mining Company (Parral).[19] ASARCO's smelter reopened after a shutdown of two years in April 1918.[20] Mineral prices, stimulated by the war in Europe, were high.[21] By 1919 one newspaper hailed a new mining boom in Chihuahua. High employment had "ended . . . working class misery. . . ."[22] The *El Paso Morning Times* claimed that Parral was better off than it had been in five years.[23]

The main economic concern for most of the population of the state during the revolutionary wars was the cost of staples. As early as March 1911 high prices caused agitation. As would often be the case in future years, many people blamed greedy merchants.[24] Two years later, after the overthrow of Madero, the resumption of hostilities again limited the availability of foodstuffs.[25] The "scarcity of articles of the first necessity" persisted through 1916.[26] Hardest hit were the isolated mining camps of western and southwestern Chihuahua, like Lluvia de Oro, where there were no jobs or food and people starved.[27] Labor shortages and transportation breakdowns drove up prices. According to one report, the price for a hectoliter of corn increased from 5 pesos in 1912 to 12 pesos in 1917 in Ciudad Juárez, and from 4.59 to 14 in Ciudad Chihuahua.[28]

Food shortages in 1917 moved the Carrancista government to urge all property owners to seed and plant all their cultivable land.[29] The new year, 1918, once again found Chihuahua in "misery." Pillaging Carrancista occupation forces exacerbated an already desperate situation.[30] Governor Arnulfo González, perhaps with an eye toward his political future, prohibited the export of *frijol* from the state early in the year.[31] But this was not enough. There were again reports of starvation in Parral.[32]

War devastated cattle raising, which was the state's leading agricultural sector before the revolution. The massive herds that roamed the state, perhaps as many as 1.2 million head in 1910, were reduced to 60,000 in 1921.[33]

The effect of the war is shown clearly in the description of Ojinaga, Cuchillo Parado, and Coyamé in the *El Paso Morning Times* in September 1919. Its reporter described Ojinaga as a "once flourishing city, today a wreck . . . [with] empty and cracked shells of buildings." Cuchillo Parado was "a town of widows and orphans, so many killed in battle, few men were left." To make matters worse, Cuchillo Parado and Coyamé were locked in a desperate feud, harking back to a long-standing dispute over land, but exacerbated by the fact that Cuchillo Parado supported Villa and Coyamé Carranza.[34]

The Political Economy of Revolution

Each of the governors and the regimes they represented balanced crucial aspects of politics and economy. Politically, they had to satisfy the demands of workers and peasants for long-postponed justice. Even the counterrevolutionary Huertistas made some effort in this direction. The revolutionary regimes also had to fight rearguard action against the Porfirian oligarchy, which twice, for short periods, actually overturned their rule. With the notable exception of Pancho Villa, Chihuahuan revolutionary leaders were not ideologically disposed toward radical transformations and therefore encountered difficulty in meeting demands from the popular classes. Equally important, each regime had to keep the economy functioning. They needed revenues to operate the government and maintain the military. They, too, had to employ and feed the people of the state.

The Maderistas were inclined to proceed cautiously. Abraham González himself stated that "the principal issues involved are local self-government, a guarantee of the autonomy of the states, free speech, a free press, and the sovereignty of the people. . . ."[35] But in Chihuahua, the new governor immediately encountered militant workers, especially in the mining camps. During the summer of 1911 there were labor troubles in Naica, Parral, Santa Bárbara, and Cusihuiriachic.[36] González promised to take steps to abolish payment in scrip and company stores. He also helped striking streetcar workers in Ciudad Chihuahua win their demands. He continued to use his influence to settle strikes throughout his term. His most strident action was to set up an arbitration procedure for those businesses with concessions or tax exemptions from the state government. When he sent troops, as he did to Santa Eulalia, in July 1911, he used them evenhandedly. Generally, workers did not win all their demands but were successful enough to return to their jobs.[37]

González proved unwilling to transform landownership radically. He did, however, equalize the tax burden on rural property, shifting more of it to the large estates. In the days just before he was deposed, the legislature considered, but did not act on, a proposal to facilitate the acquisition of land by smallholders.[38] In the end, though his efforts at reform had targeted the middle class and workers, he failed to satisfy smallholders and villagers and to defeat the old elite, and thus suffered the same fate as Madero.

The Huertistas, backed strongly by the Porfirian oligarchy and preoccupied with conducting the war against the Constitutionalists, sponsored only one actual reform for either workers or campesinos. The Huertista governor, General Mercado, approved the state's first employers' liability law.[39] As part of the agreement to win the support of Pascual Orozco and his followers, Huerta promised to appropriate land for distribution to smallholders for reasonable prices and terms.[40] There is no evidence that this was ever implemented.

Pancho Villa needed to reestablish functional government, win over the part of the population that had supported Orozco, and conduct a difficult war against Huerta and later, when he split with the Constitutionalists, against Venustiano Carranza.[41] The cornerstone of his administration was the expropriation of the land and businesses of the Porfirian oligarchy in Chihuahua, most of whom belonged to the Terrazas-Creel extended family or were its allies.[42] The revenue earned by these properties paid the expenses of government and military operations. Eventually, Villa was to divide these holdings among revolutionary veterans and the villagers from whom the hacendados had expropriated them. The general administered the appropriated property in two ways, through trusted military officers and through the Administración General de Bienes Confiscados, headed by Silvestre Terrazas. This solved the problem of maintaining production to supply his troops and satisfying demands for land reform. The policy fulfilled the first half of the equation, taking the land away from the hacendados, but delayed the second half, redistribution, until the end of the internecine wars. Villa also met the immediate needs of war widows and orphans through the revenues generated by these properties.[43] Another important reform was his eliminating the municipal land law of 1905, which had been the source of much of the unrest in Chihuahua prior to 1910, because it had deprived many pueblos of their communal lands.[44]

The Villista program went still further. Wartime demands exacerbated by speculation brought inflation. The state government stepped in to regulate staple prices.[45] Villa took even more stringent measures in mid-1915 when he ordered all foreign merchants out of Ciudad Chihuahua, then jailed Mexican merchants and confiscated their stores, accusing them of robbing the people.[46]

To fund loans to small proprietors, Villa established the Banco del Estado, with ten million pesos capital.[47] In order to insure the flow of tax revenue and create needed employment, he commanded mining and industrial companies to resume operations or he would take them over himself.[48] At times, of course, the immediate demands of war overrode those of the economy. Such was the case in 1914 when Villista recruitment caused a shortage of miners.[49]

The situation changed once the Constitutionalists defeated Villa and took over the state government. Their main goal was to reconstruct the economy, and in this their first priority was to restore the Porfirian oligarchy to its land. The more they consolidated their power, the less inclined they were toward radical reform. The exigencies of war had pushed them to it earlier, but as victory was secured, they abandoned all but the pretense of reform. The regime, propped up almost entirely by its predatory military, desperately needed allies.[50] Almost as important, Carranza had to foster the economic recovery of a devastated nation. To him it seemed the fastest and surest road was through the old oligarchy. He returned their land as quickly as possible. Despite the need to feed his soldiers, he stopped the practice of selling the livestock of intervened haciendas.[51] Four hundred mining properties in Chihuahua were returned to their owners in May 1919.[52] In the end, this was all for naught, for Carranza lost the support of his army and it overthrew him in 1920.

The new Constitutionalist government began in 1916 to return property confiscated by Villa to its original owners.[53] Guillermo Muñoz, a grandson of Luis Terrazas, despite the fact that he was labeled an "enemy" of the revolution, recovered his land in 1919, three years after his first petition.[54] Carranza, just before his overthrow, arranged for the return of the lands of Luis Terrazas.[55]

The Constitutionalists were officially still committed to agrarian reform, but it was not implemented. The law of January 1915, of course, remained on the books. The Agrarian Law of January 19, 1916, nullified illegal alienations (*enajenaciones*) of land by *jefes políticos*, all concessions made by the *secretario de fomento* since December 1, 1896, until the present, and all surveying company grants.[56] But the law of January 6, 1916 ordered residents to return property to which they had no rights.[57] Governor Arnulfo González would not permit the registration of land distributed previously that encroached on property rights or mortgages.[58] Most important, actual practice brought the return of almost all confiscated properties to the old guard. The only exception to the Constitutionalist opposition to land reform was Andrés Ortiz, who foreshadowed what was to become the policy of Obregón and Calles, when in his unsuccessful campaign for election to a full term as governor, he promised land redistribution and reform of rural taxes.[59]

The Carrancistas were not entirely insensitive to the needs of the people. Like Villa, they tried to regulate prices. They were so successful in July 1916 that merchants in Ciudad Chihuahua closed their stores in protest.[60] Again like Villa, the Carrancistas attempted to restart the mining industry through coercion with a decree in September 1916 limiting owners' leeway to close mines.[61] This, however, was not aimed at the Mexican elite, but rather at foreign companies. The Constitutionalists took these measures in their first year after establishing a precarious hold over the state.

The Municipalities

Political conditions changed more slowly on the municipal than on the state level. In many locations Porfirian bosses and their families retained power throughout the decade. This was especially true in the more isolated areas. One suspects, too, that changes had more to do with local rivalries than national allegiances. In Uruachic in the western mountains, for example, the same family that had dominated the region throughout the nineteenth century and the Porfiriato, the Rascóns, held on for most of the war years.[62] They fought, went into exile, returned, and adapted.[63]

In other municipalities instability predominated. Chínipas, in the extreme southwest, had thirty-six changes in the office of municipal president by twenty-three different people. Ciudad Juárez had forty-nine changes by thirty different officeholders. Guadalupe y Calvo in the south experienced twenty-five shifts by nineteen people. Parral was more stable, with fourteen changes by eleven men, despite its location in the middle of the war zone. Namiquipa, one of the birthplaces of the Revolution, had thirteen shifts by eleven, though only two men held the office after 1913.

Rarely did the residents of the municipalities choose their leaders. Abraham González initially appointed his allies. The Huertistas adopted their own configuration. There were no municipal elections from 1913 to 1916 in most places, so not only were the *presidentes* not responsible to local constituencies, but there were no municipal councils (*ayuntamientos*) to share power. Under Villa, the military governor named the *presidentes municipales*. They had extraordinary powers, including the power to confiscate the property of enemies of the Revolution, and were responsible for supplying cattle needed by state.[64]

The Carrancistas sought to root out their opponents from local government. Under the provisions of the decree of June 12, 1916, those who had served in a cause against the Constitutionalists could not hold public office. The question of who had fought against them was subject to some conjecture. In Allende, the new *presidente municipal* was accused of collaborating with Huerta. Alejandro Escalera purportedly took charge of the municipality in 1913 and stayed on after the coup. No proof, however, emerged, and so Escarcega remained in office. The *ayuntamiento* of Allende in 1918 included two members of Porfirian landowning families, Salvador Luján and Miguel Maynez Morales.[65] In the eyes of the Carrancistas, it was probably far better to have been a Huertista than a Villista.

Elites

At the state level, ten years of war took a heavy toll on the political leadership. The Orozquista and Villista movements indigenous to Chihuahua were defeated and their leaders dead or exiled. The old oligarchy had for the most part fled to Texas and California.

Villa's triumph in Chihuahua brought a mass exodus of "the better class of civilians."[66] "In Chihuahua . . . and in all other portions of the country there was an absence of persons of education."[67] The casualty rate for revolutionary leaders was high. Under these conditions few wartime leaders survived to achieve prominent positions after 1920. We have already seen how only two governors of the 1910 to 1920 era were important political figures in post-revolutionary Chihuahua. The most startling case of attrition was that of the Herrera family of Parral. War and Villa's vengeance put an end to a potential dynasty. The father, José de la Luz Herrera, and six sons perished.[68]

The Porfirian elite suffered considerable losses as well. They fared relatively well under the Madero administration. Although Abraham González took damaging measures to increase its taxes and diminish its stranglehold on local government, its economic holdings were not threatened. At one point, González sought to reconcile with his former enemies, guaranteeing the civil rights of Luis Terrazas and his allies if they returned to Chihuahua.[69] The old guard returned with Huerta's ascendance, only to flee again when confronted with Pancho Villa. They did not return until after 1917. Villa expropriated the properties of many of the old oligarchy and persecuted any of them who remained to protect what had been theirs.

The Terrazas, who had dominated the politics and economy of the state for a half-century and who had run the state as a family fiefdom since 1902, pursued a varied strategy from 1910 to 1919 that included conciliation, cooperation, opposition, and armed resistance. The family's leaders were undoubtedly stunned by the sudden success of the Maderistas and the depth of revolutionary sentiment in Chihuahua. At first, General Terrazas thought to arm the *gente* of his haciendas, but he quickly realized that "they would pass to the enemy armed and equipped."[70] The family's response was also handicapped by conflict with the Díaz government, which resulted in the removal of Alberto Terrazas, the general's youngest son, from the governorship in favor of Porfirista warhorse Miguel Ahumada. Alberto received no help from his fellow landowners either.[71]

Maderos's triumph could not, after some reflection, have worried them a great deal, for the Coahuilan was himself a hacendado; the Maderos were also one of the great industrial families of the era and partners of the Terrazas in several large enterprises. Furthermore, they had kinship ties with the interim president, Francisco León de la Barra. Pascual Orozco, Jr., in the fall of 1911, went so far as to help the old general in his claims for damages incurred during the revolt.[72] The most difficult problem was Abraham González, whose program of tax reform directly threatened the Terrazas's interests.

The Terrazas fought back by going around González to Madero and by undermining the governor's support in Chihuahua. In one instance, Madero responded to an appeal from Enrique Creel to quash a renewed investigation into the Banco Minero robbery which had been a cause célèbre in 1908. Most important, the Terrazas endeavored to widen the breach between González and Orozco. The family showed an interest in Orozco as early as June 1911, when one of its agents proposed him for the governorship.[73] Although for a short period in 1911 Luis Terrazas left Chihuahua for Aguascalientes and then Long Beach, California, for the most part it was business as usual.[74]

There seems to be little doubt that the "Terrazas organized, directed, and financed the Orozco rebellion," which lasted from March to September 1912.[75] One grandchild, Luis Terrazas Bobadilla (the son of Luis Jr.), served as captain of artillery for the Orozquistas and was wounded.[76] Another grandson, Francisco Terrazas (Juan Terrazas's son), held the post of *juez de instrucción militar* under Orozco.[77]

The defeat of Orozco caused the family to examine its options. The state government increased the pressure, when it embargoed the urban property of Luis Terrazas, claiming he owed 155,332.66 pesos in back taxes.[78] Enrique Creel, through his Compañía Ganadera de Chihuahua, considered selling his property in the fall of 1912.[79] A few months later, though, in early 1913, he petitioned for water to irrigate 28,000 hectares of the company's Hacienda de Orientales.[80] General Terrazas sold one of his haciendas, La Cañada, in 1913.[81]

The Terrazas enthusiastically supported the government of Victoriano Huerta.[82] This took two concrete forms. The Creels and the Banco Minero were heavily involved in the finances of the Huerta-Mercado government.[83] In addition, the Terrazas organized military forces ("un número competente de rurales").[84] Both Alberto Terrazas and Enrique Cuilty headed corps.[85]

The family suffered a major setback in September 1913 when Máximo Castillo began to distribute the lands of the Terrazas haciendas San Diego, San Lorenzo, San Luis, San Miguel de Bavícora, El Carmen, and Tapiecitas to their resident peons. He also demanded a forced war loan of 15,000 pesos a month. If Terrazas did not comply with this distribution and loan, Castillo threatened to dynamite the houses of the haciendas and behead the cattle.[86]

Two months later General Terrazas went into exile in El Paso. He moved to Los Angeles in 1919, after suffering a stroke. Pancho Villa and Silvestre Terrazas arranged for the departure of the "ancient" mother of Enrique Creel and two daughters.[87] Alberto remained until badly wounded in 1914. Luis Jr. stayed to look after the family's estates but was captured and tortured by Villa. He was freed only after a ransom payment of US$850,000.[88]

Exile did not end the family's resistance. Enrique Creel and Luis Terrazas met with counterrevolutionary Félix Díaz in October 1914.[89] After Huerta's defeat and exile, Creel was one of those who journeyed to Spain in 1915 to persuade him to return. He helped back an aborted rebellion by Huerta and Orozco that ended in the death of both in 1915.[90]

One of Villa's first acts was to expropriate the land and businesses of the Terrazas extended family and its allies.[91] The properties were operated over the next three to six years by a combination of Villista and Carrancista generals and agencies. The greatest losses occurred because both groups consumed or sold Terrazas cattle.[92] Although the Terrazas attempted to prevent this, suing the El Paso stockyard to recover the value of 349 head in 1915, for example, there was little to be done.[93] Few of the half-million head of cattle that roamed the Terrazas haciendas in 1910 were left by 1919.

The Constitutionalists hit hard at the family's banking empire. A February 1914 decree declared that the concessions of the Banco Minero, Banco Comercial Refaccionario, and the Caja de Ahorros de la República Mexicana had expired.[94] The Constitutionalists gutted the flagship bank, the Banco Minero de Chihuahua, with forced loans of more than a million pesos in 1914, and later in 1916 by confiscating its reserves.[95]

Once Villa lost control of Chihuahua and the Carrancistas moved in, the tide turned. Carranza, for both economic and political reasons, set out to restore the properties of the Porfirian elite. He saw them leading the desperately needed economic recovery and forming a crucial base of support. One member of the family did not wait around for better conditions. In 1916, according to a report in the *El Paso Morning Times,* Teresa B. de Terrazas, the wife of Luis Jr., made a sensational trip into Ciudad Chihuahua dressed as a peon and rescued the family's jewels and many valuable papers.[96]

Probably the first member of the extended family to get his property back was Carlos Cuilty, in November 1916.[97] Several of the Terrazas children received their lands in 1919.[98] Carranza returned the property of Luis Terrazas and Enrique Creel in Ciudad Chihuahua in 1919.[99] The general would have gotten his haciendas as well, but the first chief was overthrown before the deal could be implemented.[100]

The situation for the family banks and industrial companies was optimistic enough in 1918 for them to have held their stockholders' meetings to discuss future plans. The stockholders of one of these enterprises, the Compañía Minera Gibraltar y Anexas, met to explore reorganizing and hiring an attorney to retrieve its property in 1919.[101]

Not all the family's problems were resolved by any means. The general's properties were still in limbo. Enrique Creel faced suits holding him liable for his financial and banking businesses. In one case, forty thousand dollars were attached in a suit against his Guaranty Trust of El Paso in 1919.[102] Creel recognized more than 1.4 million pesos in direct and moral obligations in 1921 that he was unable to pay in cash. He maintained that he had lost 5,502,222.76 pesos in the revolution from 1913 to 1921. To offset his liabilities, he owned urban properties worth 101,944 pesos and the Hacienda de Gallina, worth 101,767 pesos.[103]

Revolution and exile were not kind to Luis Terrazas. The old general lost one son, Guillermo, and a grandson, Luis III, and saw two sons, Alberto and Luis, badly wounded.[104]

Despite their great losses, in 1920 the Terrazas had considerable resources with which to make themselves a place in the new order. It appears that Creel had sent a substantial amount of the family's funds out of the country. Family members kept a close watch on their holdings from their exile in El Paso and Los Angeles. Carranza returned much of the family's property before Obregón overthrew him. The strong family network remained. Most important, per-haps, a new generation of leaders among the general's grandchildren was ready to take the reins.

The evidence for the actions of other elite families is not nearly as plentiful. Two members of the Terrazas extended family were offi-cials in the Huertista administration. Lic. José María Luján was *sub-secretario de gobernación* in the Huerta and Carbajal cabinets. Carlos Cuilty was president of the Junta Patriótica of Ciudad Chihuahua in 1913. The Casino Chihuahuense, an exclusive elite club, publicly voted its support for Huerta in November 1913. Two Terrazas fam-ily members were on its board of directors.[105]

Alan Knight maintains that the Mexican elite in 1913 and 1914 was "neither a warrior nor an active ruling class," but rather "second generation oligarchs . . . good for the law, high finance, and diplo-macy, if they were good for anything at all";[106] and this may have been true for much of the Porfirian elite and, for that matter, much of the Chihuahuan Porfirian elite. But in Chihuahua it might more accurately be said that discretion was the better part of valor. The Terrazas, Zuloagas, Lujáns, and others at the district level knew that there were times to fight and times to negotiate or lie low. The Chihuahuan oligarchy had no recourse to arms, because, as Luis Terrazas remarked, to arm his peons would be to arm the revolution. Several important revolutionary leaders had previously been fore-men on his haciendas. It is true that they had no charismatic leader, like Luis Terrazas during the nineteenth century. But the Terrazas had purchased armed help before: they financed rebellions in th? 1890s to keep Díaz off balance; Orozco's was just one in a long line. Moreover, the villagers who had provided the troops in the wars against the conservatives, French, and Indians were now opposed.

The Terrazas, unlike many other landowners, fought. And they plotted; they were patient. Twice they overturned the revolution in Chihuahua. By 1917, with a Porfirian hacendado as president of Mexico and the son of a Terracista *jefe político* as governor of the state, the family began to recover its lost holdings.

The struggles among elites at different levels in Chihuahua, and between Chihuahuenses and the national regime, were not over by any means, nor was the conflict between elites and the popular classes. The 1920s were to be tumultuous, an era of transition, when no group, faction, or sector was strong enough to prevail.

3 Chihuahua during the 1920s

The Era of the *Caudillitos*

The new revolutionary regimes, both at the national and state levels, struggled during the 1920s with two daunting, sometimes contradictory, tasks: to establish their control and to rebuild the economy. The victorious revolutionaries in Chihuahua, like the Sonorans who ruled the nation, were first and foremost capitalists. But political reality forced them to satisfy the demands of the popular classes for labor and agrarian reforms even though these often clashed with the requirements of economic recovery to create a favorable environment for investment and production. Whatever their ideological propensities, Chihuahua's (and Mexico's) new rulers acted first to assure their own survival in the face of periodic rebellions. Challenges to their authority were met only because they could win the support of the popular classes through the adoption of such reforms, especially the redistribution of land.

Politics in Chihuahua during the 1920s took the form of three concurrent conflicts. The first, at the state level, existed between bitterly competing factions, rallied around a charismatic leader or a powerful family, which sought to capture the state government. The second took place at the local level, where municipal political bosses or influential families combatted the efforts of state governments to exert control over their bailiwicks. The third, and most important, involved the unceasing efforts of the national government to extend its hegemony over the state and the opposing efforts of state political elites to prevent these incursions. At no point during the 1920s was the central government nearly as strong as it was to become after 1940. Underlying the struggles to establish a new political regime were the state's depressed economic condition, especially in agriculture, the increasing efforts of campesinos and workers to organize, and the search of the prerevolutionary elite for its place in the new order.

The evolving interaction among the national regime, state elites, local notables, the principal sectors of the regional economy, and the popular classes provided the conditions in which the Porfirian elite survived and established its role and shaped the relationships between old and new elites that profoundly affected the path of the Revolution during the 1920s.

The Economy

In 1920 the state's agriculture, transportation, communications, and commerce were near ruin. During the next decade, the recovery of agriculture and mining, the two major sectors of the state's economy, greatly affected the political arena. A third sector, gambling, became important during the 1920s, because it directly provided the funds for Chihuahuan politics.

Economic reconstruction was slow. Despite the remarkable recovery of the state's cattle industry during the 1920s, there were only 685,000 head by the end of the decade, not much more than 50 percent of the prerevolutionary figure.[1] To make matters worse, severe drought and lost harvests struck the region in 1920, 1921, 1922, and 1929. Although harvests improved in the middle of the decade, there was only one year when all three staple crops—corn, wheat, and beans—were sufficient.[2] In that year, 1926, crops were so plentiful that commodity prices plunged, leaving farmers still in bad straits.[3]

With the exception of mining, business was generally depressed throughout the 1920s. The retail trade never recovered its prerevolutionary vitality. Money was often scarce and credit usually tight. The major Mexican-owned banks in the state failed.[4] Two of the biggest stores in the region—Krakauer, Zork and Ketelsen and Degetau—operated on the brink of bankruptcy.[5] Because of the poor economic conditions, the state government never had enough revenue. It was always behind in paying its employees.[6] Mining was the one strong sector, for it had recovered by 1918, surpassing 1910 production (in U.S. dollars) the next year. More ore was extracted and treated in Chihuahua in 1921 than at any previous time in its history. Mineral production stagnated the following year and then began a sharp rise of 400 percent from 1923 to 1926. The industry endured depression from the end of 1929 until 1934. At the height of the boom, mining employed twenty thousand in the state.[7]

The condition of agriculture and mining created crucial political issues. Disastrously erratic staple crop harvests forced the state and national governments to seek a delicate balance between promised, hard-fought-for land reform—and the inevitable dislocations it would bring—and the desperate need for increased food production. Mining presented two interrelated problems. Since the industry was the driving force in the economy, the government had to juggle the needs of mine-owners with the demands of emerging workers' organizations for better wages, working conditions, and job security. Mining was, moreover, increasingly concentrated in the hands of large, foreign-owned corporations, most importantly ASARCO.[8] This had important consequences. The companies had enormous leverage in dealing with governments and labor unions, for they could use the threat of shutting down their operations—an action that would be ruinous to the state's economy—in order to negotiate. Furthermore, the concentration in a few foreign companies and the almost total demise of small producers limited the benefits from the industry to the local economy. Mineral production was also concentrated in only four subregions of the state: Santa Eulalia, Santa Bárbara, Parral, and Cusihuiriachic.[9] Mining elsewhere was in ruins. Linkages from mining were thus restricted.

Disorder and Violence

Militarily, Chihuahua was in constant upheaval. The decade began with the overthrow of Venustiano Carranza by Alvaro Obregón (the Plan de Agua Prieta). The following year there was a short-lived uprising of three hundred Indians in the southwestern district of Andrés del Río.[10] Three separate rebellions rocked the state in 1922.[11] Adolfo de la Huerta led a nationwide rebellion in December 1923 that drew several ex-Villista leaders, such as Hípolito Villa, Nicolás Fernández, and Manuel Chao. The de la Huertistas remained in the field in Chihuahua through the spring of 1924.[12] In June the radical mayor of Santa Bárbara, Ricardo Cruz, armed twenty followers and took over the municipal government, only to be overrun by federal soldiers.[13] Nicolás Fernández revolted again in mid-July 1925 and stayed in the field well into 1927.[14] After the coup that ousted Governor Jesús Antonio Almeida in 1927, his supporters led a brief rebellion.[15] Another band of four hundred rebels operated in southwestern districts of the state in 1928.[16] Finally, Marcelo Caraveo went over to the rebellion of General José Gonzalo Escobar against Calles in March 1929.[17] Moreover, until he was assassinated in 1923, Pancho Villa was a constant source of apprehension. The continuous condition of disruption and uncertainty constrained the revolutionary elite's political options and created opportunities for the old elite (which I will discuss at length in Chapter 5).

Politics

The decade divides into political stages identified by their dominant figure. Ignacio C. Enríquez governed in close cooperation with President Alvaro Obregón in the first era from 1920 to 1924. From 1924 until he was ousted by a coup in 1927, Jesús Antonio Almeida ruled Chihuahua. Almeida, like the strongmen who arose in several other Mexican states during the 1920s, tried to build an independent political base. Marcelo Caraveo overthrew Almeida and took power until 1929, when he joined the doomed Escobar rebellion. The decade ended as it had begun, in tumult, with interim governors Luis L. León and Francisco R. Almada. It was only with the return of General Rodrigo Quevedo to Chihuahua as governor in 1932 that order returned.

Throughout the 1920s there was a dichotomy in Chihuahuan politics between the radical peasantry and proletariat and the state's political leadership, whose economic background and aspirations were essentially capitalist and relatively conservative. For much of the period, the conservatives held the upper hand. The most striking exceptions took place during the governorships of Ignacio C. Enríquez and Luis L. León, when national political considerations more than personal conviction or ideology made substantial land reforms necessary.

Ignacio C. Enriquez

The election of General Ignacio C. Enríquez as governor in 1920 marked the return of constitutional rule in Chihuahua for the first time since the assassination of Abraham González seven years earlier. His capable leadership established a measure of peace and prosperity in the state and successfully defended the new, revolutionary regime against the dangerous challenge of the de la Huerta rebellion.

Reflecting his efforts to balance the ardent demands for reform and the need to restore agriculture, his record on land reform was mixed. Chihuahua distributed 429,317 hectares of land between 1921 and 1924, more than any other states except Yucatán and San Luis Potosí.[18] Nonetheless, the convention of campesinos in Chihuahua in 1922 expressed its discontent with the slow pace of reform.[19] An official of the Partido Nacional Agrarista protested the "systematic obstruction of . . . municipal guards" against those who sought to recover land that was rightfully theirs.[20] More indicative of both Enríquez's and Obregón's attitudes and the dilemmas posed by reform was the unsuccessful attempt to sell the estate of Luis Terrazas to an American entrepreneur, Arthur J. McQuatters. The governor, with the initial approval of the president, signed the contract and campaigned vigorously for its approval, believing it to be an important step toward solving the state's perennial agricultural crisis. The agreement called for McQuatters to purchase five million acres, which he would improve and sell off in small parcels. Popular objections led first the state legislature and then the president to reject the proposal. Ultimately, the federal government purchased the properties from the Terrazas estate.[21] Enríquez and Obregón preferred small-scale private farming, but public pressures caused them to change their policies. Enríquez did not always side with the large landowners, for he ordered agricultural colonists to remain on land they had occupied on the Zuloaga family's Hacienda de Bustillos until the courts settled the matter of ownership.[22]

The balancing act of land reform was further complicated by the new revolutionary hacendados. In one case, campesinos, some of whom had lost their lands to the hacienda during the Porfiriato, occupied the Hacienda de Cienega de Mata, whose owner had fled during the revolution. General Ernesto García became involved at some point, either as the campesinos' protector or as usurper of the land. Beginning in 1919, the owner tried to regain his estate. Enríquez dispatched a hundred federal troops in 1922 to dislodge the general and his invaders.[23] There is a question as to whether the governor was defending the rights of the campesinos or a fellow general.

Political expediency was clearly evident in Enríquez's agrarian policies. In many instances, the pueblos that received lands through the land-reform laws had been originators of the revolution in 1910 and 1911. Moreover, the number of restitutions (*restituciónes*) and grants (*dotaciónes*) increased notably with the threat of the de la Huerta rebellion in 1923.[24] The government was particularly careful with the Villistas. The national government bought the Hacienda El Pueblito in 1923 to divide among Villa's division of the north.[25] An even more blatant example of the role politics played in land reform also took place in 1923. The state government called off white guards, who had killed petitioners from the pueblo of Paramo in the Guerrero district in a dispute over the lands of the Hacienda Rosario, when the villagers were needed to fight the de la Huertistas.[26] Pragmatic though it might have been, Enríquez's land reform was apparently sufficient to enable him to recruit a large number of campesinos to fight the de la Huerta rebellion.[27]

Governor Enríquez walked a similar tightrope in dealing with labor and mining. He "tempered enforcement" of the radical labor law passed by the state legislature in 1922 "by good sense," in order to maintain the industry's recovery.[28] The crucial test came with strikes against ASARCO in Santa Eulalia and Avalos, the first against the company in five years. Enríquez, who was reportedly sympathetic to the workers, responded by sending in troops to prevent violence and protect property. At the same time he encouraged negotiations that settled the conflict (though no one was pleased by his actions).[29]

Agrarians were especially dissatisfied with Enríquez's successors, who after the defeat of the de la Huerta rebellion evidently saw no need for continued reform. Rómulo Alvelais drew their particular ire, for they considered him hostile toward their interests.[30] Reinaldo Talavera was no better.[31] He employed force to evict agrarians from land awarded them by the national government.[32]

Talavera also sent soldiers to deal with a bitter strike against large U.S. companies in Santa Eulalia. There was bloodshed before the governor could supervise a settlement. During another strike in Santa Bárbara, rural guards allegedly shot workers "like dogs."[33]

ASARCO's response to its workers' demands, as it would be often in the future, was to threaten to close down its operations. This put the state government in a difficult position, for economic recovery depended on large mining companies like ASARCO investing heavily. It appears that initially the new labor law had a "decided dampening effect" on the mining companies.[34] But by 1925 employers had adjusted and found ways around it.[35]

Under Enríquez, conflict with the national regime was minimal. Obregón generally did not intervene in state politics unless there was a direct threat to his government. In the north and central states, Obregón allowed even hostile governors to rule. Only when he saw a threat to federal power, as in the case of César López de Lara in Tamaulipas, did he intervene.[36]

Enríquez was a reliable ally of Obregón, who proved his mettle by defeating the de la Huertistas in Chihuahua and acting as a counterweight to Pancho Villa.[37] In 1922 there were rumors that Villa might reenter politics (which he denied).[38] There seems little doubt Villa was killed to prevent his joining with de la Huerta. Villa's presence probably strengthened Enríquez's hand in dealing with the national regime, for eliminating him would have destabilized the state and left an opening for the old warrior.

Jesús Antonio Almeida

Enríquez, ever loyal to Obregón, showed no inclination to establish an independent power base in Chihuahua. His successor, Jesús Antonio Almeida, on the contrary, set out to build an empire for himself and his family. Almeida had risen through the ranks of the *defensas sociales,* using this as a springboard to run, with the backing of Enríquez, for governor in 1924.[39]

Jesús Antonio displayed two notable tendencies: a decided sympathy toward the old Porfirian elite and a driving ambition to acquire a fortune. He not only married into the elite (as we have seen), but enthusiastically participated in its revived social life.[40] While governor, Almeida founded an extensive economic empire that centered on lumber.

Almeida was primarily concerned with protecting private-property rights and maintaining the strong economic recovery that took place in mid-decade. His social connections and ideological sympathies led him to the side of the large landowners. He blocked many petitions for restitution and dotation, including at least three important claims against major landowners in 1926.[41] (Many of his rulings were overturned by later governors.) He approved the scheme of one of his friends, Ian Benton, to have his hacienda declared national land and exchanged for land elsewhere in the state.[42] The most politically damaging accusations involved his treatment of the Terrazas family. During his term, family members were able to repurchase part of the estate of Luis Terrazas, recently taken over by the federal government.[43] He also supposedly gave the Terrazas preferential treatment in matters of back taxes owed the state.[44] Most telling, perhaps, in the few months after his ouster forty pueblos filed petitions for land.[45]

Although Almeida generally showed little sympathy toward land reform or labor and there were no major threats to the revolutionary regime during his truncated term, he could not ignore agrarian reform entirely. An exasperated U.S. consul in Chihuahua in 1926 claimed that the Almeida administration obstructed efforts to dislodge squatters who had invaded cattle estates.[46] In the case of the Palomas Land and Cattle Company in 1926, he overturned the ruling of the local agrarian commission to deny the petitions of Puerta de Palomas and Vado de Fusiles, but then helped negotiate a deal between the agrarians and the Palomas Company, the terms of which provided that the company was to sell to the national government several thousand hectares, which were then to be turned over to the petitioners.[47] He arranged another deal in which the residents of Zaragoza (Hidalgo District) obtained water rights in return for recognizing the ownership of Federico Sisniega of the Hacienda de Bella Vista.[48] In all of these instances Almeida probably bowed to considerable public pressure. The large U.S. companies were very unpopular. Almeida, moreover, was not unwilling to condone actions against foreign competitors with his family's cattle and timber operations. Sisniega, as a member of the hated Terrazas family, was an easy target.

An emerging industrialist, Almeida also showed no sympathy toward workers, refusing to implement labor reforms passed by the state legislature and actively intervening in labor-management disputes in order to prevent strikes. The governor actually refused to publish in the *Periódico Oficial* reforms to the labor law passed by the legislature.[49] He feared that the radical new laws and strikes would jeopardize the recovery of mining.[50] His policy apparently succeeded, for the mining industry boomed during his term.

While in 1925 one commentator observed that the complicated labor legislation enacted by the states had "not yet rounded into a fair and workable form" and thus continued to cause misunderstandings between employers and employees, it was clear by 1927 that the mining companies had the upper hand.[51] Labor had made some gains on paper, but employers circumvented the reform laws and hard-won agreements with tacit support from the state and national governments. The one consolation was that mining employment rose to twenty thousand, nearly a 100 percent increase from 1910.[52]

Jesús Antonio stridently tried to construct a political dynasty, installing a brother as municipal president of Ciudad Juárez and a brother-in-law as municipal president in Ciudada Chihuahua. He initially had strong support in the western part of the state.[53] His marriage and efforts to accommodate the Porifirian elite were other important parts of his strategy. More than his predecessors, Almeida interfered in municipal politics to extend his influence.[54]

Unfortunately for him, Almeida made enemies, who organized into the Partido Liberal Progresista Chihuahuense (PLPC), led by Fernándo Orozco E.[55] Orozco allied with the new chief of military operations in Chihuahua, General Marcelo Caraveo, and with the help of PLPC members of the state legislature, overthrew Almeida on April 15, 1927. Jesús Antonio barely escaped with his life, fleeing into exile in El Paso, Texas.[56]

Almeida fell because he had no strong base, either among the peasantry, like Saturnino Cedillo in San Luis Potosí, or among the labor unions, like Adalberto Tejeda in Veracruz.[57] As an hacendado, he had little in common with or attraction for peasants; as an industrialist, he exhibited no rapport with labor. The secretary-general of the Confederación Obreros de Chihuahua opined that "Almeida had lost all popularity" because of his "inexpert, weak government."[58] *El Correo de Chihuahua* judged Almeida a "political disaster."[59] Like many of the northern middle-class revolutionaries, Almeida had more sympathy with the ideas and goals of the Porfirian elite than with the peasants or workers.

The governor also lost the regional backing so important in Chihuahuan politics. The strong support he had once enjoyed in western Chihuahua among small landowners dissipated in the agricultural depression of 1926. His other bases, Ciudad Juárez and Ciudad Chihuahua, proved unstable. His brother Alberto was popular in Juárez, but the situation there was highly competitive and treacherous. More importantly, the garrison commander there was an ally of Caraveo. Brother-in-law Socorro García proved an unpopular municipal president, because he was imposed from the outside.[60] Without grass-roots underpinning, Almeida was extremely vulnerable to any loss of confidence by the Calles-led central government.[61]

Almeida's fall marked the end of two important trends. He was the last independent political boss in Chihuahua. Caraveo, who might have established an autonomous, popular base, revolted after only six months in office. The others who followed, like Luis L. León and General Rodrigo Quevedo during the 1930s, had close ties to the national government. It was Almeida's independence that may have led Calles to support his overthrow. Almeida, in addition, represented the last gasp of western Chihuahua in state politics. Thereafter, the center of political power shifted, once and for all, to Ciudad Juárez, Ciudad Chihuahua, and Parral. The defeat of Almeida could be seen, as well, as an early effort of the national regime to prevent the cooperation of old and new elites. Almeida's close familial and economic ties to the old guard presented a threat to the national regime's goal of centralization.

Marcelo Caraveo

Fernando Orozco E. served briefly until October 1928, giving the state its "best administration in many years," spending considerable sums on school and public-works construction.[62]

The colorful Marcelo Caraveo, the military zone commander who helped overthrow Almeida, was elected governor in 1928. The U.S. consul considered Caraveo a "high type," but did not extend the kind words to the rest of his administration.[63] He had not yet served six months when he joined the Plan de Hermosillo revolt, led by Escobar, against President Portes Gil in March 1929. After the defeat of the rebellion, Caraveo went into exile in El Paso, where he lived modestly. A self-professed man of principle, Caraveo believed that Calles and his puppets had betrayed the Revolution.[64] Caraveo and Almeida, though opposed, were the last of the homegrown, independent revolutionary governors of Chihuahua.

Luis L. León and Francisco R. Almada

After Caraveo went over to the rebellion, the regime sent trusted agent Luis L. León to Chihuahua as governor. His term was to prove a watershed in state politics, for it marked the beginning of the end (but by no means the end) of the ornery independence of Chihuahuan politics, and it initiated the crucial formal alliance between agrarians and the national regime. León made state politics more responsive to the national government, and more radical, by advocating land reform. In an effort to bring Chihuahua more closely under the control of the national regime, he became the virtual boss of the state's agrarian organizations and oversaw the creation of the Partido Revolucionario Chihuahuense in 1929.[65]

As the representative of the national regime, León faced considerable hostile sentiment. Not only had the previous governor, Caraveo, sided with the rebels, but so had many members of the state legislature and the *ayuntamientos* of the two most important cities, Ciudad Juárez and Chihuahua.[66] The central government, probably quite rightly, may have perceived that a good part of the regional political elite was untrustworthy. Even if Calles and León had to work with them, they needed an alternative basis of support. This would come through the organization of the revolutionary party and through obtaining the support of the popular classes for the national regime.[67] Although he took over a state government without resources, León had to reestablish order by disarming both the large landowners and armed campesinos.[68]

His most important effort was to win over the popular classes. At the party's first convention, León vowed to end the influence of the hacendados, which had obstructed land reform. He also advocated free municipal elections to rid the people of the old bosses. The governor brought together divided campesino groups and began to reorganize labor. He treated the rebels of 1929 with magnanimity.[69] León established a program to expedite land reform, adding staff to the local agrarian commission, and to increase production, investing in public works and public education.[70] He and the head of the local agrarian commission, Carlos Terrazas, personally toured Chihuahua, listening to the pleas of the people for restitution of their lands.[71] The León administration distributed more land in his first two months in office than had been in the previous several years.[72]

Despite his advocacy of land reform, León did not favor collectivism, which he considered a foreign method unsuited to Mexico. He was a champion of smallholders, whose rights he fought to protect against the onslaught of agrarians. As a large landowner himself, León espoused the principle of private property.[73]

León foreshadowed the compromises to come when, as he departed the governorship, he called upon his opponents, "the capitalist elements," to accept defeat by the Revolution. If they would accept the new laws, he offered them guarantees and rights. They would all join to work for the reconstruction of Chihuahua.[74] This was a somewhat radical version of the Obregón-Calles modus operandi and a preview of the future political arrangements that underlay the Partido Nacional Revolucionario-Partido Revolucionario Mexicano (PNR-PRM).

Unfortunately for the political stability of Chihuahua, León spent much time out of state, spearheading the presidential campaign of Pascual Ortiz Rubio in the north.[75] Although nominally governor for ten months, he actually served in Chihuahua for only half that time. During his long absences, Francisco R. Almada served as interim governor.

Almada faithfully carried on León's reform program, instituting a new Ley de Medidas y Engenación de Terrenos Municipales that imposed high taxes on undeveloped city land. He strongly warned local authorities not to side with large landowners.[76] Under Almada there was an enormous increase in the number of petitions for restitutions and dotations of land.[77]

But Almada could not avoid the treachery of Chihuahuan politics. In 1929 he became embroiled in a dispute with the state Supremo Tribunal de Justicia that resulted in the impeachment of its chief magistrate and the expulsion of three deputies from the state legislature. The following year he was overthrown temporarily by a rival group, but was restored by the central government.[78]

Agrarian Reform: The Terrazas Latifundio

The policy of both the state and national governments during the 1920s of seeking a balance between the popular demands for land, on one hand, and ideological propensity and the practical needs for recovery of agriculture, on the other, is, perhaps, nowhere better shown than in the fate of the former latifundio of Luis Terrazas. Of the original 2.7 million hectares purchased by the federal government and administered by the Caja de Préstamos para Obras de Irrigación y Fomento de la Agricultura, as of 1930, 500 thousand hectares were transferred to *colonías agrícolas,* 1.6 million were undistributed, and 500 thousand repurchased by the Terrazas family.[79] Furthermore, the most important fortunes of postrevolutionary Chihuahua were based on the acquisition of sections of Terrazas lands from the Caja de Préstamos. The Almeida, Borunda, Carrillo, Quevedo, Russek, and Terrazas families were to lead the reconstruction of the cattle industry in the 1930s, based on their acquisition of lands from the estate of Luis Terrazas.

Through the efforts of León and Almada (added to the earlier ones of Ignacio C. Enríquez), Chihuahua had distributed more land than any other state by 1933, more than 2.5 million acres. Although land ownership remained highly concentrated—in 1930, 3.5 percent of the landholdings owned 85.7 percent of the farmland—León and Almada oversaw much progress.[80] Moreover, the balancing act seemed to have had some success. Although the statistics are incomplete and estimates vary (sometimes rather substantially), the production of staple crops recovered from 1923 to 1929 and the number of cattle increased notably.[81] The battle for the land was, of course, by no means over in 1930.

Gambling and Politics

Given Chihuahua's chronic economic depression and the state government's accompanying fiscal difficulties, the substantial monies generated by legalized gambling were at the center of its politics from 1920 to 1934. The incessant battles over legalization and the disposition of revenues are among the clearest illustrations of the tripartite political conflicts of the era. Gambling monies would prove to be the crucial factor in determining the winning factions in state politics.

Both the municipal government of Ciudad Juárez and the state authorities consistently favored legalized gambling as a way to obtain desperately needed funds to pay their bills. These revenues also provided a considerable degree of autonomy for each from the central government. Consequently, Mexico City opposed legalization. Often, particularly during Obregón's presidency, federal opposition was framed as a moral issue, but political independence was at the heart of the conflict. At times, various governors ordered gambling stopped in efforts to acquire a larger share of the revenues. The federal government used various tactics to control gambling, including pulling out the federal garrison, the city's only effective police force, from Ciudad Juárez, and closing the international bridges.[82]

Caudillitos and Revolution

Chihuahua's revolutionary leaders addressed the dilemmas of postrevolutionary political economy in accordance with the limitation of the state's peculiar economic and social forces. In some states, like Veracruz, San Luis Potosí, Yucatán, Tabasco, and Tamaulipas, the abilities and determination of individual leaders molded their economic and political development. In a number of states leaders conducted "laboratories of the revolution."[83] No powerful caudillo emerged in Chihuahua. No leader embarked on great social experiments. Unquestionably, at least two aspired to establish political fiefdoms. Two other governors espoused radical rhetoric. But Chihuahua did not replicate either of these two experiences.

Ignacio C. Enríquez would appear to have been the most likely to acquire the role of caudillo during the 1920s. An agronomist trained in the United States, he was a capable administrator, had wide expertise in agriculture, had put together two mass military organizations, and had a firm popular base among the *defensas sociales* in Chihuahua.[84] In background, Enríquez had much in common with Adalberto Tejeda, who dominated Veracruz politics during the 1920s and early 1930s.

Enríquez was initially quite popular. While governor he displayed considerable ability for popular organization: he established the state's Liga de Comunidades Agrarias and Confederación de Obreros, oversaw the first restitutions and dotations of ejidos, and set up the first *colonías agrícolas* and *colonías ganaderas*. He had a reputation for honesty. Although he had his detractors, Enríquez apparently had no strong opposition. He was certainly able to see to it that his protégé Almeida succeeded him as governor. Despite all this, Enríquez faded into relative obscurity after 1924.

There were several possible reasons for Enríquez's political demise. He had played an important role in the negotiations that led to the purchase of the Terrazas lands by McQuatters.[85] And he had, furthermore, defended the highly unpopular sale long after its cancellation. Moreover, his delicate balancing act between reform and reconstruction was bound to erode his public standing. Some critics accused him of "dilly-dallying" in putting down the de la Huerta rebellion in Chihuahua. This may have planted the seed of distrust in the minds of the national regime. Obregón may already have been leery of Enríquez's political judgment because of the McQuatters-Terrazas affair. His legacy was also limited because Almeida, determined to build his own empire in the state, proved to be an independent protégé (not the last of these in Chihuahua). Finally, there is little evidence of either driving ambition or sense of burning social mission in Enríquez.

Almeida most certainly possessed that kind of ambition, but failed to establish either widespread popular support or to obtain solid backing from Mexico City. He installed his relatives in strategic posts, but they could not establish themselves there. Almeida's opposition to labor and his tepid support of agrarian reform brought him little popularity among the masses. His marriage into and active consorting with the old elite, and his unmistakable use of his position to further his family's economic interests, eroded his backing even more. When the group led by Fernando Orozco E. and Marcelo Caraveo overthrew him in 1927, there was little public outcry. Although it is not entirely certain that Calles conspired with others to oust Almeida, he did nothing to interfere and did not restore him to office. Unlike Enríquez, and León, Fierro, and Quevedo afterward, Almeida had no experience outside Chihuahua. As a result, he had none of the personal connections so valuable in Mexican politics. There is no evidence that he had a protector in the capital (as would later governors León, Fierro, and Ortiz).

Marcelo Caraveo was the closest Chihuahua came during the 1920s to having a traditional caudillo.[86] He was a military hero with charisma. But he did not have the patience or skill to build up a wide foundation of support based on patronage, as had Saturnino Cedillo in San Luis Potosí. Instead, he sided with the ill-fated Escobar rebellion only months after taking office as governor.

Luis León was another young revolutionary who attached himself to the rising *sonorenses*. After more than fifteen years filling various offices at the state and national level, he retired to his newly acquired Hacienda de Terrenates in 1927, only to be appointed governor when Caraveo joined the Escobaristas. He assumed Enríquez's mantle of unifier and organizer of agrarian and labor groups. But León had not been in Chihuahua in many years and had no popular base. Moreover, he had a more important role to play in Mexico City conciliating factions in the wake of the assassination of Obregón. He helped Calles found the PNR in 1929. With his sights set on the national horizon, León was unable to tend closely to Chihuahua for any length of time.

None of Chihuahua's half-dozen governors from 1920 to 1929 served out their complete term. Enríquez came the closest, with three years and three weeks. There was no time to erect a substantial or lasting power base. Rodrigo Quevedo (1932–36) would be the first postrevolutionary governor to complete his term. Structurally, no leader emerged in the 1920s because the balance of Chihuahua political economy was too precarious. The competitors—various state factions and the national regime—were too evenly matched. The same struggles that dominated the 1920s continued into the next decade.

Municipal Politics

While rival revolutionary factions competed for power at the state level and the central government sought to extend its control over Chihuahua, the prerevolutionary municipal political bosses fought to retain their power. Through the 1920s several maintained their positions successfully. In isolated subregions in the western and southwestern parts of the state, the old elite dominated by virtue of its overwhelming economic power and geography. The Becerras of Urique continued to rule through mid-decade, strengthening their hold by marrying a daughter to Governor Almeida. The Rascóns of Uruachic, Rayón district, dominated local politics and economy into the 1930s. The Samaniegos, political bosses of Ciudad Juárez during the Díaz era and close allies of Terrazas, like the Becerras, extended their influence through marriage. No fewer than five postrevolutionary municipal presidents of Juárez were relations.[87]

Even in subregions where the revolution had begun or had drawn fervent backing, some of the old bosses stayed in power. In revolutionary hotbed Coyamé, the same family that held the post of municipal president in 1906–8 held it in 1929.[88] In Janos, the first pueblo to arise in 1910, essentially the same local power structure existed in the late 1920s as had in 1910. The same families (Rentería, Baeza, Echéribe) ran local politics, and the major hacendados (Baeza, Azcarate, Zozoya) kept their lands.[89] In fractionalized Guerrero district, another birthplace of the Revolution, the same families that had vied for local influence for a half-century—Casavantes, Rico, Dozal, Ordoñez, Domínguez, and Caraveo—continued to do so.[90]

The 1920s: An Assessment

To some extent, all Chihuahua reaped from a decade of civil war was another decade of turbulence. No individual, family, or party emerged from the wreckage to control state politics. No governor finished out his term, legislatures quarreled with governors, governors fought zone commanders and the courts. Even under the harsh direction of Calles, the central government was unable to bring order to the unruly state.

Beneath the disorder, however, crucial changes had begun. Political and economic power shifted decisively (even more dramatically than during the Porfiriato) toward the central core of the state and Ciudad Juárez. Ciudad Chihuahua, Ciudad Juárez, and Hidalgo de Parral came to dominate politics. The ruin of small operators concentrated mining in the central subregion from Santa Eulalia south to Parral. Juárez generated large amounts of money through gambling and liquor. There was also a generational shift. The original revolutionaries were dead, in exile, or retired. Of all Chihuahuan governors after 1920, only Ignacio C. Enríquez, Marcelo Caraveo, and Rodrigo M. Quevedo were significant military figures in the Revolution. The new leaders were less dedicated revolutionaries than "freebooters." Caraveo and Quevedo were brilliant opportunists. Last but not least, peasant and labor organizations emerged as new bases of power. In their efforts to consolidate political control, Enríquez and Obregón had started to tap them. Almeida had, to his detriment, ignored them. León brought them into a structured organization.

The Chihuahuan case points us to several conclusions about the character of Mexican politics during the 1920s. The central government had not consolidated its control over the states. Politics in Chihuahua, as in most states, were fragmented and tumultuous. One state, Nayarit, had five governors in 1925 alone. The national regime was often able to topple an unacceptable leader or group, but just as often it was unable to sustain its allies. Obregón and Calles compromised with state bosses, because when confronted with three major rebellions (de la Huerta, Cristero, and Escobar) in ten years, they desperately needed military allies. In addition, bitter conflict made coercive power paramount. It was no accident that governors Enríquez and Almeida arose from the *defensas sociales* and that Caraveo was the military-zone commander. It is also evident that the revolutionary principles of land reform and labor rights frequently gave way to expediency. Because of adverse economic conditions, political instability, lack of centralized control in the states by the federal government or in the municipalities by the state government, and unwillingness on the part of the new leadership to jeopardize their newly acquired property, reform did not proceed at a rapid pace except when a military threat made it politically advantageous.

New leaders, many of whom had come late to the Revolution, saw politics as an opportunity for self-enrichment. As landowners and industrialists, they worked against reform. Their growing alienation from peasants and workers contributed to the conflict and instability. The slowness of reform was especially evident on the municipal level, where the old bosses often retained control.

The death of Obregón, the defeat of the Escobar rebellion, the onset of the Great Depression, and the formation of the Partido Nacional Revolucionario in 1928 and 1929 heralded a new era in Mexican and Chihuahuan politics. The national revolutionary elite concluded that the violence must end. Regionalism and personalism would have to give way to a strong national state to enable the nation to develop economically. The next decade would establish arrangements to resolve the bitter conflicts between national and state elites, state and municipal elites, and elites and popular class organizations. Resolution of these sharp differences did not come easily. It would take all the combined skills of the Chihuahuan elite to bring about peace.

4 Chihuahua

during the

1930s

The Transition from Personalist to Party Rule

The major political processes of the decade, the establishment of the Partido Nacional Revolucionario (PNR), and the achievement of control over the states by the central government were uncertain and difficult. The assertion of hegemony on the part of the national regime prolonged the struggles among rival Chihuahuan factions to establish dominance, as well as the struggle for control between state factions and the national government that had dominated the previous decade. The chaos that reigned during the early 1930s reflected both the strength of Chihuahuan resistance and the weakness of the national government. During these years, no individual or group was able to establish both a firm relationship with Mexico City and a popular base in Chihuahua. Then, after mid-decade, a wary compromise emerged. Competing state factions thereafter would conduct their struggles within the PNR, later the Partido Revolucionario Mexicano (PRM). Local politics were to remain based to a large extent on personalist and family ties, but with limited independence.

Underlying the struggle at the state level was just as fierce a fight between an alliance of the prerevolutionary and revolutionary elite, on the one hand, and the popular classes, organized into peasant organizations and labor unions, on the other. Harnessing the popular classes became the crucial element in gaining political control of the state. It was through control over peasant and worker organizations that the national party finally exerted its hegemony in Chihuahua. The organized masses provided the crucial counterweight to the elite factions.

The 1930s were not merely a repetition of the previous decade. Because there were no major national rebellions and the organization of the PNR by Calles brought the state bosses under one roof, disruptions were less severe. The rift between Calles and Cárdenas, however, brought about a major realignment, which ended the temporary ascendancy of a conservative alliance between old and new regional elites and replaced it by an alliance of the national regime with state popular class organizations. Economic issues continued to revolve around the necessity for reconstruction. The recovery of the mid-1920s gave way to depression from 1929 to 1934. The downturn had a complex effect. On the one hand, it probably weakened the financial condition of some elites, and it certainly increased the desperation of campesinos and workers. On the other hand, it may have lessened the vulnerability of other elites, whose capital and expertise were even more badly needed for reconstruction, and provided political space for their survival.

The Camarazo of 1930

The decade began with an attempted *camarazo,* or coup. On June 25, 1930, discontented members of the Chihuahuan legislature, led by Manuel Jesús Estrada and Manuel Prieto, overthrew provisional governor Francisco R. Almada.[1] The Prietistas took over the government palace in the state capital, Ciudad Chihuahua, in a two-hour gun battle that killed one legislator and the chief of police. A company of federal troops finally surrounded the palace and restored order. A reconstructed legislature then impeached Almada, charging him with violating the rules of impartial conduct in the current gubernatorial election campaign, and replaced him with Estrada. The plotters enjoyed the connivance of the commander of the Fifth Military Zone (Chihuahua), General Eulogio Ortiz (in violation of his prior agreement not to involve himself in politics).[2] General Ortiz arrested more than seventy state officials. The national government of President Pascual Ortiz Rubio, after frantic negotiations, refused to recognize the coup and reinstalled Almada on June 27.[3] Although Estrada and his followers surrendered peacefully, the situation remained extremely tense. Almada and fourteen deputies slept in the government palace overnight on June 28, fearing that if they left, they would not be allowed to return.[4] The *El Paso Times* reported that many Chihuahuans were armed and that several hundred agrarians in outlying districts were "all ready for trouble."[5]

The two factions presented their cases to the authorities in Mexico City in the following days. Eventually, on July 10, the government sided with Almada.[6] Four days later, Almada resigned, replaced by Ing. Romulo Escobar.[7]

The Economy

The governors of the first half of the decade were all badly hampered by the economic depression, which reached its nadir in the years 1930 through 1932. The crash of the market for minerals caused widespread unemployment in the state. The number of unemployed in 1930 was 4,299, jumping to 6,140 in 1931, and exploding to an average of 11,211 a month in 1932. At the end of 1932 the number of persons out of work in the state was nearly 20,000.[8] The crops of 1929 and 1930 were bad; corn and bean prices doubled in 1930.[9] As the crisis worsened, the larger mining companies that remained in operation cut hours and wages.[10] There were some reports of starvation.[11] State revenues fell sharply in the deepening economic crisis. Governor Fierro had to cut the salaries of state employees 10–20 percent in 1932. There were also a large number of unemployed, repatriated workers from the United States.[12] Rodrigo Quevedo confronted a crisis in the cattle industry, which had been showing signs of recovery. High U.S. tariffs and Mexican freight charges squeezed livestock raisers.[13] There was drought in some northern cattle districts from 1932 through 1935 that caused heavy losses of livestock.[14]

The Politics of Chaos, 1930–32

Burdened with his new duties as secretary of industry, commerce, and labor in the national cabinet, León could not rule Chihuahua from long distance. To make matters worse, the new zone commander, General Eulogio Ortiz, openly opposed him.[15] Moreover, León, whose political base was among the *agraristas* to whom he had redistributed land while governor, was confronted with a new organization of landowners mobilizing to fight that very redistribution.[16] The state PNR split into rival factions: one, following Ing. Andrés Ortiz, the official candidate to fill out Caraveo's term, and León; and the other, following Eulogio Ortiz and Manuel Prieto. It was at this point that the latter group staged its *camarazo*.

The fact that the coup took place indicates that the national government did not have control of Chihuahua. It also points again to the considerable power of the conservative alliance of old and new elites. Prieto was a member of an old landowning family with intimate connections with the Porfirian oligarchy. Estrada was one of the new freebooters. The two men and their *camarilla* tried to take advantage of the weakness of the national regime, preoccupied with internal intrigues, and its Chihuahua link, Luis L. León. León simply was not strong enough in the state to dominate without assistance from Mexico City. But by the mid-1930s his base there was shaky.

The coup was also the result of a struggle for land. The big landowners, old and new, tried to eliminate León and Almada, for they had resumed the redistribution of land to agrarians. In this, León followed the pattern of other state political leaders like Adalberto Tejeda, who constructed an electoral base among the peasants in Veracruz.[17] When León began to arm the agrarians, this was the last straw for the hacendados.

The spring of 1930 brought a wave of land invasions by agrarians that authorities did not resist. The government made a large number of restitutions and grants in the first three months of the year.[18] At the same time, the Caja de Préstamos agreed to set aside 85,000 hectares of the former Terrazas estates to satisfy claims against them by ejidos.[19]

The central government was growing uneasy about the armed agrarians. The president of the *comité ejidatario* of Valle de Juárez declared that the local military-zone commander was trying "to provoke armed conflict, when all we want to do is plant our fields."[20] Another agrarian leader accused the new zone commander of "arming our enemies."[21] The landowners increasingly resisted reform, organizing *defensas sociales* into private armies to defend their haciendas.[22] Andrés Ortiz reflected the situation in his campaign for governor, promising both to carry on León's land reform and to furnish the cattle ranches with guards.[23] Ortiz tried to please both sides, but ultimately failed.

Luis L. León had no real independent power base, relying on his wits to stay on the winning side. In the twists and turns of the *maximato* (1928–34), he was inevitably to fall. Both as an hacendado who spouted radical rhetoric and organized peasants and in his efforts to blend appeal to the popular classes with advocacy of capitalist development, León previewed the eventual political compromise reached in Chihuahua by 1940. His policies were meant to establish popular support while at the same time offering an olive branch to the rich, whose entrepreneurial skills were badly needed by the revolutionary government.[24] Perhaps taking his lead from Ignacio C. Enríquez, the last Chihuahuan politician to organize both campesinos and workers, León formed the Liga de Campesinos y Obreros de Chihuahua.[25] His attempts to organize the popular classes and use them to offset his opposition failed, however, because he lost his backing in Mexico City. The fledgling peasant and worker organization was no match for the coalition of old elite and conservative "revolutionaries." It was not to be until later in the decade that Teófilo Borunda and others would harness the peasant movement into the PRM, while at the same time satisfying the requirements of the landowners.

Soon after Andrés Ortiz took office as governor in September 1930, he and León disagreed over the issues of land reform and disarming the *agraristas*.[26] León, in the meantime, had left the national cabinet, because he had allied with the losing side in the confrontation between Calles and President Emilio Portes Gil (the result of which led the latter to resign), and León retired to his Chihuahuan hacienda.[27] By this time his popularity at home had eroded as well. In December 1930 he was booed from a speakers' platform.[28] By the end of 1930, *El Correo de Chihuahua* referred to León as a "political cadaver" and "a man of water," who had "badly served the Chihuahuan public."[29]

Ortiz was caught in the middle between León and his agrarians and the federal government, which wanted to disarm them.[30] The agrarians resisted violently.[31] The León-Ortiz split provided an opportunity for the opponents of land reform led by a newcomer to Chihuahuan politics, General Rodrigo Quevedo, who clamored for

Ortiz's removal.[32] By fall 1931 Ortiz had nowhere to turn. His support among the cabinet in Mexico City evaporated when his main backers were forced out.[33] Finally Quevedo, on Calles's orders, went before the Chihuahuan legislature on October 30 to demand Ortiz's resignation; the governor left office three days later.[34]

The accusations against Ortiz were summarized by opponent Simon Puentes in a long letter to Calles in August 1931. They denote the treacherous waters of Chihuahuan politics. Ortiz, claimed Puentes, "was not in step with the revolution." An ardent Catholic and a sympathizer of the Knights of Columbus, he had allowed the church to function illegally. The governor allegedly had blocked land reform; in one specific instance he prevented the grant of land from the Zuloaga estate to petitioning peasants. Ortiz also was accused of using his office to enrich himself, obtaining rights to the stockyards in various cities and a monopoly of bus services. There was great suspicion that he had ordered the murders of agrarian leader Juan Mendoza and others. And he purportedly had used local authorities to break a strike at Santa Eulalia and had undermined the *Junta de Conciliación y Arbitraje*.[35] Ortiz clearly had satisfied no one, for he was not radical enough for the agrarians and unions and not strong enough for the Callistas.

His replacement, Colonel Roberto Fierro, one of Mexico's pioneer military pilots, a native *chihuahuense* and Leonista, was a political novice.[36] The famed aviator lasted only nine months. The state legislature impeached him in early July 1932, claiming that he had misappropriated funds and accepted bribes.[37] A deputy in the legislature, Eduardo Salido, was chosen as interim governor.

From the beginning, Fierro faced an impossible situation. The central government had evidently thrown him into the political fray in order to temporize while the Quevedos established themselves. He encountered "a series of created interests and private combinations [that] terribly prejudiced . . . the state."[38] Fierro's program of agrarian reform and his handling of gambling in Ciudad Juárez alienated powerful interests led by Rodrigo Quevedo.[39] His land reform centered on a plan to persuade landowners to give part of their lands to the state for use by agrarians.[40] The hacendados, Quevedo among them, resisted strenuously. Fierro's meddling in Ciudad Juárez gambling brought him up against the Quevedos again. Gambling revenues were financing their political rise, and they protected their interests fiercely.

Fierro tried to bring Chihuahua under control of the national government. He proposed immediately that the municipal guards be transferred to the jurisdiction of the federal chief of military operations (zone commander). Ostensibly this was to save the state the enormous expense of maintaining the guards, but it was more likely a more efficient way of neutralizing them.[41] Bringing the *guardias* under control was not meant as a move solely against agrarians, for large landowners employed the guards as private gangsters to protect their properties. The *guardias municipales* seemed to act both as radicals and counterrevolutionaries, depending on local conditions. Disarmament, then, was an effort to limit the power of both the Chihuahuan elite and the agrarians. Fierro also proposed the merger of the state committee of the PNR with the Partido Revolucionario Chihuahuense. This, too, was an effort to rein in the Chihuahuans. The state party had adamantly refused to cooperate wholeheartedly with the PNR and was not adverse to putting up opposing nominees for elections. But Fierro was only a temporary stand-in while Rodrigo Quevedo and his family established themselves as the force to be reckoned with.

The Rise of the Quevedos

The Quevedos used support from Mexico City, revenues from gambling, bootlegging, and other (allegedly) illegal activities, the backing of some labor unions, their large family, and ruthless ambition to rise to power.[42] In July 1932, Rodrigo Quevedo defeated Fernando Orozco, one of the principal plotters with Caraveo against the Almeidas and later against Ortiz, in the gubernatorial election. He served out his full four-year term, the first governor to accomplish this since the turn of the century. At the national level, Quevedo, a founding member of the so-called Revolutionary Family, had excellent connections to Calles and the national PNR. In Chihuahua, he had a family base in the western sierras and an important political base in Ciudad Juárez.

Rodrigo Quevedo began his term with considerable backing in

the countryside as well.[43] It is not clear, however, whether this meant that he had the support of agrarians or of local political bosses. In the first year of his term the governor made an effort to solicit rural backing; he distributed seeds, horses, and equipment.[44] He also enjoyed labor-union support, primarily in Ciudad Juárez.

For the most part, however, Quevedo substituted patronage for popular support, a program financed by an infusion of federal funds and by gambling revenues (until 1934). Patronage consisted of public works projects. Quevedo awarded large contracts for paving the streets of the state capital and for the Chihuahua-to-Ciudad Juárez highway.[45] He also initiated projects for potable water in Ciudad Chihuahua and Ciudad Juárez, for drainage in the Valle de Juárez, and to buy and plant trees on ejidos.[46]

As governor, Quevedo instituted a major change in the fiscal relationship between the state and federal governments. He obtained recognition from the federal government of a debt of 900,000 pesos for the state's share of tax revenues, to be paid back gradually and employed to pay for public works.[47] This most likely gave the national regime more political leverage with the power of the purse strings and eroded Chihuahuan autonomy.

The Quevedos' ascendance coincided with a resurgence of gambling as the major source of funds for Chihuahuan politics.[48] The treasurer-general of Chihuahua reported in 1932 that gambling provided 700,000 pesos for the state in 1931, almost 70 percent of all its revenues; taxes from the state's leading industry, mining, came to only 200,000 pesos that year.[49] Gambling accounted for 58,000 pesos a month in revenue to the state.

The murder of Enrique Fernández, the reputed boss of the Ciudad Juárez underworld, on the street in Mexico City on January 13, 1934, underlines both the importance of gambling in state politics and the ruthlessness of the Quevedos.[50] Fernández was, at the time, in a desperate struggle with the Quevedo clan for control of gambling in Ciudad Juárez and, indirectly, politics in Chihuahua.

The story began three years earlier, when Sonoran businessman Manuel Llantada, a front for Baja California and Mexico City gamblers, acquired a concession from the state of Chihuahua to reopen the Tivoli casino in Ciudad Juárez. The local manager, Fernández, had important ties to Luis L. León, and through León to Plutarco

Elías Calles. After his quarrel with León, Governor Andrés Ortiz pushed out Fernández and entered into partnership with Llantada. In late 1931, Governor Roberto Fierro granted a new concession to Fernández. Llantada used his influence to get the federal government to intervene to close the casino, but Fernández won this round and renewed operations. Llantada, though, entered into partnership with the newly elected (July 1932) governor of Chihuahua, Rodrigo Quevedo, and his brother Jesús, the mayor of Ciudad Juárez. State authorities closed down Fernández's casino, while Llantada reopened. For the rival factions led by Luis L. León and Rodrigo Quevedo control of gambling revenues meant nothing less than control of Chihuahuan politics. In early December 1933, assassins wounded Fernández outside a store he owned in Ciudad Juárez. He was determined to expose the criminal activities of the Quevedos in narcotic and whiskey smuggling as well as gambling. To accomplish this, the gangster went to Mexico City in January 1934, where he was murdered before he could talk.[51]

Perhaps in no other area was the interplay of local factional disputes and the relationship between state and national governments so clear. Gambling revenues meant autonomy for local and state authorities or control for the federal government. If Mexico City could not get all the revenues, the least it could do was to deny it to the state and municipality.

Ironically, the scandal surrounding Fernández's assassination ended legalized gambling in Ciudad Juárez. President Lázaro Cárdenas closed all such enterprises in Mexico after he took office in 1934.[52] This was Cárdenas's first important victory in curtailing Chihuahuan autonomy.

If public works and patronage together comprised one of the underpinnings of his administration, anticlericalism was another. Almost immediately, Quevedo "quietly and secretly" began to expel Catholic priests from the state. The state limited the number of clergy to one per hundred thousand people and ordered priests to cease all religious functions.[53] Catholic services resumed briefly in 1936 after a court order prevented the deportation of priests. Quevedo, however, retaliated, pushing the legislature to limit the number of clergy to one per religion.[54] Like Calles, Quevedo substituted rabid anticlericalism for other reforms.

The Fall of the Quevedos

As strong as Quevedo might at first have appeared, with his impeccable connections to the national regime and the enormous resources of his ubiquitous family, he faced continuous opposition. Public works patronage, in the midst of a depression, was not sufficient to silence the clamor for land redistribution and better wages and working conditions. His public works strategy put off some of his opposition for the first two years of his term.[55] There was an unsuccessful coup attempt in March 1934, headed by a group of dissident legislators and agrarian leaders, but Quevedo acted so quickly to prevent it that he could prove nothing against the conspirators and they evaded prosecution.[56]

The Quevedos were conservative capitalists (and as such reflected the Callista or *sonorense* view). As landowners, they opposed land reform. As capitalists, they were suspicious of labor unions. Consequently, agrarian and labor unions actively opposed them.[57] Agrarians complained bitterly of the stepped-up activities of the white guards during Quevedo's term.[58] Andrés Mendoza, president of the Liga de Comunidades Agrarias del Estado de Chihuahua, protested the intolerable situation for campesinos in the state and the "impositions and vexations" perpetrated by the Quevedos[59] The largest protest occurred in July 1935, when hundreds of agrarians demonstrated against the Quevedo administration, accusing the governor of being "incapable of governing the state . . . [and of] oppressing workers, [and practicing] great favoritism to capitalism."[60]

Quevedo seemed shaky in the summer of 1935, when he faced not only peasant protests, but also the split between Calles and the new president Lázaro Cárdenas. Quevedo remained noncommital until it appeared that Cárdenas would win and then jumped on the Cárdenas bandwagon.[61] The general apparently accomplished his switch of allegiances with some grace, for unlike another Callista state boss, Tomás Garrido Canabal of Tabasco, he was able to retain both the governorship and his influence after leaving office.[62] As his term came to a close, Quevedo confronted an opposition consisting of *agraristas,* labor unions, and the remnants of his political enemies like Fernando Orozco.[63] None of these groups, either alone or to-gether, was sufficiently powerful to overthrow him, however.

Rodrigo Quevedo, despite the support of his large family, his growing riches, the alliance of the old and new landowner class, and strong connections in Mexico City, was not destined to establish permanent control in Chihuahua. Cárdenas simply could not permit an independent, conservative political coalition between old and new elites to maintain power in Chihuahua.

The national regime took the opportunity presented by the pressing need to satisfy the demands of popular organizations for land redistribution and workers' rights to establish these organiza-tions as a counterweight to the conservative alliance. Neither the national government nor the national party nor local agrarian or labor groups individually were strong enough to take on the Quev-edos. But the various popular organizations clamored ever more forcefully. Quevedo resisted, but his successors, adapting to Car-denismo, were to capture the masses for the party, unable any longer to hold off reform.

The labor unions achieved their gains even before Quevedo left office. Since his family's fortune was land-based and the most im-portant industry, mining, was mostly foreign-owned, he was more likely to make concessions. The U.S. consul maintained in late 1935 that "native leaders in this district are becoming all powerful through their labor syndicates. . . . The time is nearly at hand when either control of the profits of the business of mining com-panies must be given to labor or the plants shut down. . . ."[64]

When Rodrigo Quevedo left office in 1936, there was "jubila-tion, immense rejoicing, because at last members of the 'sinister' Quevedo clan will cease to oppress and exploit the state."[65] One critic complained to President Cárdenas that the Quevedos were "killers and thieves."[66]

As he had in the cases of other state bosses, Cárdenas moved carefully in Chihuahua in order to allow mass organizations to gain strength. They were to prove the foundation of the next two state administrations.

Gustavo L. Talamantes

Ing. Gustavo L. Talamantes succeeded Quevedo. His nomination was evidence that the unions and peasant organizations had reached a high degree of influence. Quevedo and the PNR in Chihuahua initially favored the candidacy of General Lorenzo Muñoz Merino, who had been the chief of staff of the Mexican army. Although Muñoz Merino was closer to Quevedo in his conservative outlook, in practical terms the opposition to his candidacy by campesino and labor groups probably pressured the party to select Talamantes.[67] If Quevedo thought Talamantes would continue his conservative policies or act as his agent, his mistake soon became apparent.

The old and new governors quickly were at odds. Talamantes provoked a major confrontation when he ousted José Quevedo as *presidente municipal* of Ciudad Juárez in April 1937. But in order to take control of the crucial border city, he required the assistance of federal troops.[68] Talamantes also went after the Quevedos' gambling empire. Cárdenas appears to have been unwilling to back either side to the hilt, preferring to keep them warring. As a result, the PNR accepted all of the Quevedo slate in the May 1937 elections, including Guillermo Quevedo who stood for federal deputy. (He won.)[69] Talamantes, however, held on to Ciudad Juárez, when his new ally, former Quevedista José Borunda E., won the election for municipal president in July 1937.[70]

The Quevedos fought back. On March 12, Rodrigo, his brother José, and three companions encountered two virulent political opponents, federal senator Angel Posada and Narciso Talamantes, brother of the current governor, on the street in Ciudad Chihuahua. In the shooting that followed, General Quevedo killed Posada.[71] Less than three weeks later, on April 1, another ally, the mayor of Ciudad Juárez, José Borunda, was blown up by a mail bomb in his office. There were more shootings in the following weeks. Again, the Cárdenas administration refused overtly to take sides in order to maintain a delicate balance of power.

In the face of Quevedo's opposition, Talamantes ruled with the support of the state's labor unions.[72] The governor consistently took the side of labor in disputes with employers. He raised the salaries of schoolteachers and public employees.[73] Of the two popular movements, agrarian and labor, the latter had the best chance of obtaining its demands—first, because the mining industry was recovering, and second, because it was controlled by foreign companies, notably ASARCO. Foreign-owned extractive companies would, of course, in the wake of the oil expropriation, become excellent targets.[74] Mining had begun to emerge from the depression. With increased employment and profits there was more to give workers without resistance from the large companies.[75] Talamantes's relations with labor were helped by a considerable improvement in their plight after 1935. The recovery of mineral prices in 1935 resulted in a 75–100 percent increase in wages.[76] He also presided over the second of two major revisions to the state labor law during the decade, in May 1937. (The first was in March 1932.)[77] Provisions included the mandatory construction of homes, operation of schools, and provision of medical care for workers of large firms.[78]

The power of the unions also reflected their growing membership. All industries of over twenty employees had a union.[79] By 1939, the U.S. consul reported more than twenty thousand unionized workers in Chihuahua, most of them miners.[80]

There were major efforts on the part of popular organizations in 1936 to cooperate among themselves, but this was not entirely successful, because the labor unions in Chihuahua were divided in their loyalties between the Confederación Regional de Obreros Mexicanos (CROM) and the Confederación de Trabajadores Mexicanos (CTM). Their failure to consolidate probably resulted from their resistance to central control. The divisions among the unions did not seem to impede labor reform to the extent that they obstructed agrarian reform.[81]

Talamantes's record on agrarian reform was not as clear, for it reflected the more complex situation in the countryside, where he faced not only a resurgent group of large landowners but divisions among campesinos. Nonetheless, he resolved hundreds of cases of land *restituciónes* and *dotaciónes* for ejidos. The U.S. consul in Ciudad Chihuahua summed up the change in the political balance under Talamantes (and Cárdenas):

> Local unions in combination with more or less loosely organized campesinos (small farmers) have become politically powerful in the

state of Chihuahua. An aspirant to state office solicits their support by word and deed (expenditure of money) and any intimation, true or false, that may show the politician to hold views lukewarm to labor and labor interests, will injure or even destroy his chances politically. The present Governor of Chihuahua, Gustavo L. Talamantes, is just now continuing to hold office, despite alienation of powerful political interests here, by catering to the demands of laborers and agrarians as against entrepreneurs and capital interests.[82]

That Talamantes was willing to confront even the most powerful on behalf of land reform was indicated by the fact that in 1938 the state agrarian commission ordered the return to an ejido of an hacienda owned by the Quevedos.[83]

But under Talamantes land reform had political limitations. Justino Loya, the general secretary of the Liga de Comunidades Agrarias del Estado de Chihuahua, saw little progress after eighteen months of Talamantes's term. The promised rural schools and improved roads were not forthcoming. Far worse, the land distributed to ejidos was "of the worst quality."[84] He claimed that the latifundists kept their best lands. Moreover, administration of the land reform was in the hands of the most extreme reactionaries. Evidently, Talamantes at some point recognized the political and economic power of the landowners.

The governor, perhaps because of pressure from large landowning interests (both pre- and postrevolutionary) or because he attempted to rein in the independent popular organizations, encountered tremendous opposition from agrarian groups. One critic called him "a little dictator who took over the powers of the legislature and judiciary" and characterized his administration as "disastrous and criminal." A letter from the *mesa directiva* of the Liga de Comunidades Agrarias del Estado de Chihuahua in March 1938 reflected its disillusionment. It had supported the candidacy and election of Talamantes with "all moral force" and "ardor and faith." But although Talamantes had offered great promises a year and a half ago, he had fulfilled none.

The bill of particulars for his "odious administration" was long. First and foremost, he allegedly ordered the murder and imprisonment of several important agrarian leaders. Other agrarian leaders were said also to be in jeopardy of their lives. Campesinos in Casas Grandes, Parral, San Francisco del Oro, Santa Bárbara, and Juárez were killed by the special police and white guards. Despite his earlier reform efforts, critics claimed that Talamantes favored latifundists in the majority of his decisions. Moreover, the land grants he approved were for great extensions of parched, uncultivable land. Latifundists kept the best land upon which to raise cattle. Supposedly, he also employed reactionaries in his administration like Francisco Chávez Holguín, Angel Martínez, Alfonso Talamantes, and Demetrio Ponce, all of whom held high posts. He reduced the autonomy of municipalities, overthrowing all the *ayuntamientos* that had campesinos and workers as members: Cusihuiriachic, Casas Grandes, Ciudad Delicias, Valle de Zaragoza, and Cuauhtémoc.[85] There was not one agrarian deputy, *presidente municipal,* or high-echelon administrator in state government. As if to prove it all, when campesinos offered a precandidate for the legislature from the third district, comprised almost entirely of ejido members, Talamantes instead offered a candidate thoroughly unfamiliar with the region, who was a Knight of Columbus and from Mexico City. In the ninth district campesinos put forth their own candidate, but Talamantes countered with his relative, Santos M. Ponce, who exerted "brutal pressure" on local authorities to assure his success. In the eleventh district, when a former official of the Balleza Liga, a candidate supported by all the local agrarian groups, was put forth, Talamantes immediately countered with a bureaucrat without local connections and knowledge. Finally, in the fifth district Narciso Talamantes, the governor's brother, a known enemy of workers and campesinos, was the official candidate. Widespread fraud prevailed in the municipalities. "Los caciquillos," it was charged, returned to enthrone themselves as in the days of the Porfiriato.[86]

From the documents available it is not entirely clear what was happening. Talamantes had served as president of the state agrarian commission from 1920 to 1924 under Governor Enríquez. He had thus supervised one of the most extensive land reforms in state history. Yet it was the agrarian groups that protested the most loudly against him in 1937 and 1938. It might have been a problem of unachieved high expectations. More likely were two other possibilities. Talamantes may have been under orders to curtail the political independence of the agrarians at both the state and local levels. Governor Ortiz in 1931 had endured sharp criticism from agrarian groups because he had tried to limit their independence by disarming them. Talamantes also faced stronger, more organized opposition from landholders. After 1937 the national government became favorably disposed toward the cattle barons, apparently with the idea that livestock raising was in need of protection and nurture, which gave added weight to the landowners' position. A presidential decree amended the agrarian code so that those lands necessary for livestock enterprises would not be subject to dotation for twenty-five years. To be eligible for "unaffectability" a property had to have five hundred head or three hundred milk cows, or the equivalent in sheep or goats. The maximum that could be free from dotation was fifty thousand hectares.[87] It is very probable that a number of powerful landowning generals influenced the president to rescue the cattlemen.

Another possibility is that Talamantes had to deal with a split in agrarian ranks between the older recipients of land redistribution, who were mostly smallholders, and latecomers, who made up ejidos, whose demands encroached on the earlier group's holdings. If Talamantes sided with the latter, it might account for the bitterness of the criticism. Some of the worst violence in the countryside was not latifundists against peasants but peasant pitted against peasant.

Although to a more limited extent, Talamantes, like Quevedo, sought to establish a dynasty; he attempted to install family members in important posts around the state. His brother Narciso was elected mayor of Hidalgo de Parral from 1940 to 1941.[88] Brother-in-law Demetrio Ponce was the tax collector of Parral and ran unsuccessfully against Teófilo Borunda for the mayoralty of Ciudad Juárez in 1939.[89]

By the end of the decade the alliance of old and new elites reached a stalemate with the popular organizations. Alfredo Chávez, a former tax collector and legislator, was elected governor in 1940. Chávez, "a member of a pioneer Chihuahua family," received strong support from the CTM.[90] The new governor, a rancher and member of an old-line family, a career politician with popular support, represented the final Chihuahuan revolutionary arrangement. But relative peace did not mean a lack of violence or political machinations. Chávez, a henchman of Talamantes, had done a lot of the dirty work against agrarians. He stood as the candidate of the local PRM, while the national PRM put up Fernando Foglio, who was also backed by the Quevedos.[91] Foglio would win the governorship four years later.

Conclusion

By 1940 the worst of the Chihuahuan political wars had ended. They yielded a compromise that had begun with Luis León's attempts to organize and incorporate the popular classes into an alliance with the national revolutionary party and coalesced in the successful candidacy of Alfredo Chávez for governor.

The ultimate compromise required the elimination of autonomous political leadership. Thus, only one major leader from the 1920s, Luis León, continued to contend for power in the 1930s. But León had come on the Chihuahuan scene only in 1929 and, moreover, had close ties to Plutarco Elías Calles. Other Chihuahuan leaders of the 1920s, such as Andrés Ortiz, Fernando Orozco, and Manuel Prieto, were too independent to obtain backing from Mexico City.

The major political contenders—Luis León, Rodrigo Quevedo, and Gustavo Talamantes—represented the different stages that Chihuahua went through in reaching the final political compromise. León introduced the national revolutionary party into Chihuahua and initiated the incorporation of labor and campesino organizations into it. He moved too quickly for the Callista national regime, because Calles sought primarily to strengthen the loose coalition of regional caudillos, not the influence of the popular classes. Quevedo and his family were representative of the opportunists who used the Revolution to make their fortunes and sought in the 1930s to protect their gains. They allied with members of the surviving, prerevolutionary landowning elite against populist reforms. It was left to Talamantes to incorporate workers and campesinos into the revolutionary party. Under the leadership of the Borunda family after 1937, the PNR moved leftward, while at the same time taking steps to reassure large landowners.

The national regime by 1940 had tipped the balance of power in its favor. Land and labor reform had weakened both old and new elite in Chihuahua just enough for the PRM coalition with its strong national ties to establish firm control. Personalism was not dead but, rather, subsumed in the party. Families and *camarillas* continued to play crucial roles but, again, within the limits of the party.

The political economy of the decade presented the same dilemma for the revolutionary elite as it had during the 1920s. Chihuahuan leaders had to balance the needs of recovery from economic depression with the demands for reform from the popular classes. But the political terrain was altered. The national government, bolstered by the PNR, strengthened itself as the decade progressed. Campesino and labor organizations proliferated and grew stronger. They looked increasingly to the national government rather than regional leaders for support in obtaining their demands. The forces that opposed the national party and popular class organizations also grew stronger. Important families like the Almeidas and Quevedos developed economic interests that closely coincided with those of the Porfirian elite. Old and new elite joined in opposition to land reform.

To complicate politics further, popular organizations were divided. In the first rounds of land redistribution in the early 1920s, many rural people were ineligible to participate. (Resident peons on the haciendas were the most important sector thus excluded.) Once the franchise was widened, newcomers sometimes sought land already given to the earlier agrarians.[92] This created bitter conflicts. The labor movement was also split between the CTM and the CROM.

Unanswered questions about Chihuahuan and Mexican politics during the 1930s abound. We need to know more about the formation of peasant leagues and labor unions: whether they were locally based, state based, or encouraged by the national regime; or whether they were initially independent and their leadership later coopted by Cárdenas. Many of the questions involve the surviving elements of the old oligarchy and the new postrevolutionary elite. It is to these elites that we turn in the next three chapters.

The Old Elite

One of the least studied and perhaps most intriguing aspects of the history of revolutions is the fate of the members of the elite of the old regime. Did the old elite or some portion of it survive the revolution? If so, which elements persisted and why? What strategies did the old elite use to defend and maintain itself? What were the relations between the old elite and the new, revolutionary elite? Did the revolutionaries accommodate the old elite, and why? And finally, what effect did the accommodation between old and new elites have on the course of the revolution?

Albert Saboul has noted for the French Revolution that it destroyed the "formerly dominant class, the landed aristocracy (though exactly to what extent is open to question)," by eliminating the bases of its power: feudal rights, tithes, and access to national lands. Yet he also observes that a "great many nobles lived through the revolution without coming to much harm and kept their property intact. . . ." Saboul goes on to argue that even those elements of the landed aristocracy who persisted transformed their economic organization to meet the challenges of bourgeois capitalism.[1] In his study of the old regime in Europe after the French Revolution, Arno Mayer warns that "There has been . . . a marked tendency to neglect or underplay, and to disvalue, the endurance of old forces . . . and their cunning genius for assimilating, delaying, and neutralizing, and subduing capitalist modernization. . . . The Forces of the old order were still sufficiently willful to resist and slow down the course of history, if necessary by recourse to violence."[2] In both these views of the French Revolution there are lessons for historians of the Mexican Revolution, for they point out both interesting parallels and the complexity of the phenomenon of old elite survival.

There is some considerable difference of opinion about the extent to which the Porfirian elite survived the Mexican upheaval. One view holds that the Revolution gradually eliminated the landowning oligarchy from 1920 to 1940 by redistributing its land.[3] A second view postulates that "the old Porfirian oligarchy had not disappeared physically, but a good part of its capital had been lost or taken outside the country; as a group it was divided and disarticulated by its political defeat and lack of power." The landholders "never recovered their power, and little by little, they negotiated their subordination to the state in return for economic gains and sinecures."[4] A third view ranks the old elite as one of the "three distinct groups" that vied for power after the Revolution.[5] While at first glance these appear to be widely disparate interpretations, they are, in fact, only differing perspectives on the same complex process, which—and this is crucial to understanding the aftermath of the Mexican Revolution—varied according to time and region.

Consideration of various regional case studies permits us to construct some order out of these conflicting interpretations. It will become clear from a review of these that a significant element of the old elite did survive the Revolution. The pertinent questions, therefore, will concern not whether the old elite persisted, but who, how, why, and to what effect. A study of Chihuahua from 1920 to 1940 will point to answers to these inquiries.

A Comparative Overview

Recent investigations of Aguascalientes, Guerrero, Hidalgo, Michoacán, Morelos, Nuevo León, Puebla, San Luis Potosí, and Yucatán that study all or part of the period from 1920 to 1940 enable us to construct a model of old elite survival.[6] It is possible to posit both a typology and a chronological pattern of old elite persistence.

We can classify the members of the old elite according to their economic bases. The more diverse their economic holdings, the more likely they were to endure the Revolution; the more dependent on landholding, the more vulnerable the elite over time. Thus, Arturo Warman found in Morelos that the "old, dominant class, above all the narrow group in which the Porfirian hacendados dominated, had not been liquidated, but they had lost their strength. . . . They were a defeated group.''[7] This group, however, fought hard, and at times successfully, to retain its properties. In areas such as Veracruz the hacendados maintained the upper hand well into the Cárdenas era.[8] On the other end of the continuum were the Monterrey elite. Its members had never relied on landholding as their base. They were, both before and after the Revolution, the most important industrialists in Mexico. It was thus no accident that the Monterrey elite emerged in the late 1920s and 1930s as the strongest foes of the revolutionary regime, defying even Lázaro Cárdenas.[9] The old landed elite of the Huasteca region, enriched by oil royalties, held the Revolution at bay in open rebellion, led by Manuel Pelaez, until 1920.[10] The smartest, most capable of the old elite changed with the times, diversifying their economic assets.

We can also construct a general chronological pattern for the plight of the old elite. From 1910 to 1913 they were virtually untouched. The government of Francisco I. Madero sought no percipitous change in the countryside.[11] Many hacendados abandoned their property from 1914 to 1917, some as the victims of revolutionary expropriations, but primarily because of adverse economic conditions during the upheaval's most violent period. In these circumstances the landowner either turned the property over to an administrator or rented it out. A few of the landed elite had commercial or financial interests in the larger cities or abroad, which they tended.[12] After 1917 Carranza encouraged many hacendados to return in an effort to increase food production and find political allies.[13] For the next decade, those of the old landed elite who remained battled the Revolution to a standstill. During the era, they found new allies among the revolutionaries, many of them generals who had themselves become hacendados.[14] They were strengthened by the continued and widespread economic and political crises that pushed aside reform in favor of expediency. In Veracruz in the early 1920s, for example, the old landlords joined with General Guadalupe Sánchez, the military-zone commander, to neutralize agrarian reform.[15] The landlords, using local political bosses and militia, suppressed agrarian reform in Naranja, Michoacán, through the end of the decade.[16] Yucatecan landed elite joined the de la Huerta rebellion in 1923 and ousted radical Felipe Carrillo Puerto.[17] The old elite suffered at the hands of the federal government when, during major revolts—de la

Huerta, 1923–24, Cristero, 1926–29, and Escobar, 1929—agrarian reform became a condition of the latter's survival. Land reform was the price the regime had to pay for the military support of the rural population. The depression years from 1929 to 1934 eroded the power of the old elite because they could not operate profitably. Moreover, although there was no notable sympathy for agrarian reform during the presidencies of Pascual Ortiz Rubio and Abelardo Rodríguez, during the early 1930s campesino and labor organizations sprung up in many areas that demanded agrarian reform and were willing to fight for it. Ultimately, the old landed elite was nearly dealt a death blow with the massive reform administered by Cárdenas. Even then, however, a strong segment remained.

Each element of the old elite, to whichever era it lasted, survived through a combination of the weakness of the revolutionary regime at all political levels (local, state, and national), the growing compatibility of economic and political interests with the emerging new elite, and the considerable skills and sound strategies of its own members.

The decade of civil war and foreign invasion had left Mexico in ruins. Not only had a million people perished, but the nation's communications, commerce, and transportation were nearly destroyed. The most pressing matter for the triumphant northerners, led by President Alvaro Obregón, was to consolidate their political power. As Linda Hall has amply demonstrated, land reform, the crucial threat to the old elite, was strictly a means to this end.[18] The Revolution had by no means won a full victory even by the end of the 1920s. The northerners needed political allies on the local and state levels. They were more than willing to work with local bosses, some of whom were left over from the Díaz era, in order to consolidate their power. This was true of even the most radical revolutionaries, like Felipe Carrillo Puerto in Yucatán.[19]

Ideologically the victors were more compatible with the old elite than with the agrarians or workers. For the most part, they were capitalists with a firm belief in private property. They had participated in the Revolution in order to obtain their fair share of the spoils of economic development and politics. New and old elite would prove useful allies in preserving and protecting their respective property and privilege.

In the prevalent unstable economic and political situation, the old elite resisted the radical aspects of the Revolution with every resource at its disposal and forced the revolutionaries to compromise. Members of the elite employed several strategies, including violence, legal maneuvering, fraud, cooptation, bribery, and exertion of pressure through interest-group associations.

Violence was endemic in the Mexican countryside throughout the period from 1920 to 1940. Landowners hired private armies, variously called *guardias blancas, guardias municipales,* militias, or *rurales,* which murdered agrarian leaders and terrorized rural populations. In Veracruz, General Guadalupe Sánchez armed these irregulars, financed by the landowners.[20] The governor of Guanajuato used the state militia in 1926 to kill peasants who had the affrontery to ask for higher wages.[21] In Michoacán, hacendados used the militias to intimidate and suppress "incipient local reforms."[22] Mayhem was as often as not committed by or with the tacit agreement of local, state, or federal authorities. Federal troops were actually stationed on the Hacienda de Cantabria near Naranja, Michoacán.[23] Many state governors during the 1920s were notoriously opposed to agrarian reform. The Figueroas in Guerrero, for example, provided troops to protect landowners.[24]

The old elite also used the law—especially the new agrarian laws—to resist. Elite members fought expropriations in the courts; countless writs of *amparo* (injunctions) were obtained to forestall land takeovers by landless campesinos. In one district of Veracruz alone, from 1929 to 1931 twenty landowners got *amparos.* The elite cleverly divided its lands to fall within prescribed acreage limitations.[25] Pepe Landero, the owner of the Hacienda de Hueyapan, subdivided all his property in 1925 and 1926 among his sisters, nieces, and friends of the family, but continued to operate it as one unit.[26] At the same time, the proprietor of the Hacienda de la Primavera in Aguascalientes divided his lands similarly to avoid expropriation.[27]

Other landholders sold or leased their properties to avoid their loss. Porfirio Rubio, the longtime boss of Pisaflores, Hidalgo, for example, sold off his property to tenants or other farmers to sidestep the land reform.[28] Pepe Landero also sold off bits of his land to tenants.[29] Selling land to tenants or other smallholders in advance of the land reform was proven, successful strategy, for it created a vigorous group of opponents of future reforms. These small owners bitterly fought the agrarians to protect their own property.

According to Gilbert Joseph, Yucatán's old landed elite employed passive-aggressive resistance. They bribed local agrarian reform officials, laid off workers, paid workers in scrip, and removed fields from production and did not replant.[30]

Beginning in the late 1920s, the old elite, often allied with the new revolutionary hacendados, exerted pressure through various organized interest groups like the Chamber of Commerce, cattlemen's associations, and the Chamber of Mines. These organizations lobbied state and national governments to block detrimental legislation and adopt favorable measures. In addition, the old elite financed local and state political opposition to the revolutionary regime. Later the old elite would found the Partido Acción Nacional (PAN).

Chihuahua

Chihuahua presents an instructive case for studying the old elite's strategies for survival in revolutionary Mexico. Its Porfirian elite, headed by the Terrazas-Creel family, was one of the strongest and most homogeneous state elites in Mexico. The Mexican Revolution began in Chihuahua and won its first victories there. Some historians maintain that the first revolutionaries fought more against the Terrazas than against dictator Porfirio Díaz; perhaps more than any other group, this family symbolized the old order against which the revolutionaries stood. Revolutionary Chihuahuenses deeply resented the Terrazas. Moreover, one of the leading revolutionary leaders, Pancho Villa, waged nearly a decade-long campaign against them. If the family and its henchmen retained even a semblance of their old power, what conclusions can we draw about the Revolution?

Like the nineteenth-century conservatives who had collaborated with the French, the great Porfirian bosses and their families were now completely discredited politically. They could not hold public office, except on the local level, generally in isolated communities. This did not mean, however, that they lost all their influence. On the contrary, they exercised enormous economic power to assure them-selves of a say in public affairs. In many instances they formed alliances, often through marriages with members of the revolution-ary elite, which in the factionalized politics of Chihuahua could not be scornful of potential allies. Through much of the era, revolution-ary officials had to negotiate the best possible deal with entrenched local leaders and other repentant or unrepentant Porfiristas. This, of course, limited the possibilities for profound change on the state or local level.

The chaos of state politics and the depression of the economy created an environment well suited for the survival of major families of the Porfirian elite. The 1920s in Chihuahua were, in many re-spects, a throwback to the tumultuous days before the Porfiriato. State politics were torn by factionalism and rebellion. The state's proximity to the United States border made it a hotbed of conspira-tors of every persuasion. Villa's presence, until he was assassinated in 1923, made the region potentially even more explosive.[31] The old Porfirian elite, with their still substantial resources—capital, local political influence, family connections—took advantage of these conditions and the weakness of the revolutionary regime to survive and prosper.

The Terrazas-Creel Family

The history of the Terrazas-Creel family from 1910 to 1940 fits the general outline for the survival of the Porfirian elite and provides some instructive illustrations of elite strategies. While the Terrazas-Creels never regained their political omnipotence, they managed to reorganize and eventually expand their economic interests. Given the circumstances of the 1910 revolution in Chihuahua and the sub-sequent ten years spent as constant targets of the revolutionaries, theirs is a remarkable story.

The political and economic empire of the Terrazas-Creels was unparalleled in Porfirian Mexico. Family members or close allies filled nearly every important political office in state government. The Terrazas-Creels owned fifteen million acres of land in Chi-huahua, where the nation's leading cattle exporters controlled a nationwide banking enterprise with assets of 200 million pesos (1 peso = US 0.50 dollar), and owned innumerable mining, industrial, and commercial concerns. They had a stranglehold on crucial areas of the state's economy such as meat packing, flour milling, public utilities, and local transportation.[32]

As we saw in Chapter 2, the Terrazas used a wide range of strategies to maintain their empire during and after the Revolution. In its initial stages the Terrazas-Creels played a double game of conciliation and resistance, taking advantage of business and kinship ties with the Madero family while at the same time fighting the revolutionary governorship of Abraham González in Chihuahua and backing the rebellion of Pascual Orozco against Francisco Madero in 1912. The family later supported Huerta. Even the general's sons and grandsons actually fought against the Revolution. The experience of the Terrazas thus differed from elites elsewhere because they had to deal earlier with revolutionary reforms. Unlike most of their contemporaries, the Terrazas had to fight—and did—almost from the beginning of the Madero regime.

The revolution took a heavy toll on the Terrazas's economic empire. Villa expropriated the family's landholdings, banks, houses, mines, and personal effects in 1913.[33] The Constitutionalist government gutted the family's banking enterprise with forced loans and confiscations.[34]

The history of the Terrazas' landholdings illustrates much about the strategies employed by the old elite to maintain itself and also explains a great deal about how the revolutionary elite regarded the issues of property and the relations between old and new elites. The story of the Terrazas's lands, too, says much about the limits of the Revolution.

After Villa expropriated the family's land in 1913, the Villista governor of Chihuahua, Fidel Avila, distributed the land to the Division of the North and handed over the most prosperous Terrazas haciendas to Villista generals Máximo Márquez and Porfirio Ornelas. Other properties were administered by the Agencia de Confiscaciónes.[35] In an effort to avoid expropriation, the Terrazas sold the Hacienda La Cañada in 1913.[36] By 1919 the Terrazas haciendas were "completely abandoned, despoiled of all equipment and livestock."[37] That year General Terrazas nearly regained his estates, reaching agreement with the Carranza government, but the deal was never consummated, because the First Chief was overthrown before it could be implemented.[38] Carranza at that point was desperate for allies and looked to the Porfirian hacendados for backing.

Two years later, Luis Terrazas arranged to sell the preponderance of his landholdings to an American mining entrepreneur, Arthur J. McQuatters, who was to improve the land and then resell it in small parcels. Initially, both the state and the federal government enthusiastically welcomed the transaction. Governor Ignacio C. Enríquez, a close ally of President Obregón, signed the contract and defended it as beneficial to Chihuahua. Obregón wrote in December 1921 that he welcomed "the noble efforts which you and your group . . . are putting forth" and said that the government "proposes to impart the greatest facilities possible to you, offering its entire moral support and, besides, the most ample guarantees conceded by our laws."[39] McQuatters was to pay a peso per acre and made a down payment. The deal hit a snag when it was made contingent on the exemption of the Terrazas estate from the new agrarian law then pending in the state legislature.[40] At first, the legislature seemed willing to go along, but a growing number of deputies opposed selling to a foreigner, and soon the popular outcry against the sale forced its rejection.[41] Governor Enríquez campaigned hard both in Chihuahua and Mexico City for acceptance of the transaction.[42] In April 1922, Obregón ended the controversy by expropriating all of the Terrazas landholdings not then under cultivation.[43] Luis Terrazas then sued to prevent the expropriation.[44] In June a settlement was reached whereby Terrazas was to sell all his land, except Quinta Carolina, to the Caja de Préstamos at 1.25 pesos per acre for 5.5 million acres. McQuatters was to be reimbursed for his expenses plus 900,000 pesos. The government was to pay two million pesos in cash and the rest in guaranteed bonds. The total price was 13.5 million pesos.[45] The bonds were originally to be repaid over fifteen years at 5 percent interest by the Caja de Préstamos, but eventually the federal government had to incorporate it into the public debt because the Caja could not pay.[46] Despite protests that the deal was illegal and the Terrazas were overpaid, the affair was settled.[47]

The deal with McQuatters was a brilliant strategy because it

adjusted to the circumstances of national and state politics and economics. The estates had virtually no livestock left after years of
Villista plundering. Three years of drought had rendered much of
the semiarid pastureland worthless, especially since there was little
hope of restocking the range quickly. It would be decades before the
family would need this pasture again. Selling to a foreigner ensured
that Obregón would have to proceed very carefully. The president
was reluctant to expropriate foreign landholders, fearing that this
would discourage foreign investment that was badly needed for economic recovery.[48] In the beginning at least, the project was an attractive addition to the Obregonista reconstruction program. Nearly
a decade later Enríquez still defended the McQuatters sale in these
terms.[49]

The government purchase included only the property of Luis
Terrazas, no other family members' land. In fact, not all the general's estate came into government hands. Quinta Carolina was specifically excluded from the deal. By 1926 it had regained its former
splendor.[50] There is also some question as to whether or not the
estate kept other haciendas as well.[51]

The most remarkable aspect of the Terrazas strategy, however,
lay ahead. During the 1920s and 1930s, the family repurchased the
best of its landholdings. The estate of Luis Terrazas bought San
Isidro, San Ignacio, and five other haciendas in the southern region
of the state, and parts of Encinillas and El Carmen in the northern
part. In addition, Amanda Terrazas de Sisniega bought the Hacienda
de Aguanueva. The total of the repurchases was nearly 500,000 hectares (1,235,000 acres), or a little less than 20 percent of the original
landholding. It was approximately the same amount of land from
the Terrazas estate that had been granted to agricultural colonies and
ejidos combined by 1930. The family paid somewhat more per hectare for the land than it had received, but it bought back the best
land.[52] Family members continued to buy large chunks of the estate
in the early 1930s. (Members obtained more than 60,000 hectares in
1932.)[53]

Since resale to the Terrazas was handled through the Caja de
Préstamos, an organization administered by the federal government,
it is clear that it was national policy to allow them to return as large
landowners in order to reconstruct the Chihuahuan cattle business.

That this was the highest priority of the Obregón and Calles government is made clearer by the fact that 1.6 million of the 2.7 million hectares of the Terrazas estate were still not distributed by 1930 and that only 20 percent of the land was distributed to ejidos or *colonías agrícolas*.

The family members who recovered their lands faced a long fight to retain them. Enrique Creel first incorporated his haciendas into the Compañía Ganadera de Chihuahua and then divided them up, beginning in 1923, in order to comply with the state agrarian law of 1922.[54] The conflicts with local villages were unceasing for the next two decades. The Creels apparently kept the upper hand despite some adverse rulings until the Cárdenas era, when they lost at least 38,000 hectares to various ejidos in the Ojinaga region.[55] The Creel heirs suffered consistent losses in agrarian reform during the 1930s. Petitioners took 1,500 hectares in 1934 and another 4,600 in 1937. Angela Terrazas de Creel lost 3,700 hectares of her Hacienda de Zapien in Parral in 1938. The City of Chihuahua expropriated prime land in the center of town in 1939.[56]

One property owned by the Banco Minero, the Hacienda La Gallina in Jiménez, was occupied by agrarians in 1923 by virtue of a presidential decree, but the Creels won a ruling nine years later that ordered federal troops to expel them.[57] Agrarians took 9,100 hectares from Quinta Carolina's 22,000 in 1937.[58]

The Terrazas were willing to compromise. In 1926 Federico Sisniega, Jr., agreed to sell enough water to small farmers to raise their crops and donated two small plots of land to the municipio in return for recognition by residents of the Valle de Zaragoza that he was the legitimate owner of the Hacienda de Bella Vista. The Local Agrarian Commission had ruled three years before that the village was entitled to 12,000 hectares of the property.[59] Enrique Creel Terrazas loaned money to the *ejidatarios* of Coahuayana in order to clear and sow cotton so that there would be no interruption of work during the grant process.[60]

Even the repurchased haciendas were targets of land-hungry agrarians. San Isidro, for example, lost nearly 4,000 hectares to an ejido petition in 1940.[61] The pressure was so great two years later that the family leased a part of the property to another cattle company.[62] In 1940 Teresa Bobadilla de Terrazas wrote to President

Cárdenas asking him to help her son Juan sell the Hacienda de San Isidro, which she claimed was the only property left from the legacy of Luis Terrazas. After losing some of her children and her husband, she wanted to return to her land from exile in Los Angeles.[63]

The enormous urban properties of both the Terrazas estate and Enrique C. Creel were untouched by Obregón's expropriation decree. Before the Revolution each had owned hundreds of lots and buildings in Ciudad Chihuahua alone. When the state's economy began to recover in 1924, the Terrazas estate began investing in new construction and remodeling and repairing existing properties. The U.S. consul reported in 1926 that the current upturn in the state's lumber industry was owing to these new investments by the Terrazas estate.[64] These holdings were so extensive that one citizen complained to President Calles that the Terrazas family was "determined to bring ruin and desolation to the state" and "continued their wicked work without respect to society and its laws."[65]

The Terrazas economic comeback was led by Luis Terrazas's grandchildren, Ing. Miguel Márquez, Salvador Creel, Luis Laguette, Carlos Sisniega, and Federico Sisniega. Márquez, Laguette, and the Sisniega brothers emerged as leading cattlemen in the late 1920s and early 1930s.[66] Márquez was also the head of one of the state's biggest construction companies.[67] Salvador Creel was president of both the Compañía Eléctrica y de Ferrocarriles de Chihuahua and the Compañía Rastro de Torreón.[68] Federico Sisniega was also a prominent lawyer.[69] The family based its economic activities on old strengths—landowning and cattle raising, real estate, textiles, banking, and utilities—to which they added a new business, construction.

The Terrazas by no means had an entirely smooth road during the 1920s. There were still revolutionaries with long memories, who sought retribution for old abuses, especially in banking and insurance. The Terrazas were also vulnerable to damages caused by fluctuations in the national economy, political instability, and the new militancy of workers. During the 1920s at least two family members were investigated for alleged illegal banking activities.[70]

The three Terrazas banks—the Banco Minero, the Caja de Ahorros de la República Mexicana, and the Banco Comercial Refaccionario—were involved in endless litigation and government proceedings.[71] The Banco Minero had over twelve million pesos in assets in 1924 and its stock still traded on the Mexico City exchange in 1925. Moreover, it held a number of substantial mortgages and owned land and a textile factory.[72] The bank went into liquidation in 1927, a process that continued into the next decade.[73] The Caja de Ahorros de la República Mexicana was an object of particular popular venom. The government claimed that its original concession was illegal, for the interim governor who granted it, Joaquín Cortazar, Sr., was the father of one of the owners. The bank, which owned six hundred houses in Chihuahua City, was accused of many abuses, including "despoiling widows and orphans."[74] A further investigation alleged that the Terrazas had illegally combined their three banks.[75] The Caja de Ahorros continued to operate into the 1930s and was in liquidation in 1939.[76] The Banco Comercial went into liquidation in 1922 and was embroiled in this process as late as 1927. It was under constant siege by its creditors and government regulators.[77]

The Terrazas did not give up their role in Chihuahuan (or national) banking, despite the tribulations of the banks they founded during the Porfiriato. Francisco C. Terrazas was assistant manager of the Chihuahua Investment Company in 1928.[78] More important, Miguel Márquez and Carlos Sisniega were founders of the Banco Comercial Mexicano as partners of a rising entrepreneurial family, the Vallinas, in 1934.[79]

Several members of the family were jailed over "an old matter" concerning "La Equidad," an insurance company. Juan A. Creel, Enrique's brother, could not return to Chihuahua for some time for fear of arrest in this affair. Enrique C. Creel finally settled the problem by buying the assets of the company and paying its policyholders. The federal government ordered the company liquidated in 1926.[80]

The family's industrial interests were, of course, hard hit by the Revolution. Some operations were abandoned, others were leased to other entrepreneurs. The Terrazas's textile interests were struck by downturns in the economy and labor difficulties. The Fábrica Río Florido, for example, was closed in 1921, reopened, struck by labor troubles in mid-decade, and then went into liquidation in 1926.[81] The factory apparently continued to operate under the management of the heirs of the original founders until 1930.[82] The Banco Minero–

owned Fábrica de Hilados y Tejidos "La Amistad" was closed in 1926 and its equipment leased.[83] Another mill was hounded for back taxes.[84] Revolutionaries took over the Bella Vista factory, owned by Federico Sisniega, in 1913 and operated it for four to five years.[85] Still another, La Paz, was evidently sold to Tomás Alvarez y Compañía, a mercantile firm in Camargo.[86]

The Terrazas brewery company ended its operations but leased its facilities in 1924.[87] The Compañía Harinera de Chihuahua was run by revolutionaries with some success through the 1910s. It was managed as late as 1934 by the same group that ran the brewery.[88] The family continued its involvement in meat packing. Salvador Creel was president of the Compañía Rastro de Torreón, S.A.[89] The Terrazas sold their Compañía Telefonera de Chihuahua to a large foreign company.[90] Family members remained heavily involved in mining. Both Creel brothers, Enrique and Juan, owned a considerable number of mining properties. They were particularly adept at leasing them to foreign corporations.[91] The Creels remained in control of the Compañía Eléctrica y Ferrocarriles de Chihuahua into the 1930s. The electric railway of Ciudad Chihuahua was out of service from the early years of the Revolution and, as a result, its equipment and roadbeds were dilapidated. In 1924 the Río Conchos Agricultural and Electric Power Company took over the old electric plant. In the early 1920s the company was embroiled in litigation with the city over water bills allegedly worth 325,000 pesos. The company's board spent most of its time trying to pay its bond and mortgage holders.[92]

The Terrazas were especially vulnerable to government claims for back taxes. In 1924 the state sued Luis Terrazas, Jr., for taxes in Ciudad Chihuahua.[93] Four years later some officials claimed that the Terrazas estate owed 1.9 million pesos. There were claims after Almeida's overthrow that he had afforded the family favorable treatment to the detriment of the state.[94] In 1930 there were more claims for back taxes.[95]

Clearly, no Terrazas family member could hold public office in the 1920s. Instead, the clan exerted influence in indirect ways. Enrique Creel returned from exile during the Obregón administration and became an important advisor on monetary policy. He had enough influence, on the personal level at least, to gain the release of his nephew from prison in the United States through the intervention of Obregón.[96] In the early 1930s, however, Juan Terrazas was elected *regidor* of the *ayuntamiento* of San Buenaventura and Luis Terrazas *regidor* in Ascensión.[97] These were minor offices, to be sure, but they point to the fact that the Terrazas were once again accepted in the public sphere (though probably not welcomed).

Even more important, family members took active part in influential interest groups, particularly the state's cattlemen's association, the Rotary Club, the Chamber of Commerce, and the Chamber of Mines.[98] In 1924 Eduardo C. Creel was an alternate on the board of the Confederación de Cámaras de Comercio.[99] Jorge Muñoz served similarly six years later in the Chamber of Commerce.[100] The cattlemen's group was especially active and successful as a lobbying organization: for example, in 1927 its protests achieved a substantial reduction in the proposed increase in cattle export taxes.[101] Carlos Sisniega was treasurer of the Cámara de Ganadera de Chihuahua in 1929.[102] In 1933 Miguel Márquez became its president.[103] Márquez and Laguette would thereafter play prominent roles in this group. When the first Mexican Mining Congress met in June 1930, Enrique Creel was named to the three-man board of control.[104]

Socially, the Terrazas had made a comeback by 1925, perhaps ushered in by the Almeidas. In 1925 the women of the family became very active in the Red Cross.[105] Two years later its *señoritas* organized and helped run the fashionable Club Sirosis.[106] The women (most importantly María Luján de Terrazas) continued their social concerns, in 1930 organizing the Committee to Help Poor Children.[107] Amada Terrazas de Sisniega founded the Casa de Regeneración de la Mujer the same year.[108]

The men made their entrees through businessmen's social clubs. Jorge Muñoz, for example, was president of the Casino Chihuahuense, the foremost men's club, in 1928.[109] Luis Laguette was vice president of the Rotary Club in 1928–29.[110] Francisco Terrazas, Benjamín Márquez, and Lic. Luis Laguette were officers of the fashionable Club de Tiradores.[111] The clubs Sirosis and Tiradores indicated that the new generation stood at the top of Chihuahua society. Public acceptance continued apace with the appointment of a Terrazas Cuilty to the Junta de Beneficia Privada in 1932.[112]

Despite their notoriety, the Terrazas returned to Chihuahua during the 1920s and began to rebuild. Damaged as it was, their economic power was formidable. Even Obregón felt compelled to conciliate them. Blessed with a talented new generation of leaders, the family emerged from the decade as a potent force.

The extent to which the Terrazas retained their place in Chihuahua was indicated in a letter by Sergio Sánchez to the editor of *El Correo de Chihuahua* in 1928: "the powerful House of Terrazas confronts a worthy adversary to its power and riches: the Chihuahuan people."[113] The extent of the family's rehabilitation even as soon as 1928 was indicated on the pages of *El Correo de Chihuahua*, which had fought them for twenty years. That year the newspaper praised General Luis Terrazas for his actions during the French Intervention.[114] The following year the family donated to Ciudad Chihuahua a fifteen-ton marble monument to Luis Terrazas put up in the Sanatario Guadalupe. No protest arose.[115] The obituary of Enrique C. Creel in 1931 in *El Correo* made no mention of the fact that the Revolution had erupted against his rule.[116] In an article in *Excelsior* in 1939, Luis Vargas Piñera raised the Terrazas once again to high esteem in the national press.[117]

The Lujáns, Zuloagas, and Falomirs

The Lujáns, Zuloagas, and Falomirs, all part of the Terrazas-Creel extended family, survived the Revolution's violent years and struggled, for the most part successfully, to reestablish their old wealth and prominence in the 1920s. A distinguished family of legislators, magistrates, congressmen, local government officials, and governors, the Lujáns in 1910 owned a half-million acres in the state. Along with their relatives, the Terrazas, their lands were expropriated by Pancho Villa in 1913. Carranza, however, restored most of their property. Not everything went smoothly, however, for Ramón F. Luján, probably the family's largest landowner, fought unsuccessfully to keep his Hacienda de Salaices. By 1924 he was in a state of "ruin and desperation" in his attempt to defend it against the onslaught of local agrarians. His property had been intervened by various revolutionary governments since 1913. He regained possession only in the early 1920s. In order to try to save Salaices, he sold off extensive holdings in the Comarca Lagunera in Torreón, Coahuila, at what he claimed to be a 750,000 peso loss. Luján had an enormous mortgage, contracted just before the Revolution to upgrade the hacienda's irrigation system and to divide the land for colonization by smallholders. A million-peso investment was in ruin. In 1922 the local agrarian commission began to dismember the hacienda. Neighboring ejidos stole its water. The national government agreed to purchase the land in 1924, but there were difficulties in agreeing on the price. Luján valued the hacienda at 3,181,000 pesos, but the Caja de Préstamos valued it at 2,125,272 pesos.[118] In 1926 the Lujáns had hopes for administrative or judicial resolution, with the case pending in the supreme court.[119] By 1927 they had lost Salaices to the banks.[120] The new administrators leased it out and forced out the sharecroppers.[121] In 1934 the Hacienda de Salaices was the property of the Banco Nacional de Crédito Agrícola, the successor to the Caja de Préstamos.[122] The family's other major hacienda, Santa Gertrudis, was attacked by rebels in 1911.[123] The Caja de Préstamos acquired the property in 1919 in return for the debt of owner José María Luján (857,287 pesos).[124] By that time the *casco* was ruined, the irrigation system destroyed. There were only six hundred animals of all types, and wolves everywhere.[125]

Despite these disasters, the Lujáns did not surrender their dreams easily. From exile in California, José María inquired about forming a colony from the lands irrigated by the Boquilla dam.[126] In 1928 Abraham Luján Z. was vice president of the Compañía Agrícola y de Fuerza Eléctrica del Río Conchos, S.A., which operated that dam.[127] Less economically diversified than the Terrazas, the Lujáns suffered proportionately more from the Revolution.

Aside from Ramón Luján's unsuccessful struggle, family members were active in the local chamber of commerce and in community public service. Their widespread family connections in Jiménez district in southern Chihuahua—they were related to the Acostas, Maynez, Mendozas, Chávez, Sotos, and Villegas—assured them extensive influence in local politics. Through these branches the family participated in state and local government.[128] José L. Luján, for example, was municipal treasurer of Jiménez during the early 1930s.[129] Jesús Muñoz L. served as president of Comité de Servicios de la Comunidad.[130]

Like the Terrazas, the Lujáns were active in state business groups. Jesús Muñoz Luján was president of the Cámara de Comercio de Chihuahua and general agent in Chihuahua of the Compañía

Mexicana de El Aguila, S.A.[131] In 1930 Abraham Luján Z. was vice president of the Chamber of Commerce.[132]

Most of the family was in exile well into the 1920s. Manuel L. Luján, who married one of General Terrazas's granddaughters, lived in Caléxico, California, between 1916 and 1918, where he was *consultor general* to the government of Colonel Estebán Cantú. Lic. José Mariá resided on the Paseo de la Reforma in Mexico City and then moved to Santa Ana, California. Ramón was in El Paso.[133]

The Zuloagas were among Chihuahua's oldest and most prominent families. They had been the state's leading political and military figures of the first half of the nineteenth century, gaining fame as Indian fighters. At mid-century they led the Conservatives in Chihuahua. Discredited by collaboration with the French, the family quietly exerted influence through its familial and financial alliance with Luis Terrazas. The Zuloagas were, after the Terrazas, the largest native landowners in Chihuahua, with more than a million acres in 1910. Like the Terrazas, they followed a strategy of fighting hard to keep their land through the courts and manipulation of the law, then sold part of it to foreigners. This gave the family at least temporary respite, and it kept the preponderance of its lands.[134] In the early 1920s the family fought expropriation on the ground that it had not divided the land among the heirs of Carlos Zuloaga. The Zuloagas claimed that the agrarian law could not apply until the division.[135] When pressures from agrarians grew so strong that expropriation looked inevitable, they sold their largest hacienda, Bustillos, to the Mennonites (whose large colony flourishes to this day).[136] Like the Terrazas, the Zuloagas were related to virtually every important family in Chihuahua, Coahuila, and Durango, and this assured them of continued standing.

The Zuloagas did not waste much time in seeking to reestablish themselves. In 1917 family members Kraft and Madero imported ten thousand sheep to restock their herds.[137] They fought incursions on their land. They sued to prevent the formation of a *colonía agrícola* at San Antonio de Arenales through a local agrarian commission decree of restitution.[138] To comply with the provisions of the May 25, 1922, agrarian law, the Zuloagas divided their lands among six heirs. The estate voluntarily formed a *colonía,* with 10,000 hectares of its best land chosen by the governor and another 6,000 expropriated for formation of an ejido. But the deal did not go through because the governor proceeded before the estate was divided.[139] In the face of agrarian petitions, the Zuloagas sold parts of Bustillos to the Mennonites.[140] The Casa Zuloaga donated 1,500 hectares to fifty families of *aparcieros* and *arrendatarios*, along with 10,000 pesos to move them to new land, and promised to invest 50,000 pesos more in a dam, school, and granary, as well as to establish a *banco refaccionario* that would extend credit to smallholders. The offer was accepted. This, of course, did not stop the wave of reform, for two other awards totaling 25,000 hectares went to San Antonio de Arenales, which had previously obtained 7,300.[141] The pressure was enormous. In 1926 people were leaving San Andrés to colonize Bustillos because of its fertile land.[142] In another case, the government took 3,200 hectares in 1923 to form an agricultural colony on Bustillos. The Zuloagas obtained an *amparo,* but were unable to stop the occupation by colonists. Five years later the federal government awarded 6,435 hectares and legalized the colony (the price for land was to be negotiated).[143] In 1931 the *colonía* got an additional 4,434 hectares from Bustillos.[144] The family suffered the loss of more than 10,000 hectares to petitioners during 1928 and 1930.[145] But it continued to resist. In an effort to forestall the inevitable, Luz Zuloaga de Madero sold land to Lorenzo Crosby in the Bachíniva-Cuauhtemoc region.[146]

In 1931 the Zuloagas won out against a petition from San Carlos, San Andrés.[147] But mostly they lost, often a few hundred or a thousand hectares at a time.[148] The family tried to sell land they rented to the residents of Chocachic in 1931 (the arrangement had begun in 1922), but the tenants, who had developed the land, refused to leave. Eventually they obtained 1,507 hectares.[149] The Zuloagas did not always contest the petitions, as in the case of La Cruz in 1931.[150] Sometimes the court proceedings had their effect. A 1932 *amparo* purportedly did "grave harm" to agrarians in Cuauhtémoc.[151] Perhaps the most innovative strategy took place in 1932, when the Zuloagas exchanged the entire Hacienda Bachimba for lot 46 of the Hacienda de Encinillas, which was part of the former Terrazas estate administered by the Caja de Préstamos.[152] The Cárdenas years brought larger losses. In 1936–37 Margarita Prieto de Maíz, Elena Prieto de Treviño, and Pedro Jesús de Prieto lost a fourth of their property.[153] In 1939, 18,000 hectares of Bustillos was lost to ten pueblos.[154]

Like the Terrazas, the Zuloagas returned to Chihuahuan society in 1925, when Pedro Zuloaga became vice president of the Club Ariel, a new club for culture and arts.[155] Various of their extended family, such as Dr. Ruben Prieto Maíz, would also hold local political offices.

The Falomirs were large landowners, important businessmen, and local political officials during the Porfiriato who worked in close association with the Terrazas. Villa expropriated their land in 1913; but, like many of their contemporaries, they reacquired a large part of their properties from 1916 to 1919 under Carranza. Family members had long been associated with the Terrazas banking enterprises. Under the revolutionary regime, Jesús J. Falomir was manager of the Banco de México in Ciudad Chihuahua. To their great advantage, the family intermarried with one of the rising postrevolutionary entrepreneurial families, the Vallinas.[156]

The Falomirs rose from the ashes, led by Jesús J. and José María Falomir.[157] Each engaged in a number of enterprises, including mining and banking.[158] Members remained in close association with the Terrazas. Jesús J. was manager of the postrevolutionary Banco Minero.[159] He was also secretary of the Compañía Mexicana de Inversiones.[160]

The family's property included the Hacienda de Dolores (Chihuahua), San Ignacio, and Rancho Viejo in Aldama.[161] The Rancho Viejo was the target of persistent petitions from the residents of Aldama, which in their 1922 plea sought 29,000 hectares.[162] Martín, Jesús J., José María, and Dolores Caballero de Falomir lost 2,668 hectares in 1927, 2,210 in 1936, and 5,680 in 1940 (all to the *ejido* Maclovio Herrera).[163] The hacienda had only 28,091 hectares in 1936.

Although the Falomirs were hardly of the same stature as the Terrazas in the revolutionary pantheon, when Jesús J. Falomir was named manager of the Chihuahua branch of Banco de México in 1926, protests arose. He was accused of being an "enemy of the Revolution," who had demonstrated ineptness in the management of the Banco Minero, the Banco Refaccionario, and the Caja de Ahorros de la República Mexicana, and had been jailed in the "La Equidad" scandal.[164] He was also purportedly a "noted reactionary and Knight of Columbus," and was sustained only by being a relative of the wife of General Obregón.[165]

Family members were active in local interest groups. José M.
Falomir was treasurer of the Cámara Ganadera de Chihuahua, and
Jesús J. a *vocal suplente* in 1930.[166] Jesús J. Falomir Vallina was a
member of a committee of the Chamber of Commerce studying the
municipal land law.[167]

The Cuiltys seemed to have survived well enough until the
mid-1930s, when they sold off two 40,000-hectare chunks of their
Hacienda de Corral de Piedra.[168] From 1935 to 1939 they lost at least
35,000 hectares to the agrarian reform.[169] The Horcasitas, who
owned the Hacienda de Mápula, also managed to avoid the full brunt
of land reform until the 1930s, though they had to fight in the years
before.[170] But they maintained their position as important cattle
raisers. In addition, Antonio Horcasitas became a representative of
the Mines and Metals Securities Company, S.A.[171] Pablo Horcasitas operated the Chihuahua city *rastro* (slaughterhouse).[172] In
1932 Pablo was secretary of the Compañía Transportes de Chihuahua, S.A.[173] The family must have maintained considerable influence, for both the *rastro* and the transportation company required
concessions from the state government. Both were potentially lucrative monopolies.

From observing the experiences of the extended Terrazas family
we can see a pattern of strategy of survival similar to that of the old
elite elsewhere in Mexico. The old elite used the courts and the law
to stall agrarian reform as long as possible. When expropriation of at
least part of their lands became unavoidable, they would sell off a
large part to foreigners. In the cases of the Terrazas and Zuloagas the
strategy worked well. The estate of Luis Terrazas brought thirteen
million pesos, which it used later to buy back some of the estate. The
Zuloagas sold to the Mennonites property that was under siege. All
five families used marriage and blood ties to maintain their influence
in local politics and society. The most successful survivors, the Terrazas, were the most economically diversified.

Land Reform

The crucial factor in the survival of the largest part of the Porfirian elite was land reform. As we have noted in Chapters 2 and 3,
agrarian reform was used by national and state governments as a

political tool to win over the support of the campesinos. But as we have also observed, most of the land for redistribution in the 1920s came from national lands and the expropriated estate of Luis Terrazas. This changed, however, from 1934 to 1938, under Lázaro Cárdenas.

The Terrazas, of course, were not the only elite to employ various strategies to protect their properties. Selling to foreigners was a favorite ploy throughout the era. In 1913 Juan María Salazar sold 78,000 hectares in Zaragoza to Paul Ginther, who in turn sold it to the General Investment Company of Mexico two years later.[174] Marcos Russek in 1939 sold his 147,000-hectare Santa Clara to Fomento Industrial y Agrícola, owned by Spanish exiles.[175] Another strategy was to offer compromises. Gabriel Saénz was willing to cede 500 hectares of his Hacienda de Rosales in Pedernales, Guerrero, in 1929 rather than the 1,298 that agrarians sought, a claim which he believed would ruin his property; the governor would not consider it.[176] Enrique Beckman tried to get each petitioning *ejidatario* to sign a contract giving up their rights to Punto Alegre on the Hacienda Corral de Piedra, but they were unwilling to comply.[177] In 1929 several Hacendados agreed to cede a great extension of land to unemployed campesinos and workers.[178] Legal obstructions were manifold. Sabás Murga divided up the Hacienda de San José near San Andrés and obtained an *amparo* against a grant because the petition asked for land from an entity that no longer existed. Sabás Murga also argued that the agrarian census included too many people who were not residents.[179] The Prieto and Muller families obtained injunctions against the expropriation of half their lands to the *pueblos* of Galeana and Cruces in 1923.[180] Landowners also used violence. The state secretary of *gobernacion* ordered white guards against petitioners who sought the land of the Hacienda de San Rafael as a favor to his cousin the latifundist Guillermo Porras.[181] The *presidente municipal* forced the *ejidatarios* out of their houses.

Conclusion

Several circumstances thus sustained the Porfirian elite during the 1920s and 1930s. First, especially for the Terrazas and elites in isolated regions, their economic resources were formidable. Much of their land was returned during the latter years of Carranza's administration. Others generated money through land and mine sales and leases. With Mexico in the throes of a severe economic crisis that lasted most of the decade, the old elite's business and agricultural expertise was badly needed. Obregón, for example, was unwilling to go too far beyond political expediency in expropriating land. Second, given the unsettled political situation in much of Mexico, the old elite, where it had survived the violent revolution, was a valuable potential ally for competing state factions as well as the national government. If the price for the old elite's cooperation was protection of its property, the new elite found the alliance was worth the cost. The Porfirian elite of the western mining communities of Chihuahua was additionally protected by the difficulty of transport and communication into the region. Third, the old elite was bolstered by old and newly acquired family ties. As in the cases of the Lujáns and Samaniegos especially, if one branch of the family was discredited, another went forward or a new one was added. It was a tried-and-true method that worked for the benefit of the revolutionary elite, too, giving them social status, instant allies, and economic support. Fourth, the new revolutionaries, like the Almeidas, were not radicals. They believed in private property and were not comfortable with expropriations. Many had seized land and riches during the Revolution and sought to protect their new wealth—a goal they held in common with the old elite. Finally, the Porfirian elite proved enormously resourceful and capable. They adapted to shifting situations with innovative strategies, taking advantage of the weaknesses of the new regime. They adjusted to the new changes that emerged at the end of the 1920s. When new loci of political power—like labor unions, campesino organizations, and political parties—emerged, the elite formed businessmen's groups and corporations. In other words, the old elite found new strategies and alliances to deal with the radicalism of the 1930s. The Porfirian elite created a place for itself in the new order alongside that of the new, revolutionary elite, which welcomed it, for the most part, as a partner.

The New Elite

At the same time that the Revolution discredited the Porfirian elite in the political realm yet allowed it a place in the new economic order, a new elite rose from the ruins and turmoil. New people emerged to lead state and local politics and to dominate the region's economy. This chapter examines the creation of postrevolutionary political and economic elites at the state level. The main questions revolve around the composition of the new elite, its geographic and class origins, its members' paths to power and riches, and how they interacted with the overshadowed Porfirian elite. It is also important to discern to what extent, if any, the new elite's methods of governance and domination changed from those of the old.

There is apparent agreement among historians that the Revolution transformed the Mexican elite. Alan Knight maintains that "one of the main achievements of the revolution was the break-up of . . . entrenched political monopolies and their replacement by a younger, more dynamic, shifting elite."[1] Peter Smith concludes similarly, but more cautiously, that "the revolutionary group differed from the prerevolutionary elite in several discernible ways."[2]

But there is a basic consensus only on the point that some form of transformation occurred, not on its substance. Knight concludes that "the Porfirian political elite was replaced by a new, revolutionary elite that was younger and more plebian."[3] Smith argues that the Revolution "did not lead to any major change in the class basis of political leadership," for "political elites have come mainly from the middle class—before, during, and since, the Revolution." As a political movement it "hastened the removal of upper class elements from high governmental office, [brought about] . . . the consequent separation of political and economic elites . . . [and] redistributed political power among relatively dispossessed segments of

the nation's middle class." Smith characterizes the Revolution as a
"struggle between two elements of Mexico's middle class: the ins
and the outs."[4] His data indicate that the new group had its origins
more in small towns and cities than in either the population as a
whole or the metropolitan Porfirians. He concurs with Knight that
they were younger. Camp goes a step further, identifying a "revolutionary generation" born between 1880 and 1899.[5] There seems to
be less doubt that the emergent elite was far more fractured than the
less-than-homogeneous Porfirian elite and that the separation between economic and political elites was more structured than during
the Díaz (Terrazas) era.

The process of elite formation took time. Recruitment and composition changed with circumstances. As the revolutionary regime
grew stronger after 1920, for example, there were alterations in the
makeup of the Chihuahuan elite. According to Knight

> over time, the criteria for advancement—initially military prowess,
> popular appeal, youth and machismo—necessarily changed, as warfare
> gave way to political stabilisation and economic reconstruction. The
> old criteria were no longer functional to the increasingly civilian, ur-
> ban, bureaucratic society of post-revolutionary Mexico, and more ap-
> propriate criteria evolved (or were revived): wealth, education, techni-
> cal and administrative expertise. Popular rebels were rarely endowed
> with such attributes. . . . Increasingly the political elite was drawn
> from the university educated, cosmopolitan, professional classes, most
> of them lacking individual or family claims to revolutionary sta-
> tus, some of them deriving from old-prerevolutionary elite families
> . . . . The post-revolutionary entrepreneurs, who were to play a
> growing part in Mexico's development, emerged from well-to-do
> backgrounds—often apolitical, sometimes Porfirian, less often revo-
> lutionary—and they did so because they possessed skills, attitudes (and
> sometimes capital) which survived the Revolution and stood them in
> good stead thereafter.[6]

Nor is it clear just how a new elite emerged and how it related to
the old elite. Knight finds that "while the political elite certainly
underwent change, therefore, it does not seem legitimate to talk of a
new, revolutionary bourgeoisie supplanting the old, at least as re-
gard personnel." At best, there was a "syncretisation of old and
new."[7] To the contrary, Smith discovers a different pattern: "There

has been . . . a slow and steady transformation, at least regarding social composition. . . . The upper class has faded from the scene, the lower class has assumed a (minor) role, and the middle class has (if anything) strengthened its control of public office."[8]

It becomes crucial not only to identify the composition of the new elite and how it changed over time, but to examine the relations between old and new elites, and to what extent political and economic elites were separated and how they related. The Revolution most certainly altered the relationship between economic and political elites. Most historians concur that under Díaz the economic oligarchy, despite the dictator's attempts to prevent it, monopolized politics as well.[9] Evidence from regional studies certainly supports this conclusion. Roderic Camp maintains that "the economic oligarchy's influence prior to 1910 was substantially more significant than since 1920, at least in the immediate postrevolutionary decades." The Revolution lessened the "pool of economic elites holding national political office." Moreover, "in the postrevolutionary period, some of the outstanding builders of the private sector reaped their original fortunes in public life, but they were exceptional, as were their private sector peers willing to contribute to national political leadership." Camp argues that the Revolution, for the most part through the tone set by the Constitution of 1917, created an unfavorable attitude toward business. "Businessmen were not recruited into Mexican political leadership, which, if possible, flaunted its popular origins, even if after 1920 most politicians were actually middle class and urban." After the formation of the PNR, they were excluded from formal relations with the regime.[10]

These generalizations for Mexico, while certainly appropriate for the post-1940 Mexican national government, do not work as well on the state and local levels for the era from 1910 to 1940. The original revolutionaries in Chihuahua were a heterogeneous group of middle-class "outs" or, as I have defined them, the "entrepreneurial" or risk-taking middle class; so-called rancheros, roughly defined as small landholders; and some elements of the working class, particularly miners. There were no dissident elites, unlike in other northern states. Class definitions are especially difficult to form, however, for in Chihuahua (and we increasingly discover elsewhere, including Morelos) many people were in transition. How does one categorize the small rancher who also contracted to transport ores and other materials to the mining camps or who labored in the mines in the off-seasons? What of the small rancher or farmer who crossed the U.S. border, became exposed to union organizing and ideology, and returned home and set up a small store? Social fluidity was not confined to the lower and lower middle classes.

Abraham González and Ignacio C. Enríquez present us with another side of the definitional problem. González's family had competed for and won political power against the Terrazas during the 1880s, only to lose out in the 1890s. But its economic resources never came close to matching those of its foes. González himself never attained anything other than modest wealth. Yet some of his relatives were large landowners. The definition of a large landowner in the sierras of western Chihuahua, where his family resided, hardly matched the size of the vast estates of the landed elite of the central part of the state. Enríquez's father was one of the Terracista *jefes políticos* against whom the revolutionaries protested. Was Enríquez one of the "outs"? The list of contradictions and anomalies is long.

The Formation of a New Elite

The formation of the new elite followed a rough chronology. The diverse middle class described above led the Revolution in 1910, with substantial support from small landholders centered in the former *presidios* in northeastern and western Chihuahua and miners from central and western sectors. Once the Maderistas won, the middle-class–dissident-elite (the latter elsewhere but not in Chihuahua) leadership of the movement rejected further lower-middle-class and lower-class participation, leading to unrest and rebellion in 1912. Much as the Zapatistas had rejected the temporization of Madero's government on land reform, the lower-middle-class Orozquistas sought their share of the political and economic spoils. Madero passed over many military leaders from more modest origins in favor of civilians (his choice of Abraham González over Pascual Orozco is the most telling example), thus forestalling participation of these groups in the new elite. From 1913 to 1916 the small landowners and workers held center stage, led by Pancho Villa and

Emiliano Zapata. Upward mobility through the battlefield predominated. With the complete breakdown of the old order by 1914, and the total failure of any order in 1914 and 1915, opportunities abounded. Leaders such as Villa, Manuel Chao, the Arrieta brothers of Durango, and the Herreras of Parral seized the reins. After the triumph of Carranza and during the three years of his presidency, the middle-class–dissident-elite alliance tried to push aside those of humbler origins. The First Chief, as we have seen, made concerted efforts to obtain the support of the Porfirian landed elite. His generals sought to create their own wealth by thwarting the aspirations of the lower classes. The promulgation of the Constitution of 1917 and the overthrow of Carranza three years later were evidence enough, however, that the middle class could not win without lower-class support. The serious rebellions that marked the 1920s assured that the northern middle class of Obregón and Calles had to take into consideration the demands of the lower classes, who demanded a price for their military assistance.

The military was a crucial base of power during the 1920s. In Chihuahua the leadership of the *defensas sociales,* a local militia, provided two governors. Two others were federal army zone commanders. Despite the upward mobility provided by the military, middle-class civilians were the most radical leaders in Chihuahua in the postwar decades. Luis L. León, Francisco R. Almada, and Gustavo L. Talamantes, middle-class politicians or bureaucrats, were the most favorably disposed toward land and labor reforms. The colonels and generals were far more acquisitive and ideologically conservative.

During the 1930s, economic interest organizations obtained considerable political influence. Labor, campesino, commercial, and landowner groups vied. However, unlike in the class-mobile days of military dominance, there does not seem to have been extensive upward mobility in politics through these interest groups. Labor and campesino organizations were brought into the official party during the 1930s, but their leaders did not cross over to high political office, though they did win office on the municipal level and election to the legislature. Their influence was primarily exercised through the PNR and its successor, the PRM. They served as important members of the party's state executive committee. Local chambers of commerce exerted a considerable measure of influence in the big cities, Ciudad Juárez and Ciudad Chihuahua.[11]

Political turnover was high. There were several benchmarks in Chihuahua: 1912, 1916, 1920, 1923, and 1929. Those who sided with the losing Orozquistas, Villistas, Carrancistas, de la Huerstistas, or Escobaristas (respectively) usually, but not always, lost either their lives or their political careers. The attrition was, of course, highest prior to 1920. Few leaders survived the civil wars to participate in state-level politics in the 1920s. Few people were able to sustain their influence over a long period.

Geographically, the dominant governors and personalities of the era either were born in or sunk their political roots in western Chihuahua. Ignacio C. Enríquez, though born in Ciudad Chihuahua, based his political strength on the control of the *defensas sociales,* which were strong in the western sierras. Jesús Antonio Almeida came from Bachíniva, Guerrero district. Marcelo Caraveo was also from Guerrero. Rodrigo M. Quevedo was from Casas Grandes. Two other governors, Fernando Orozco E. from Santo Tomás and Roberto Fierro from Ciudad Guerrero, also came from the sierras. By the end of the era, however, Parral had gained dominance. Talamantes came from Matamoros near Hidalgo de Parral, and Alfredo Chávez was from Parral itself. Andrés Ortiz and Reinaldo Talavera came from Ciudad Chihuahua, but they were merely interim governors. Although Ciudad Juárez grew in population, it did not provide a governor until Teófilo Borunda (1956–62) and Oscar Flores (1968–74). This trend reflected economic, demographic, and political transformations that had begun in the latter years of the Porfiriato. The economic center of the state moved away from the agricultural western districts, populated by small farmers, to the cattle lands and mining camps between Ciudad Chihuahua and Parral. The construction of dams and irrigation works on the river system in the state's southeast quadrant intensified this shift. The concentration of mining in the great camps of Santa Eulalia, Parral, and Santa Bárbara, overshadowing the less accessible, smaller operations in the west, brought more people to those areas. Politically, the *sierrenses* of western Chihuahua lost out to heavy *ejido* and labor-union backing of the revolutionary party in the central part of Chihuahua.

The composition of the new elite changed over time. Generally, upward mobility in class was more likely in the earlier years, as a result of opportunities available through the military. There were few civilian political leaders who arose from the lower class in the aftermath of the 1911 overthrow of Díaz. One of them, Manuel Molinar y Rey of Santa Rosalía, Camargo, won election as municipal president in 1913. "An honorable worker of good habits, devoted to family, good conduct that was a rare model for the working class," he soon allowed power to corrupt him, to the detriment of his community.[12] He, of course, would not be the last.

If some, like Molinar, fell victim to their newfound status, and others, like the Herreras, were sacrificed to the brutality of the civil wars, there were a few instances of leaders who arose from the working class, survived the violence, and gained prominence in the postrevolutionary years. Jesús Lugo of Parral was one example. An antireelectionist in 1908, he ran for the legislature from Parral in 1911.[13] He was later a leader of the CROM in Chihuahua during the early 1920s and was secretary-general of the organization in 1925.[14] Jesús had served as vice president of the board of directors of the convention of workers and campesinos in Chihuahua in 1922.[15] Eight years later he acted as president of the state Congreso Agrario.[16] At one time he ran for governor.[17] Jesús Lugo, however, was an exception. Few of his fellow working-class antireelectionists either survived or retained political influence into the postrevolutionary era.

A lower-middle-class (white-collar) civilian leader who survived the 1910s to occupy a position of leadership in the 1920s was Juan B. Rosales. As a young man, he worked as a bookkeeper for a foreign mining company and for various haciendas in Durango and Chihuahua. Rosales came to Parral in 1904, eventually finding employment with Henry Nordwald, a retailer. An early antireelectionist, he founded the newspaper *El Voz del Pueblo* and was elected to the state legislature in 1911. He was the only legislator who objected to the body's adhesion to the Orozco revolt, for which he was imprisoned by Orozco. Rosales edited a series of revolutionary newspapers from 1913 to 1915 and served in Governor Chao's cabinet in 1914. In 1925 he remained politically active as Centro Director de la Alianza de Partidos Políticos in Chihuahua.[18]

The new ruling class, however, rose predominantly from the

middle sectors of rural and urban society. They joined the revolution to obtain power and wealth.

The Plunderers

Two Chihuahuan governors, Jesús Antonio Almeida and Rodrigo M. Quevedo, and their families epitomized the opportunistic leaders who emerged from the chaos and violence of the postrevolutionary era. They followed a pattern well laid out by the Terrazas. Each had large extended families to whose members they entrusted important political and economic roles. They both used their political positions to enhance their economic holdings.

The Almeidas emerged in the mid-1920s, when they attempted and failed to establish a political dynasty.[19] Resilient, the family recovered from the coup that toppled them in 1927 and went on to become important cattle ranchers and entrepreneurs. The foundation of their economic empire was laid during Jesús Antonio's governorship.

The Almeidas had their roots in Bachíniva, in the district of Guerrero in western Chihuahua. Jesús Antonio Almeida flirted briefly with the Orozquistas in their rebellion against Madero in 1912. He gained prominence in 1917, when he joined the *defensas sociales* to battle Pancho Villa. Shrewdly, he sided with Obregón against Carranza in 1920. During the governorship of Ignacio C. Enríquez, Jesús Antonio rose through the ranks to head the *defensas,* and he used this as a springboard to run, with Enríquez's backing, for governor in 1924.[20]

Brother Alberto B. Almeida became a well-known businessman and politician in Ciudad Juárez. His first deals occurred during the early years of the Revolution, when in 1913 he registered mining claims on the Hacienda de Encinillas. The *Periódico Oficial del Estado de Chihuahua* recorded Alberto as an *empleado* and a *vecino* of Encinillas.[21] It is not clear if he actually worked for the owner, Luis Terrazas, or merely had taken advantage of Terrazas's temporary exile to claim mining property. In 1915, he was the director of a foundry in Camargo.[22] He also resumed his mining activities in the late 1910s and early 1920s.[23] Alberto reappeared in the early 1920s as a member of the firm Cuarón, Almeida y Compañía, customs agents in Ciudad Juárez. His associates in the business, Raymundo S. García, T. G. Cuellar, Ulises Irigoyen, and Ignacio Rodarte, would become members of the city's economic and political elite.[24]

Alberto was *presidente municipal* of Ciudad Juárez from March 1926 to April 1927, when he fled the coup that also ousted his brother as governor. He served briefly in the same post in April 1929, August to November 1930, and November and December 1931. In 1938 he was *presidente municipal* of Villa Ahumada. According to *juarense* historian Armando B. Chávez M., Alberto was "honest, energetic, constructive, and active." The extent of his popularity and esteem was indicated by the fact that, despite his brother's fall, he was thereafter called upon on three occasions to take over the municipality in times of crisis.[25]

The family's agent in Ciudad Chihuahua was brother-in-law Socorro García. He was first noted as a member of the city's Junta Patriótica in 1918.[26] Governor Almeida imposed him as *presidente municipal* in 1925. The U.S. consul accused him of being a lawyer of "unsavory" reputation, a drunkard, and unscrupulous.[27] He was suspended from office for six months on vague charges by the *ayuntamiento* in 1926.[28] García reassumed his post in January 1927, only to be ousted by force in April. By 1929 he had returned to politics as a member of the Partido Socialista Democrático "Alvaro Obregón" that opposed the fledgling PNR.[29]

The Almeida family enterprise was centered in mining, cattle, and lumber. The largest investment in mining was at Mosqueteros. Originally the Almeidas were in partnership with two foreigners. Alberto had claimed the property in 1918, then worked it for four years, after which he incorporated it as an Arizona company. In 1925 the Peñoles Company took an option on it, but gave it up. Almeida and his partners invested 100,000 pesos in the mines. Alberto had another large investment, 50,000 pesos, in the Los Aztecas silver mine near Villa Ahumada, which he also organized as an Arizona company.[30] The largest investments took place when Jesús Antonio was governor.

The family's cattle empire was based at least in part on the purchase of lots 27 and 29 of the Terrazas estate (Encinillas) from the Caja de Préstamos in 1932.[31] It is likely that this was facilitated by the then governor Roberto Fierro, who was a cousin.[32] The Almeidas also came into possession of the Hacienda La Quemada, with over 40,000 hectares.[33] The family's livestock interests were subsequently incorporated into the Compañía Ganadera del Norte.[34] Estebán and Casímiro would play important roles in the state cattlemen's association, the Cámara Nacional de Ganadera del Estado de Chihuahua.

The Almeida family entered the lumber business in the mid-1920s when, employing the power of the governorship, it acquired the properties of two foreign-owned companies, the Chihuahua Lumber Company and the Cargill Lumber Company.[35] The American managers of both these firms accused Almeida of using the state's agrarian law to force them to sell. They also claimed that he had stolen timber from their property before purchasing it.[36] Their Compañía Maderera y Manufacturera, S.A., had a large mill at Bocoyna.[37]

The governor was not adverse to using his position in more direct ways to augment his fortune. The U.S. consul alleged that Almeida had entered office a man of modest means, but had accumulated US$300,000 to obtain the two lumber companies and US$25,000 to build a fine house in Ciudad Chihuahua. The money supposedly came from his rake-off from gambling in Ciudad Juárez and from protecting ore thieves.[38] Other critics accused him of stealing from the state treasury.[39]

The Almeidas were opportunists of the first order. But their ambitions in the end overreached their political support. The Quevedos, formed from the same mold, were more ruthless and more successful at politics. These eleven brothers and innumerable family members were reminiscent of the Terrazas, who by virtue of their enormous family controlled state politics from top to bottom. Like the Almeidas, their fortune derived directly from their political power.

The leader of the family, Rodrigo M. Quevedo, according to United States Intelligence, had worked his way up from farmhand to "manager" on a Terrazas hacienda. (They characterized him as "rough" and having "little military knowledge or education.")[40] He joined the opposition to Porfirio Díaz in 1908. He was a Maderista in 1910. Two years later he sided with Orozco against Madero.[41] It is most likely that he served with the Huertistas under General Mercado in 1914.[42] Quevedo was later captured by civil authorities in El Paso, who accused him of being one of the leaders of a band of Huertista filibusterers who committed depredations in northern Chihuahua and in New Mexico.[43] Rodrigo was with Rosendo Salazar in February 1917 when he occupied the Mormon colonies in Chihuahua. At the time he was purported to be a Villista chief. In the spring, Quevedo went over to the Constitutionalists.[44] Rodrigo was subsequently active in defending the regime against the major rebellions of the 1920s. He served at various times as chief of military operations in Morelos, Guanajuato, Puebla, and La Laguna.

His brothers, Jesús, Jr., José, and Lorenzo, held a number of local political posts in Casas Grandes and Ciudad Juárez. Jesús and José had criminal records. Jesús was *presidente municipal* of Casas Grandes in 1920; a member of the state legislature, 1922–24; tax collector of Ciudad Juárez, 1924–25; city councillor in Ciudad Juárez in 1930; and mayor of Juárez in 1930 and 1932–33.[45] As tax collector of Casas Grandes, Jesús was accused of embezzling 8,928 pesos in 1927.[46]

José Quevedo was *presidente municipal* of Casas Grandes in 1911; tax collector of Casas Grandes, Villa Ahumada, and Ciudad Juárez; and *presidente municipal* of Ciudad Juárez in 1936–37. At one point he was accused of theft and embezzlement as tax collector, for which he was imprisoned.[47] There were constant reports that José was deeply involved in the underworld. One opponent wrote to President Cárdenas that "it is public and notorious" that José Quevedo devoted much of his time to illegal activities.[48]

Lorenzo Quevedo was *presidente municipal* of Nuevo Casas Grandes at the time Almeida was ousted in 1927. Because he had collaborated with Almeida, Lorenzo was forced from office and had to leave the state in 1928. He returned as a propagandist in the campaign of Manuel M. Prieto for the governorship two years later. Fearing for his life, he fled again.[49] When his brother became governor in 1932, of course, Chihuahua was once more safe for him.

Like the Almeidas (and perhaps even more so), the Quevedos' fortune was founded on their use of their public positions and influence. Jesús and Guillermo owned the Compañía de Luz y Fuerza de Ciudad Juárez, which supplied the city's light and power. When

Jesús was both municipal president (1932–33) and president of the company, he supposedly had the municipality pay for the installation of light-generating equipment for the firm. He also used municipal street-cleaning trucks in the construction of his electric plant. The family acquired the concession for the municipal slaughterhouse and allegedly skimmed off 80 percent of the profits due the city government.[50] A city cleaning contract with the family produced thousands of pesos more.

The biggest money generators were public works and gambling. The construction of the highway between Ciudad Chihuahua and Ciudad Juárez was "a rich vein of gold" for the Quevedos and their supporters.[51] Gambling, both before and after it was made illegal in 1934, was a huge revenue producer. José managed the largest casino, the Tivoli.

The Quevedos acquired a large cattle empire as well. Rodrigo purchased land from the Terrazas *latifundio,* Agua Caliente, Los Aparejos, Corralitos, and the estate of the Martínez del Río family.[52] To care for the cattle, he reportedly organized white guards. He used government bonds to buy the land. The face value of the bonds he used to pay was 280,000 pesos, but they were actually worth only 10 centavos to the peso.[53] In 1941 Rodrigo Quevedo and William W. Wallace bought the famed Corralitos ranch from a U.S. company for US$100,000.[54]

There were additional accusations of criminal involvement. One charged that in Ciudad Juárez there continued "all class of evil," all of which was abetted by *presidente municipal* Jesús Quevedo. It was "well-known" that José associated with all sorts of illegal businesses: drugs, counterfeiting, and gambling.[55] The Quevedos, summarized his critic, were a "band of thieves," supported by "el pulpo [octopus] Chihuahuense."[56] In 1934 there were between thirty and forty murders in Ciudad Juárez to attest to the extent of criminal activity under their auspices.[57] Allegedly, in his first year as governor, Rodrigo Quevedo acquired two million pesos in property, livestock, and other businesses.[58]

The plunderers thus emerged as an important part of the new economic elite, joining with the vestiges of the old guard, notably the Terrazas. Like their predecessors, they based their fortunes on the land. The breakup of the estates of Luis Terrazas provided their best opportunity to establish themselves as cattle ranchers. The *lati-*

fundio of Luis Terrazas formed the basis of several new cattle fortunes, not only those of Quevedo and Almeida, but of Borunda and
Caballero (and probably Guerrero) as well.

The Almeidas and Quevedos arose from the small landholder
class of the western sierras. Jesús Antonio Almeida had not left
Chihuahua during the Revolution. That he survived was amazing in
itself. Rodrigo Quevedo, similarly, endured. By luck or cunning, he
avoided the treachery of Chihuahuan politics in the 1920s and returned to become a formidable presence in the state for a decade.
Both families believed in private property and individual initiative.
They thus furnished little more than grudging, politically expedient
support for either agrarian or labor reform. In ruling they applied the
same techniques—nepotism and use of public position for private
gain—as had the Porfirian elite. If anything, the Quevedos were
more violent than either the Almeidas or the Terrazas. Categorizing
them as to class is, given the complexities of Chihuahuan society
discussed previously, not without difficulty. Both families came
from rural areas, and the older brothers probably began as small
farmers who were also day workers. The younger ones, however,
do not seem to have started so modestly. The Almeidas and Quevedos perhaps provide the best examples of the rising, entrepreneurial
middle class that won the revolution and molded it to their vision of
Mexico.

The Civilians

The other men who rose to political power as governors of
Chihuahua between 1920 and 1940 were middle-class civilians, with
the notable exceptions of General Ignacio C. Enríquez, General
Marcelo Caraveo, and Colonel Roberto Fierro. Reinaldo Talavera,
interim governor during 1923 and 1924, came from Aldama, an
agricultural town east of Ciudad Chihuahua. He graduated from
New Mexico A&M, returning in 1910 to the state capital, where he
managed a ranch and later was a representative of a U.S. hardware
company. Talavera entered politics in 1918, when he was named to
the *ayuntamiento* of Ciudad Chihuahua. After his governorship he
served as *presidente municipal* of Chihuahua in 1930 and 1931.[59]

León, a native of Ciudad Juárez, was educated at the National

School of Agriculture in Mexico City, where he became a student leader. Initially a journalist in Sonora, he was appointed by Plutarco Elías Calles as the head of the local agrarian commission in 1915. León was, subsequently, a federal deputy from Sonora and a legislator in Chihuahua.[60] He was founder and first president of the Comisión Nacional de Irrigación, founder and first president of the Comisión Nacional Agraria, and founder of the Banco de México and the Banco Nacional de Crédito Agrícola y Ganadero. In 1923 he was subsecretary of the Hacienda y Crédito Público. Calles named him secretary of agriculture in 1928.[61] During a brief retirement from politics in the late 1920s, León attempted unsuccessfully to become a cattle baron. He, like Governors Almeida and Quevedo, purchased a part of the former Terrazas estate, the Hacienda de Terrenates. But it was relatively poor land and he never was able to make a go of it. León's roots in Chihuahua were not deep. He went south after Quevedo took control of the state and was ousted along with Calles in 1935.

Unlike almost all the other Chihuahuan political elite of the era, León played an important role in national politics. He was a member of the original organizing committee of the PNR and was in on all the negotiations that followed Obregón's assassination.[62]

Fernando Orozco E. was a cattle buyer for a Mexico City firm who worked closely with the Hearst interests. He was intensely concerned to rebuild the cattle industry.[63] Francisco R. Almada was a schoolteacher who rose quickly from the municipal presidency of Chínipas, through the state legislature, the federal congress, and then the legislature again, to the governorship. Although he came from an old, well-to-do family with ties in both Sonora and Chihuahua, Almada was perhaps the most radical governor of the era. Andrés Ortiz was the son of a journalist from the state capital who was trained as a hydraulic engineer. A state legislator in Chihuahua, he emerged as a compromise governor appointed by Carranza to mediate the rivalry between Ignacio Enríquez and zone commander Murguía.[64] In a less flashy manner, Ortiz was as politically nimble as Caraveo or Quevedo. He was ousted as governor in 1919, having been accused of misappropriation of funds and political repression. With Carranza almost to the end, he escaped from Mexico dressed as a workman in May 1920.[65] Nonetheless, he adhered to the PNR and

León in 1930, and staged a remarkable, if short-lived, comeback. Along the way he acquired the Hacienda La Joya in Valle de Allende.[66]

Born near Parral and educated as an agrarian engineer, Gustavo L. Talamantes was the first revolutionary bureaucrat to rise to the governorship. After a term as municipal president of Ciudad Jiménez in 1916, he became the president of the state agrarian commission from 1920 to 1924. During the 1910s and early 1920s, he was a busy mining engineer and owned several properties. He also held a number of government and party posts, including federal senator, before he became governor in 1936.[67]

The men who were governors during the 1940s began their careers only the decade before. Alfredo Chávez, born in Parral and educated at the agricultural school in Ciudad Juárez, was one of three politically prominent brothers. Their father, Manuel Chávez Valdez, was *jefe político* of Parral and proprietor of the ranch El Mirador. Alfredo entered the political arena in 1931 when he ran for municipal president of Parral. He was subsequently inspector general of police in Ciudad Chihuahua, tax collector in Parral, state legislator, and interim governor. Among some he earned a reputation for "honesty [and] irreproachable principles." As one might expect of someone whose political base was in Parral, Chávez was "popular with the working class" with the support of the CTM.[68] Brother Gustavo was municipal president of Parral.[69] Brother Arturo was president of the state legislature, interim governor, and finally municipal president of Ciudad Juárez from 1943 to 1946.[70] The family had extensive cattle and commercial interests in the Delicias region. Fernando Foglio Miramontes (1906–), a native of Temósachic, also graduated from the Juárez Agricultural College. He held various posts in the federal government during the 1930s. He was also a large landowner.[71]

The Military Men

The son of an hacendado and longtime *jefe político* during the Porfiriato, Ignacio C. Enríquez joined the Revolution late, tending to his family's estate until the overthrow of Madero. As a soldier he was a loyal Carrancista, who fought variously under the command of Alvaro Obregón and Pablo González, working his way up to the rank of brigadier general by the time he was thirty. Enríquez held a number of important administrative posts for Carranza, including consul-general in New York, organizer of the red batallions, and municipal president of Mexico City, in addition to his stints as governor of Chihuahua.[72] Unlike the freebooters Almeida and Quevedo, Enríquez did not (at least from the available evidence) use his position to enrich himself.

Marcelo Caraveo, positioned between Almeida and Quevedo, came from the same mold. Born in western Chihuahua in 1884, he joined the Revolution at its beginning in 1910. He initially fought under Pascual Orozco, becoming successively a Huertista, Zapatista, Felicista, Pelaecista, and Obregonista, emerging in 1920 as a brigadier general. He served in various military posts until 1925 when he was named military-zone commander for Chihuahua and Durango.[73]

Called "bolder, more cruel, and more unprincipled than Zapata," the general was really a failed freebooter.[74] While military-zone commander, for example, Caraveo and two partners used their influence to obtain mining property from a Japanese company.[75] There were also rumors that he got 500,000 pesos from the Chihuahua Investment Company when he rebelled with Escobar.[76] Like Almeida and Quevedo, Caraveo began in humble circumstances in western Chihuahua and used the Revolution to rise.[77] In 1929 he simply guessed wrong and ended up in exile.

The other military figure, Roberto Fierro, was too young to have fought in the Revolution and spent his youth in El Paso. Although born in Guerrero, he had few ties to the state.[78]

Other Political Leaders

Perhaps the leading unsuccessful political figure of the 1920s and 1930s was Manuel M. Prieto. A Carrancista, he became municipal president of Ciudad Juárez in 1915 and served several months in the post while Enríquez was governor. He was subsequently administrator of frontier customs, federal senator, and head of the Calles presidential campaign in Chihuahua. After leading a troop of peasants from Guadalupe, Bravos district, against the rebels in 1929, he ran unsuccessfully for governor in 1930. He held a number of posts outside the state thereafter.[79]

The state's secondary political figures were overwhelmingly middle-class, though a few agrarian and labor leaders emerged during the 1930s to exert important influence. The effective behind-the-scenes politicians of the era dabbled in everything while seeking to increase their influence and their fortunes. Luis Esther Estrada (?–1934), a business partner and political backer of Jesús Antonio Almeida, was a merchant in Miñaca in the 1910s. With two partners, Juan F. Treviño and Primitivo Enríquez, he was a stockholder in the Compañía Madreria Agrícola, S.A. During the 1920s, he was involved with the Almeida brothers in a number of ventures, including the Negociación Manufacturera de Maderas in Durango. Although he became a federal senator from Chihuahua, he was not popular. Union and agrarian groups protested against his activities, accusing him of being "only dedicated to plotting." He was politically adept enough to recover from Almeida's fall, supporting Quevedo in 1931.[80] He was president of the state PNR in 1931.

Nicolás Pérez (?–1932), a former preacher, one of the signers of the Constitution of 1917, was also one of the plotters against Almeida in 1927. A large landholder (the Hacienda de Agua Caliente in San Francisco de Borjas, with more than 60,000 hectares) and mining entrepreneur, during the mid-1920s he was in charge of the immigration department in Ciudad Juárez, a federal congressman from 1926 to 1928, and president of the congress in 1927.[81] He was the leading Callista in Chihuahua.[82] Angel Martínez was a businessman and politician first in Parral and then Ciudad Juárez, whose career spanned from the 1920s to 1940. Originally a merchant in Parral, he became a large landowner in northern Chihuahua. He was president of the Cámara de Comercio in Ciudad Juárez during the 1930s.[83] An early opponent of the Quevedos, he became a member of Governor Talamantes's cabinet.[84] He was notorious among Talamantes's henchmen for corruption. Although biographical material on these three men is limited, they all seemed to rise in the aftermath of the Revolution to considerable wealth, accumulated in great part through the use of their political positions.

There were a few cases of prominent political figures who began as businessmen. Pantaleón E. Meléndez, for example, headed a banking house in the early 1920s.[85] He was elected municipal president of Ciudad Chihuahua for 1925 to 1926 as a strong supporter of the Almeidas.[86] He survived the coup against them in 1927 and became a leading figure in the opposition to the PNR, first as an officer of the Gran Partido Socialista de Chihuahua.[87] Meléndez was president of the Partido Independiente del Norte (formerly Obreros del Norte), which backed Aaron Sáenz in 1929. He helped organize the Prieto gubernatorial campaign in 1930, again in opposition to the PNR. Although he backed the losing side on three occasions, he obtained a position as chief of the federal office of labor in Monterrey in 1931.[88]

Julio Ornelas obtained political position through his work in the Cámara de Comercio in Ciudad Chihuahua, which he founded in 1916 and of which he was manager from 1921 until 1930. Ornelas was elected municipal president of Ciudad Chihuahua in 1916.[89] He was still active in city politics in 1925, when he ran for a seat on the *ayuntamiento*. His son was elected governor of Chihuahua in 1980.

No major worker or campesino leader was elected governor, but a number played important roles in state politics. For instance, Eugenio Prado, who reportedly controlled the workers' movement in Chihuahua, was a founder of the local PNR. He was elected to the legislature in 1934, served as interim governor, was a federal congressman from 1937 to 1940, and president of the committee on administration of the national chamber of deputies. He was also municipal president of Ciudad Chihuahua. It was primarily through his efforts that opposing factions in the 1940 gubernatorial election, when Foglio Miramontes opposed Alfredo Chávez, were reconciled. He was a federal senator from Chihuahua from 1940 to 1946.[90] Justino Loya, who was secretary-general of the Liga de Comunidades Agrarias in 1936 and 1937, subsequently became an important official of the PRM in 1939.[91] Being a leader of a popular organization could be dangerous. Andrés Mendoza, president of the Liga de Comunidades Agrarias in the early 1930s, attained so much power that Governor Ortiz allegedly had him assassinated in 1931.[92] Mendoza began his revolutionary activities as a teenage participant in an uprising in San Andrés in 1906. After a long career as a Villista, he organized campesinos, threatening especially the holdings of the Zuloaga family (the Hacienda de Bustillos).[93] Another radical schoolteacher in the mold of Francisco Almada was Manuel López Dávila, who was a powerful influence on local politics as the municipal president of Ciudad Chihuahua in 1936 and 1937.[94]

Small landholders and small businessmen found a representative in Cruz Villalba, a former legislator, who was secretary of the Veteranos de la Revolución in 1935. He was also a board member of the Cámara de Comerciantes e Industriales en Pequeño and the Cámara Nacional de Comercio e Industria de Chihuahua and president of the Sindical de Comerciantes y Detallistas. Obviously opposed to the radical Cardenista program, whose agrarian and labor policies threatened his constituents, he joined the Partido Constitucional Democrático Chihuahuense, which backed Juan A. Almazán's candidacy for the presidency in 1939. Villalba was a retail grocer.[95]

It is evident from the careers of the leading state politicians that Knight's pattern holds true. Upwardly mobile freebooters like Almeida and Quevedo, who had made their way through the military, gave way in the late 1930s to better-trained middle-class (in the case of Chávez, probably upper-middle-class if not upper-class) career politicians. Indicative of this was the discernible new pattern in education. The later leaders were better educated. Several of the governors graduated as engineers from the Agricultural School in Ciudad Juárez. Others were educated in the United States. Talamantes, the agrarian bureaucrat, who succeeded Quevedo, the bandit-turned-general, epitomized the transition from lower- to middle-class leadership and from personalism to party rule.

Turnover in Political Office

One method that historians have used to measure the mettle of the revolutionary regime has been to evaluate the turnover in political office. Peter Smith discovered in the national government a high degree of turnover in comparison with other democratic nations.[96] In Chihuahua, there was no reelection to the governorship; but this was not true for the state legislature or for other offices. There is, of course, some question as to the importance of turnover in a system dominated by informal influences and a political party that was virtually inseparable from the government. During the 1920s, there were many reelections to the legislature but rarely a third term. The only three-term legislators were Francisco R. Almada and Manuel Jesús Estrada, each of whom had broken service. In other instances, there was no individual reelection but families kept the position. The Acosta (Acosta y Plata and Acosta Rivera) family had a representative from Jiménez district in the legislatures elected in 1911 and 1920–26. The Hasbach brothers, Bernardo R. and Federico, were deputies from Guadalupe y Calvo for two terms each during the mid-1920s. Reelections were curtailed severely after the formation of the PNR in 1929. Only eight individuals served more than one term during the 1930s; and, of those, only one served more than two terms.

The lesser extent of reelection coincided with a distinct deterioration of the legislature's power. Members of the body had overthrown governors in 1927, 1931, and 1932 and attempted to unsuccessfully in 1930 and 1931. In the years of chaos from 1927 to 1932 (which paralleled the unsettled period surrounding Obregón's reelection and assassination and the formation of the PNR-Maximato compromise nationally), the legislature had gained considerably more influence than it had under more forceful governors before or afterward.

The Businessmen

No one family would ever dominate Chihuahua's economy in the postrevolutionary era as had the Terrazas prior to 1910. And in the ten to fifteen years after the end of the civil wars, the state's economy was in such turmoil and disrepair that there was probably no small group of individuals or families that stood above the rest. But gradually a handful of families emerged to acquire great wealth and lead Chihuahua, for the most part after 1940, to substantial prosperity. As we have seen in the preceding chapter, a number of branches of the Terrazas and Zuloaga extended families could be counted among them. The Almeidas and Quevedos were included as well. More important, perhaps, were three other families, the

Vallinas, Bermúdez, and Borundas. Each took advantage of the vast opportunities offered by the state's enormous resources.

The demise of the Terrazas as the predominant bankers and landowners of Chihuahua provided opportunities for others to make themselves rich. Other possibilities were created by the breakup of Terrazas monopolies in flour milling and meat packing. The curtailment of the vast landholdings of others than the Terrazas also furnished possibilities.[97] These opportunities were precisely those for which many of the original Chihuahuan revolutionaries had fought. Ultimately, after reconstruction from war and depression, they achieved their goals.

The family that was to become perhaps the richest and most powerful of all rose from humble but ambitious Spanish immigrants. They arrived in Mexico in the Porfiriato with their father, a mining superintendent.[98] They went to the United States in 1914 to avoid the Revolution. The brothers Eloy and Rafael Vallina settled in El Paso, Texas, in 1919. (Eventually a third brother, Jesús, joined them.) They studied banking at a local business college and then went to work in local banks. Eloy rose to head the loan department of the First National Bank. Rafael married Delfina Fernández Campo, the daughter of another Spanish immigrant, an industrialist in Chihuahua, Tomás Fernández Blanco. The three Fernández brothers—Tomás, José, and Ramón—operated a flour-milling business and leased the Compañía Cervecera de Chihuahua, formerly operated by the Terrazas.

Building on the partial ruins of the Terrazas, the Vallina brothers parlayed their expertise in banking and a good marriage into one of the greatest fortunes in Mexico. With their in-laws' financial backing, they started the Banco Mercantil in 1925. As they would do in many of their enterprises, the Vallinas brought together various elements of the Chihuahuan elite and foreign investors in the bank.[99] After a series of bankruptcies of rival financial institutions and their takeover of the Ciudad Juárez and Chihuahua branches of the Banco Nacional in 1932, their bank enjoyed a virtual monopoly of banking in Chihuahua. Moreover, Vallina reported that the Banco Mercantil had not suffered during the depression: 1931 was a better year than 1930.[100] In 1929 Rafael started the Compañía Mercantil de Inversiones, which operated an ice factory and refrigeration plant for fruits and vegetables.[101] In 1928 Eloy married into another prominent family with large industrial holdings when he married María Laguera Zambrano.

The Vallinas' most successful enterprise was established in 1934, when Eloy united the Chihuahuan elite in the Banco Comercial Mexicano to be "an instrument of regional progress that would make [it] possible to overcome the crisis and open new horizons to the economic life of Chihuahua."[102] Its offices were (no small irony) in the old site of the Banco Minero de Chihuahua.

The bank brought together a wide range of the Chihuahuan elite: Simon L. Gill as president; Edwin P. Ryan as vice president; board members: Ing. Miguel Márquez, Lic. Ramón Gómez Salas, Arturo Wisbrun, Eloy S. Vallina, Ricardo Hernández; and alternates: Lauro C. Alvarez, Walther G. Gibbe, Jacobo L. Castro, Lic. Carlos Sisniega, Enrique N. Seyffert, José Costemalle; *comisario:* Manuel Rivero y Mier.[103]

After the Banco de Londres y México set up a branch in Chihuahua in 1948, the Vallinas engineered a merger of the smaller banks in the region in order to better compete. Eventually the family established a nationwide banking system. The Banco Comercial became the foundation of the economic development of Chihuahua after 1940.

The Vallina brothers' careers were startlingly like that of Enrique C. Creel during the Porfiriato. He, too, at a young age had married well and used his father-in-law's capital to found an important regional bank. Like Creel, Eloy Vallina went on to establish an even larger bank into which he incorporated foreign and local capital. Using the bank—as Creel had with the Banco Minero—as a base after 1940, the Vallinas, in conjunction with their long-standing partners, branched out into industry. Like Creel, Vallina had wider ambitions, extending his banking network nationwide. Like the Terrazas-Creels, the Vallinas had links to other northern enterprise groups. Each had an insurance company. Each experienced a large bank robbery, Creel in 1908 and Vallina thirty years later. The Vallinas, like the Terrazas-Creels, also bought the telephone company. In fact, not surprisingly, the Terrazas family was one of Vallina's most important backers. Ing. Miguel Márquez, in particular, was involved in almost all the Vallina businesses.[104]

Antonio J. Bermúdez built his fortune on supplying liquor to the tourist trade in Mexico and to bootleggers across the border during the Prohibition era in the United States. Starting out as a liquor wholesaler, he expanded his business by purchasing the D&W Distillery and an ice plant in the 1920s. He attained social prominence when he and other family members married into old-line families such as the Mascareñas, Luján, and Zuloaga. Bermúdez constructed a parallel career as an influential member of the Cámara de Comercio de Ciudad Juárez. He was president of that organization in 1926 and was regarded as "young and progressive."[105] Bermúdez was municipal president of Ciudad Juárez in 1942 and 1943. From 1946 to 1958 he headed Petroleos Mexicanos. Like his contemporaries, he acquired part of the Terrazas estate. In 1931 he bought Los Aparejos.[106]

José Borunda, a native of San Onofre, Satevó, was secretary of the Acción Obrera and Organización Industrial in 1935, secretary of the state committee of the PNR, and president of the Partido Revolucionario del Norte. He was a member of the *ayuntamiento* of Ciudad Juárez in 1929 and then a state legislator from Guerrero district during the early 1930s. He was elected a federal deputy and became secretary-general of the PNR. He headed the Bloque Izquierdista del Norte in Chihuahua in the mid-1930s. After he was elected municipal president of Juárez in 1937, he was assassinated by a mail bomb.[107] His nephew Teófilo, also born in San Onofrio, rose in his footsteps to become a dominant force in Chihuahuan politics in the 1940s and 1950s. He held his first political office in 1932 as a *regidor* of the ayuntamiento of Juárez. He was elected mayor in 1940, governor in 1956. Borunda married well; his wife was Hortensia Flores, the daughter of one of the leading political families in Ciudad Juárez.[108]

Like the Almeidas and Quevedos, the Borunda family based its landholding on the acquisition of sections of the former Terrazas estate. At least four members acquired lots of the Hacienda de Encinillas in 1934.[109] There is little doubt that they used their political connections to acquire the properties from the Caja de Préstamos.[110]

The leading attorney of the era was Guillermo Porras. He was the Terrazas family's representative who handled the disposition of Luis's estate in 1922. He was related by marriage to the Zuloagas, whom he also represented in their litigation against the implementation of the agrarian reform.[111] A landowner himself, he was a spokesperson for the state's livestock raisers, becoming president of the cattlemen's association, the Unión Ganadera Regional de Chihuahua, in 1939 and 1940.[112]

There were fortunes to be made, as during the Porfiriato, in representing foreign companies. Ramón Gómez y Salas and Manuel Prieto, for example, represented ASARCO.[113] Manuel Prieto, Jr. (1892–) attended Georgetown Law School and represented a number of other large companies.[114] He, like Guillermo Porras, was tied to the Terrazas family and its enterprises. He was secretary of the Compañía Eléctrica y de Ferrocarriles de Chihuahua and also of the Cámara Nacional de Mineria del Estado de Chihuahua.[115] Prieto had extensive ties to the most important, surviving Porfirian elite families.[116] Arguably, both Porras and Prieto are better categorized as members of the old elite. But they were illustrative of how, while one branch of a family may have found itself stymied, another branch rose to prominence.

The breakup of the old *latifundios* gave chances for others to become large landowners and cattle barons. Juan F. Carrillo owned the Hacienda de Samalayuca in partnership with an heir of the original owners, Señorita Mariana Ochoa.[117] Carrillo also leased the San Isidro hacienda in Jiménez.[118] The Raynal family (Manuel, José Angel, and María E. de Raynal) obtained part of the Zuloaga's Tres Hermanos. Manuel had started his career as a merchant and miner in the mid-1920s.[119] Prieto also owned the Hacienda de Esteban.[120] Both Carrillo and Raynal were important figures in the state cattlemen's association during the 1930s.[121] Several revolutionary military leaders obtained lands too. Colonel Ignacio Almada grabbed part of the Hacienda El Charco, only to lose it when he went over to the rebels in 1929. General Antonio A. Guerrero, one-time zone commander in Chihuahua, seized the Hacienda de Ojo Caliente. General Claudio Fox acquired El Refugio.[122]

The most colorful entrepreneur of the era was David Russek. The son of immigrant businessman Marcos Russek, who had married into the prominent family of Manuel Gameros, he controlled, through his wife's inheritance, the vast estate of Enrique Muller, which included the Hacienda de Santa Clara. Through the 1920s, Russek schemed unsuccessfully to build an empire in banking and landholding. In 1923 his bank required special treatment from Governor Enríquez to gain a moratorium on its 500,000-peso debt to Ciudad Chihuahua merchants. He also promoted one venture to colonize Santa Clara and another to build a railroad line from Agua Nueva to Santa Clara. He had fallen into such great difficulties in 1924 that an irate creditor bombed his house. In the early 1920s, Russek leased a portion of the hacienda to the United States War Finance Corporation to graze its cattle. He was still negotiating to sell the estate in 1932 to a colony of Doukhobors (Russians). His allegedly preferential treatment by the state government caused successive scandals.[123]

Old and New Elites

Old and new elites came together most crucially in the state cattlemen's association and in the formation of the Vallinas' flagship bank, the Banco Comercial Mexicano, S.A. The board of directors of the Union Ganadera Regional de Chihuahua in 1942 included: Lic. Luis Laguette Terrazas, president; Ing. J. Carlos Ochoa Arroniz, secretary; Juan Salas Porras, treasurer; Esteban L. Almeida, Rodolfo Quevedo, Ing. Manuel O'Reilly, and Ing. Carlos Barney, board members; and Ing. Federico Terrazas, Ing. Jesús J. Corral, Manuel Raynal, on the vigilance committee. Laguette and Terrazas were members of the Terrazas-Creel family. The Almeidas (Almeida and Barney) and Quevedos were also represented, as were Ochoa and Raynal.

The board of directors of the Banco Comercial included, in 1940: Simon Gill, Esteban L. Almeida, Eloy S. Vallina, Arturo Wisbrun, Edwin P. Ryan, and Ing. Miguel Márquez.[124] Gill was a prominent entrepreneur from Ciudad Chihuahua. Almeida, of course, represented his family, as Márquez did the Terrazas. Wisbrun was a merchant and politician from the state capital.[125] Ramón Salas Porras was president of the bank. Vallina acted much as had Enrique C. Creel during the Terrazas era. As the state's leading banker, he brought together old and new elites and foreigners in important ventures.

Perhaps indicative of the outcome of the process by which a new elite emerged and how it melded with the old was the makeup of a commission formed in 1937 to push construction of the highway between Ciudad Chihuahua and Ciudad Juárez. Its president was Jesús Muñoz Luján, an agent of the Cía Petroleo del Aguila, S.A., and representative of the rotary club. Muñoz was probably the son of Jorge Muñoz and Rosa Terrazas Luján, which meant he was a great-grandchild of Luis Terrazas. The vice president was Lauro Alvarez, representative of the local chamber of commerce, who had for many years been the private secretary of Enrique C. Creel and had managed the state's first automobile agency. The secretary was Antonio Hernández, a prominent real-estate dealer and representative of the Chamber of Proprietors. The treasurer was Eloy Vallina, representative of the Chamber of Commerce and manager of the state's largest bank. The board of directors consisted of Estebán Almeida, the head of a lumber company, J. Refugio Sandoval, owner of El Progreso clothing textile factory, Gabriel Chávez, a Parral merchant and representative of the Chamber of Proprietors, and Angel Martínez, the state treasurer.[126] Almeida and Sandoval represented the cattlemen's association. The commission was geographically balanced between the major urban areas and business interests. It had representatives from both old and new elites. It was as if Creel were still ruling Chihuahua's enterprise.

Rising entrepreneurs, economic and political, quickly recognized the value of social ties to the old elite. When Antonio J. Bermúdez married Hilda Mascareñas, the wedding party rivaled that of the Almeida-Nesbitt gala. Old elite like Creel and Terrazas rubbed shoulders with the new, such as Cuarón, Adame, Almeida, and Martínez.[127]

Conclusion

The new elite that emerged from the ashes of the revolutionary civil war in Chihuahua was far less homogeneous than the group that had dominated the state in the last two decades of the Porfiriato. (Although if we make the comparison with the Chihuahuan elite in its formative stage from the 1860s through the 1880s, of course, there was far more heterogeneity.) The Terrazas family included nearly all the prominent figures in government in the first decade of the century. Moreover, the small ranchers and businessmen who rebelled in 1910, in order to break the economic and political hegemony of the Terrazas family, formed the core of the new elite but by no means monopolized it. There was, too, almost a complete turnover in the people who ruled Chihuahua in each succeeding decade after 1910. The devastation and attrition wrought by war and fierce internecine political competition exacted a heavy toll. Because of the almost constant rebellions, Chihuahua was highly militarized until the early 1930s and, consequently and unsurprisingly, drew its political leaders from army or militia ranks (Enríquez, Almeida, Caraveo, Fierro, Quevedo). Personalism and family ties were essential throughout the era, even after the formation of the PNR.

The geographical origins of the elite changed. During the Díaz era, the cattle barons of the state's central region defeated the small ranchers of the western foothills for political hegemony in the state. The Revolution altered this situation. Competition arose from four areas: Ciudad Chihuahua, which continued to represent central cattle interests; Hidalgo de Parral, the major mining region; Ciudad Juárez, a growing commercial entrepot whose legalized gambling generated large sums; and the western region encompassing Guerrero district and the Casas Grandes area, heavily populated by small ranchers.

The great fortunes in Chihuahua that were made after 1920 had three bases: the expropriated estates of Luis Terrazas; the vacuum left by the absence of Terrazas banks; and the opportunities provided by gambling and bootlegging prior to 1934. In addition, the separation of political and economic elites was never very clear in Chihuahua. The dominant family of the 1920s, the Almeidas, and that of the 1930s, the Quevedos, used each sphere to augment the other (as had the Terrazas before the Revolution). Of the important economic elites of the 1930s and afterward, only the Vallinas steered clear of open participation in politics; as they had been born in Spain, politics was out of the question. But the Bermúdez and Borundas followed the same prescription as the Almeidas and Quevedos. Lastly, the alliance between old and new elites flourished, particularly after 1930. Jesús Antonio Almeida had begun the process of reconciliation and cooperation. The Vallinas had mastered the technique. They invited the full participation of the Terrazas and other old elite families in their enterprises, much as Enrique C. Creel had welcomed the participation of the Zuloagas and other conservatives in the late nineteenth century.

The alliance of old and new elites solidified over the years. In the 1988 election for the governorship of Chihuahua, the inner circle of the very strong PAN candidate Francisco Barrio Terrazas was comprised of Federico Terrazas, Guillermo Villalobos Madero (the Zuloaga family), Archbishop Adalberto Almeida y Merino, Francisco Villarreal (Quevedo), and Guillermo Prieto Luján.[128]

The clearest evidence of the diversity and complexity of the consequences of the Revolution lies in local politics. It was there that the interplay of national regime, state elite, and local elite was perhaps fiercest and most important for the daily lives of Mexicans. Only recently have historians of Chihuahua begun to unearth the documentary record that will enable us to reconstruct the history and offer an interpretation of these politics. This chapter is meant to provide a working framework for these endeavors. It sketches, from evidence available mostly from national and state sources, an outline from the top down. At the heart of this skeleton is the case of Ciudad Juárez. Although as a small bordertown it was in some respects an aberration, Ciudad Juárez, perhaps better than anywhere else, illustrates the three-dimensional construction of Chihuahuan political history. It also furnishes a concise picture of how new elites arose and new and old elites interacted. The outline nevertheless leaves us with many questions, especially about the roles played by local agrarian and labor organizations and local military groups and the composition of their leadership.

Local politics often played out independently of, though not without reference to, national and state issues, loyalties, and ideology. Municipal (and village) factions battled with their own "logic": to control economic resources such as land, taxes, and patronage. During the 1920s, the national regime rarely exhibited the power to other than occasionally exert its influence at the local level. Warring factions at the state level created considerable space in which municipal ruling groups could operate. In this way the 1920s were a throwback to the era of internecine strife from the 1820s through to the 1880s. The advent of the official revolutionary party in 1929 did not immediately lead to hegemony for the national regime. It took some time for the PNR, through the Quevedos, to establish itself. The split between Calles and Cárdenas, manifested in Chihuahua to some extent by a similar falling out between the Quevedos and Talamantes, further delayed national control. It appears that even in the last years of the Cárdenas administration neither the party nor the national government was strong enough to impose its authority completely and unilaterally in the municipalities.

In order to bring the municipalities (and the state) under control, the national regime required either one of two resources: money or force. During the tumultuous 1920s and the depression-ridden 1930s, the former was in short supply. The latter, in the face of periodic, dangerous rebellions in the 1920s and the downsizing of the federal army in the 1930s, was often more needed elsewhere. The economic boom after World War II enhanced the financial resources of the national regime, which then, over time, constrained municipal autonomy. Subsuming popular organizations and local bosses alike into the national party obviated the need, in most instances, for institutional force.

As we have seen in earlier chapters, the national regime, even in a weakened condition, was not without influence in state politics. Similarly, state elites were not without consequence in the municipalities, particularly in the larger ones. State governments often exerted veto power over local elections. Governors obstructed agrarian and labor reforms.

Underlying the three-tiered structure of political conflict was the struggle of prerevolutionary elites to maintain their positions and new elites to establish themselves at the local level. It is in the municipalities that we see just how long it took the Revolution to come to Mexico, how strong was the resistance it met, and how varied was its outcome.

In discussing the old and new elites at the municipal level, it is useful to introduce the term "local notable." Barnett Singer uses the phrase to differentiate between the *grandes notables,* or the nobility, and the mayors, schoolmasters, and priests who controlled local politics in France both before and after the revolution of 1789.[1] By definition these local elites had limited, if any, ambitions or influence beyond their home municipalities. French local notables owed their appointments to department prefects. During the nineteenth century in Chihuahua, a local notable occasionally challenged for statewide political office. The Becerras of Urique, for example, tried their hand at state politics in the 1870s, lost out, and retired from the fray. The Papigochic group of Guerrero district actually wrested power from the Terrazas from 1884 to 1892, with the support of Porfirio Díaz, but faded thereafter. The others kept to their home grounds. During the Porfiriato, they exerted influence through political alliances with the Terrazas or the latter's opponents. After the Revolution, the importance of a local base for statewide politics diminished over time. Governors Enríquez and Almeida obtained strong support in the western sierras, but this was more a military than a political base. The local notables were not nearly a match for state-level elites in terms of wealth or breadth of political influence. Neither would qualify them for elite rank. Nonetheless, they constituted the municipal ruling class. In Mexico generally and in Chihuahua specifically, all politics began at the municipal level, and so the notables must be taken into consideration.

French and Chihuahuan local notables had a number of similar characteristics. Some French families, for example, held the mayoralty among their number for a century or more. In the more stagnant areas there was little possibility of change. Likewise, in Chihuahua, the Becerras and Rascóns ruled their bailiwicks for an equal length of time. French and Chihuahuan notables alike were "repressive [and] authoritarian." Both were continuously accused of electoral abuses.[2] After 1940, with the growing penetration of the national party, Chihuahuan notables became the tools of higher authority, as had been the French.

There were, perhaps, five categories of municipalities in the postrevolutionary era: relatively isolated enclaves where the Porfirian notables, after some initial setbacks, reestablished their political and economic preeminence at least through the end of the 1920s; areas where the old elite remained prominent, often through intermarriage with emerging families, and held local political office but did not dominate; revolutionary centers in which there was considerable continuity in political leadership; municipalities where a new group or groups arose; and finally, major urban areas—Ciudad Chihuahua, Parral, and Ciudad Juárez—where political competition among new groups was fierce and the state elite (and at times the national elite) more influential. In each category circumstances changed over time. Isolated enclaves became less insular. Some dominant families held on until 1930 but faded thereafter. Others made comebacks after a decade or so out of power.

Although membership of the local elite may or may not have changed, many aspects of elite behavior and strategies did not. Complaints of arbitrary and capricious actions on the part of municipal presidents and police continued unabated, if local newspapers and the correspondence to the national government are any guide. Electoral fraud was a constant problem, both before and after the advent of an official party. State-level officials, as they had before the Revolution, continued to interfere in municipal politics whenever the opportunity offered itself. Almost every governor overturned some results of municipal elections.[3] Corruption was commonplace.

Isolated Enclaves

There are two outstanding examples of the first category of municipality, isolated communities in which Porfirian elites remained dominant through at least the 1920s. In the first, the Rascóns were the political bosses, leading mine-owners, and most important merchants of Uruachic, a southwestern mining town, from the late eighteenth century. During the thirty years preceding the Revolution, they came to control virtually every mining claim of any value in the region, as well as its largest haciendas. The family dominated local politics to such an extent that in 1908 its members held eight of ten seats on the Uruachic *ayuntamiento*. Family patriarchs Enrique C. and Ignacio Rascón acted as state legislators and *jefes políticos* during much of the Porfiriato. They allied themselves with Luis Terrazas from the time when they joined him in opposition to Porfirio Díaz in the 1870s. The Rascóns emerged from the Revolution with their mining and commercial interests intact. Like the Terrazas, they had backed the Orozquistas in 1912 but evidently avoided exile because they kept a foot in both camps. When Orozquista Guillermo S. Rascón was ousted as *presidente municipal,* another Rascón was his *suplente* (alternate). Guillermo was eventually pardoned by Villa. During the 1920s, the family dominated the local *ayuntamiento* once again and a family member was *presidente* in nine of the thirteen years between 1918 and 1931. After being out of power through the 1930s, the family installed one of its own as municipal president in 1940 and 1941.[4]

In the second example, the Becerras ruled Urique during the Porfiriato much as the Rascóns had Uruachic. Juan N. Becerra moved to the region in the early years of the nineteenth century, becoming an important mine-owner and political official. His sons, Buenaventura and José María, expanded the family's economic holdings. Buenaventura, in particular, grew rich selling mines to foreign companies and died a millionaire in 1907. The brothers briefly tried to obtain statewide office in 1877, when José María ran in and lost the gubernatorial election. Thereafter they allied with the Terrazas. Marriage linked them to foreigners, who operated their mining enterprises, and to local political officials. During the Revolution, one Becerra, Rafael, was *jefe político* during the governorship of Abraham González, leading to the conclusion that the family played both sides during the years of upheaval. The Becerras continued to mine and ranch in Urique through the 1930s. Relatives served in the state legislature from western districts. The family's political rule was challenged in 1924, when angry opponents ran local boss and family member Alfredo S. Monge and his son from town. The family strengthened its position, at least temporarily, when Susana Nesbit Becerra married governor Jesús Antonio Almeida in 1925.[5]

Prominence or even dominance did not assure that the Revolution would not affect local notables. The Becerras lost a substantial amount of land to agrarian reform from 1920 to 1940.[6] In one dispute, Buenaventura's son Rafael (presumably the same appointed *jefe* by González) ended the long tradition of allowing the pueblo of Piedras Verdes to occupy a tract of land rent-free. Rafael used local authorities to enforce his decision. But the agrarians fought back and petitioned for a grant and restitution of land under the reform laws.[7]

Not all of the enclaves remained as stable as Uruachic and Urique. The political history of two of the larger, isolated western mining towns, Chínipas and Guadalupe y Calvo, differed rather substantially from these old elite bastions. Chínipas, the mining and commercial center of Arteaga district, had sixty-seven changes in the office of municipal president, with thirty-six different men in the post between 1911 and 1941. Over half the changes (thirty-four) took place between 1911 and 1919. Only six people held the office for more than one term.[8]

Guadalupe y Calvo, in southern Chihuahua, Mina district, another old mining center, had sixty-nine changes in the office of the municipal presidency, with forty-six different people serving. Four individuals or families seemed to vie for the post through the early 1920s.[9] Thereafter only Francisco Olivas Peña (1924–25, 1928–29, 1939) and Manuel Chávez Palma (1932, 1936–37) had more than one term. No family seemed to have obtained predominance, let alone a monopoly of important political posts.

The Old Notables: Active But Not Dominant

Perhaps the most visible example of the second category of municipality, where an old elite extended family retained considerable influence and openly participated in local politics, was in Jiménez. Members of the Acosta, Estavillo, Luján, Muñoz, and Soto families served in the *ayuntamiento* and as municipal presidents. Although these families provided a basis of continuity, political turnover was high: there were fifty-seven changes in municipal president, with fifty-one people in the position from 1910 to 1940.[10] The Lujáns' influence spread over a wider area, for three of their number were municipal presidents of Villa López from 1930 to 1940. The Acostas, Estavillos, and Lujáns were important cattle ranchers.

Former Terracistas were not necessarily excluded from local office elsewhere. Vicente N. Mendoza became municipal president of Santa Isabel (later General Trías) despite his backing of Luis Terrazas. In Zaragoza, the Alvidrez family made a comeback after the Revolution, regaining the post of municipal president, which it held during the Terrazas era (1903), in 1936 and 1937.[11]

Revolutionary Centers

Ironically, in several areas where the Revolution had spawned, Porfirian landholding and merchant families continued to have great influence. In Coyamé the Ramírez family, merchants who had dominated the office of *jefe político* under the Terrazas, continued to do so in the 1920s.[12] The three families that were central to politics before the Revolution in Janos retained their positions afterward. The Baeza, Echéribel, and Renterías kept their hold through the 1920s. The Renterías were members of the *ayuntamiento* into the 1930s. In Bachíniva, the Estradas, who had served on the *ayuntamiento* during the Terrazas era, survived, and family members held the municipal presidency for four years in the 1920s. The same families that had dominated the *ayuntamiento* of Ciudad Guerrero before 1910 held sway through 1940: the merchants Casavantes, Estrada, and Saenz. In Namiquipa an old Porfirista *presidente* (1902–3), Eligio Muñoz, was president under the Revolution from 1913 to 1917.[13]

The persistence of the old notables in revolutionary municipalities is persuasive evidence that local issues were paramount. National labels and trends were not necessarily decisive. Past alliances with the Terrazas-Creels did not preclude important positions in the postrevolutionary era.

New Notables

In many municipalities modest merchants and landholders rose to political power, if not riches, in the aftermath of the Revolution. Little is known of their prerevolutionary or revolutionary activities. In several instances single families or individuals predominated for periods of time. In Balleza, the Medinas, a family of merchants and cattlemen, occupied the municipal presidency for five of nine years between 1926 and 1934. Members of the González and Pérez families occupied the post in Bocoyna almost every year between 1925 and 1940. One family, the Licóns, came to exert great political influence in five villages in a cluster southeast of Ciudad Chihuahua and northeast of Parral: Camargo, Delicias, La Cruz, Meoqui, and Rosales. Married into important landowning families, the Maynez and Urrutia, they were particularly prominent in the politics of Meoqui and Rosales. The merchant Salidos of Guazapares held the municipal presidency four times between 1919 and 1939. Eduardo Salido was municipal president of Chínipas, a state legislator, and acting governor in 1932.[14]

Methods of Rule

No matter which category of municipality, neither new nor old notables seemed to change the old ways of ruling. Many of the complaints against local authorities that had precipitated agitation before 1910—such as nepotism, arbitrariness, election abuses, and corruption—were reprised in complaints in the 1920s and 1930s. Nepotism still flourished. *El Correo* complained in 1926 that in Ocampo the municipal presidency and three other important appointed local offices were in the hands of the Juárez family.[15] Once a family established itself, it was difficult to dislodge. The same family ran Guadalupe, Bravos district, from 1938, when Jesús Aguilera M. was elected municipal president, through the 1970s. From 1950 to 1973 Antonio Gallegos Aguilera ruled the pueblo, serving for fourteen years as president of the *comisariado ejidal* of Guadalupe and three times as *alcalde*.[16]

It was not just families or individuals who maintained themselves against popular sentiment. The revolutionary party perpetuated its henchman as well. Temósachic, for example, endured the party's imposition of Baldomero García as municipal president in 1935 over the objections of workers and campesinos.[17] Similarly, in Janos in 1938, Pedro Hernández was accused of political manuevering to impose a successor as president of the *comité comisariado* against the wishes of the *ejidatarios*. In 1940 there were protests against the intervention of federal forces in favor of the PRM candidate in Bocoyna.[18]

Petty tyrannies abounded. The year 1930 brought complaints against municipal presidents: of "hostility and vengeance" in Cusihuiriachic, arbitrariness in San Andrés, tyranny in Ojinaga.[19] During the 1930s there were chronic complaints against the police and judiciary in Batopilas.[20] The "ignorance and apathy" of the municipal and judicial authorities oppressed Madera, where the municipal president had awarded himself an auto and a 50 percent salary increase.[21] Camargo's municipal president, Manuel Chávez M., drew protests against his arbitrary actions in 1935.[22] Satevó found itself still victimized in 1937 by local boss José Borunda E., who threatened individual rights and property and jailed and humiliated local citizens. Residents were further terrorized by the local municipal guard, which enforced the will of local landowners through murder and intimidation.[23]

During the mid-1920s there were allegations of electoral abuses in municipalities such as Ciudad Juárez, San Ignacio, Guadalupe, and San Lorenzo.[24] In a rare upset, Lorenzo L. Quevedo defeated an attempt by outgoing municipal president Andrés Campa to impose his brother-in-law Juventino Chávez in Casas Grandes in 1925. Campa allegedly had turned his post into a "feudal domain." Norberto Acosta, the boss of Ojinaga, allegedly used extortion to get elected.[25]

As was their prerevolutionary custom, municipal officials also stole their constituents' land. In 1935 the municipal president and chief of police of Bocoyna took land from the Tarahumara. Local authorities in 1940 tried to steal the harvest in Guerrero.[26]

In sum, the practice of democracy left much to be desired. Boss rule predominated. Despite recurring federal and state meddling, the practice, if not the practitioners, of politics and government at the local level remained, for the most part, unchanged from the Porfiriato.

This brief overview, with only selected examples, leaves many questions as to why some Porfirian local bosses retained their power and others lost it. Moreover, it is not clear if these were patterns for the emergence of new local notables. There is not enough information to tell us definitively how new notables rose or from what they derived their power. Undoubtedly, research in the archives of the smaller municipalities will yield many more answers.

There is, however, sufficient evidence to draw some speculative conclusions. Many local leaders, especially in the 1910s, came from the military, most often in Chihuahua from the *defensas sociales.*[27] Their successors—white guards, *acordadas,* and municipal guards— probably continued to supply leaders through the 1930s. What is not evident from the materials at hand is whether there were parallel structures in the municipalities. An understanding of the relationship between local militia chiefs and municipal presidents, if they were not the same person, awaits documentation. Another group of local leaders arose from agrarian politics. They started as officials of ejidos and crossed over to municipal politics. How common this was is not evident. The relationship between *ejido* and municipal governing bodies is unexplored.

There are additional questions about the role of union leaders in local politics. It would seem likely that there was some union participation in the mining camps like Parral, San Francisco del Oro, Santa Bárbara, and Santa Eulalia. It is not clear, except in the case of Ciudad Juárez discussed below, how politics changed after the organization of the PRN. We need to know to what extent the party made inroads into the municipalities and over what period of time. Little is known about the relations between the national party and local bosses. We do not know whether local notables opposed or cooperated with the PRN, and why.

There apparently was less of a separation between business and politics at the local level than Camp, for example, has discovered in national politics for the era.[28] The Licóns were only one case of merchants who translated mercantile success into political power. In Parral and Ciudad Juárez, certainly, businesspersons became involved in local politics through Rotary clubs and chambers of commerce. Several prominent political leaders rose through the ranks of these organizations in both cities.

Wielding unseen but surely felt power were the large landowners, new and old, who often had the means of coercion or could easily purchase them. The hacendados often had family representatives on the *ayuntamientos* of the larger municipalities like Parral, Jiménez, and Ciudad Chihuahua.

The Cities

The state's three major cities, Ciudad Chihuahua, Parral, and Ciudad Juárez, furnish a somewhat different perspective on the effect of revolutionary change than the smaller municipalities. Control of the cities and their wealth was crucial for control of the state. Ciudad Chihuahua, the capital and largest city, was the center of state politics. Parral was the most important mining center. Ciudad Juárez, the port of entry to the United States border and a gambling and bootleg liquor center, was the principal source of funds for state politics. Although I will touch briefly on the other two cities, the main focus for the remainder of this chapter will be Ciudad Juárez, for the funds it generated were the linchpin of Chihuahuan politics. Moreover, nowhere was the interplay of municipal, state, and federal politics and the evolution of local notables better illustrated.

Politics in Ciudad Chihuahua and Parral were somewhat less tumultuous than in Ciudad Juárez. In the state capital there were thirty-three changes in the office of municipal president between 1912 and 1941, with twenty-six different men serving in the post. With the exception of the rebellious years of 1927 and 1929, the city's *presidentes* completed their two-year terms. None were reelected. The city council was not a stepping-stone to higher office. Only one city council member, Reynaldo Talavera, moved up to be *presidente municipal*. One, Gustavo L. Talamantes, became governor.

Parral had only twenty-two different municipal presidents from 1912 to 1941. More than in Ciudad Chihuahua or Ciudad Juárez (as we shall see below), the *parralense* Porfirian political elite continued to hold office.[29] Ignacio Corral, for example, was prosecretary of the Club Reeleccionista de Porfirio Díaz in 1910, and then *presidente municipal* in 1921 and 1922.[30] Two members of the Domínguez family were officers in the same club. This did not prevent Enrique A. Domínguez from becoming *presidente* in 1926–27.[31] A third *presidente,* Rafael Sepúlveda (1936–37), very likely had a Porfirian ancestor as well. As was true for Ciudad Chihuahua, the city council provided little opportunity for upward mobility in one's political career. Only one municipal president, Valente Chacón Baca, served in the legislature (for two terms, 1928–29 and 1930–31), and only Enrique Hernández G. rose from the local body to become *presidente* (1928–29). The *ayuntamiento* was comprised mostly of local business people.[32] Parral shared some political characteristics with the isolated mining enclaves discussed above, at least through the early 1930s. Two important factors differentiated it from the others, however. First, the railroad tied it to the state capital and Mexico City. Second, it was a substantially larger and relatively more prosperous mining camp, with many more workers, a considerable labor-union presence, and significant foreign investment. When mining recovered during the late 1930s and, at the same time, unions took on a more influential role in state and national politics under Talamantes and Cárdenas, Parral assumed more importance as well.

Ciudad Juárez

All the crucial elements of postrevolutionary politics were in place in Ciudad Juárez from 1920 to 1940. The constant, bitter, brutal struggles between various local and state political factions and the national regime mirrored similar conflicts in Chihuahua and throughout Mexico, perhaps magnified in intensity by the extent of the riches involved. The money generated by the city as a port of entry and the center of bootlegging, legal and illegal gambling, illicit drug smuggling, and tourism was the fuel of Chihuahuan state government and politics. The ebb and flow of the control and resistance of each of the three levels of elites against those above is particularly well exhibited here. The deal-making and shifting alliances, it seemed, never ceased. *Juarense* politics, moreover, illustrated well the emergence of the postrevolutionary elite. The five families that intermittently controlled the city—Almeida, Bermúdez, Borundas, Flores, and Quevedo—typified the new rulers and their methods.

Paso del Norte (renamed Ciudad Juárez in 1888) was a dusty backwater until the last decades of the nineteenth century. Although it had been a trading center on the Camino Real from Santa Fe to Ciudad Chihuahua before the war between Mexico and the United States (1846–48), it counted for little in state politics and society. The balance of economic and political power in Chihuahua, however, gradually shifted from the agricultural districts of the western sierras and the southern mining districts to Ciudad Chihuahua, the capital, and Ciudad Juárez after the completion of the major north-south railroad, the Mexican Central, in 1884. The growing influx of foreign investment in north Mexican mining and burgeoning cattle exports from Chihuahua to the United States increased the importance of Ciudad Juárez as a commercial center.[33]

This process accelerated during the Revolution. While the rest of the state lost population from 1910 to 1920, Ciudad Juárez's population rose by 83.2 percent. In the succeeding decade it more than doubled. Growth slowed during the 1930s, but the number of inhabitants still grew by more than 20 percent. During the Revolution the city was a bustling center of arms and munitions trade, migration, and transportation.[34] As a port of entry it was an attractive target for various revolutionary armies, which coveted the funds from its customs collections. The city was of considerable symbolic and strategic significance, too, as was evidenced by the fact that its capture by Pascual Orozco in 1911 led to the overthrow of Porfirio Díaz.

But Ciudad Juárez also suffered enormously from the Revolution. Eight times from 1911 to 1920 it fell to rebel armies, the last time in June 1919, when Pancho Villa besieged and captured it before United States army units routed him. Moreover, the city found itself the temporary home of hundreds, sometimes thousands, of migrants fleeing the destruction to the south. This transient population was a constant drain on its resources and a threat to its stability.

The return of peace left the city with few prospects. Aside from a handful of clothing factories and railroad repair facilities, there was little industry in Ciudad Juárez in 1920. As we have seen, Chihuahua as a whole was in ruins. The Revolution had destroyed the state's cattle industry, for which Ciudad Juárez had been the major entrepôt. The area's mining industry never recovered. Commerce was in the doldrums, the result of the postwar recession in the United States and the still uncertain political conditions throughout northern Mexico.

Gambling, Liquor, and Narcotics

Two economic opportunities presented themselves after 1918. The prohibition of the sale of alcoholic beverages in the United States in 1920 provided a potential bonanza for Ciudad Juárez. Its liquor stores and saloons served customers who came from across the border. The location of El Paso on the major east-west railroad made its sister city an accessible tourist attraction. Proximity to the border and transport also proved an advantage to *juarense* distillers and wholesale liquor distributors, who legally sold their products to smugglers. At the same time, some *juarenses* sought to reintroduce and expand legalized gambling. Chihuahuan political leaders saw potentially enormous revenues for their bankrupt municipal and state governments from taxes on gambling.[35]

There were definite costs, especially in the long term. It was inevitable that liquor and gambling would attract criminal activity.

As a border town, Juárez had always had a rough reputation, but the 1920s elicited cries of modern-day "Sodom and Gomorrah." Conventional merchants, eventually allied with the more respectable liquor elements, split with gambling proponents. The former became leaders of the local chamber of commerce (Cámara Nacional de Comercio de Ciudad Juárez). Periodically they led local reform movements.[36] The substantial economic stakes added to the bitterness in municipal politics.

The city's businessmen moved quickly to take advantage of Prohibition. Many United States distillers shipped their stock across the border in order to avoid confiscation after the passage of the Volstead Act. *Juarense* wholesalers reaped large profits from distributing this liquor. Antonio J. Bermúdez, who became one of Chihuahua's most respected civic leaders, amassed his fortune as a liquor wholesaler.[37] Local entrepreneurs began construction of a distillery within months after Prohibition.[38]

The liquor trade, though legal on the Mexican side of the border, had its unsavory aspects. Local newspapers occasionally reported shoot-outs between smugglers and police. Flourishing saloons attracted sharpsters, extortionists, muggers, and pickpockets, who preyed on tourists. The most important illicit enterprise, however, was corruption. State and local officials demanded bribes or secret partnerships for themselves or relatives. One favorite ploy was the requirement that cantina owners hire "special police," off-duty city officers, to protect their establishments.[39]

Legalized gambling had begun in Ciudad Juárez before the Revolution under the auspices of one of Luis Terrazas's sons. The Madero government closed the first casino, the Tivoli, in 1911. Municipal officials and federal authorities began what was to be a long series of clashes over gambling policy, when the local federal army commander jailed the mayor because he did not close down the gambling establishments fast enough. Dictator Victoriano Huerta reopened them, receiving large license fees for his government. They remained open for most of the time from 1913 to 1920. By the end of the decade, optimistic *juarenses* talked of making the city into another Monte Carlo.[40]

For the next fifteen years, the Tivoli and other casinos were caught in a tug-of-war between municipal and state officials, desperate to find revenues for bankrupt governments or eager for lucrative bribes, who favored legalization, and national leaders, who, seeking to limit local autonomy, stood against it. Although the issue was often framed in moralistic terms, political autonomy, made possible by gambling revenues, was the real stake.

During the early 1920s, governors Enríquez and Talavera promoted legalization in the face of stern opposition from Obregón. At one point, after the Chihuahuan government permitted the casinos to reopen, the president withdrew the federal garrison from Ciudad Juárez in protest, leaving the city virtually without any police. On other occasions the federal government forced the state and city to comply by closing or threatening to close the international bridge that connected Ciudad Juárez with El Paso, an action that shut down the city's economy.[41]

Casino licenses became a lucrative and bitter source of rivalry. The vicious struggle between Enrique Fernández and Manuel Llantada between 1930 and 1934 was indicative of the competition. Twenty men, including Fernández, were killed in gangland wars in the first two years (1932–34) of Governor Quevedo's term. And the stakes were high. In 1926, the recently reopened Tivoli took in 250,000 pesos a month.[42]

This battle illustrates in starkest terms the characteristics and composition of the three-dimensional aspect of politics. Fernández allied with Luis León, who in turn was closely tied to Calles. Llantada joined with León's successor as governor, Andrés Ortiz. Eventually the Quevedo family, allied with Llantada, won control of the casinos and the state government. Cárdenas finally ended legalized gambling in 1934.[43]

A third lucrative commerce, in illegal drugs, also emerged during the early 1920s. The *El Paso Times* declared in December 1922 that Ciudad Juárez had become the "gateway" for morphine shipped from Germany and Switzerland to Los Angeles.[44] There were periodic attempts to eradicate the narcotics trade. In February 1923, for example, police seized US$20,000 worth of narcotics in Ciudad Juárez, the "biggest ever" drug bust. Another effort followed the scandal over the murder by an El Paso police detective of a Mexican army major on undercover assignment to investigate the drug business.[45] But these efforts never lasted very long. There were constant rumors and allegations that influential *juarenses,* such as Enrique Fernández and brothers José and Jesús Quevedo, were involved in the trade.

Chronic political instability and economic depression in the years from 1920 to 1940 magnified the importance of the money derived from gambling, liquor, and drugs. Other sources of economic opportunity and patronage in Juárez and the rest of Chihuahua were limited.

Politics

Local government was in constant turmoil. In the two decades after 1920, forty-two men served as *presidente municipal* of Ciudad Juárez.[46] In 1921 the office changed hands eighteen times, with seven different occupants. There were eleven changes involving five men in 1931. Eight men held the post in 1930. In August 1930, there were three different municipal administrations in forty-eight hours. In contrast, Parral, of equivalent size, had only thirteen municipal presidents during the same period.[47] Political campaigns were rough, violent, and fraudulent. Riots were commonplace. Most election days brought murder. At times losing candidates refused to recognize defeat and set up rival governments. The state legislature frequently intervened to settle these disputes.

The 1920s began in confusion, when the state legislature overruled the municipal electoral commission and awarded victory in the election for municipal president to Francisco G. Rodríguez. Incumbent mayor Alberto Delgado thereupon refused to give up his post and for a while the city had two administrations. This would not be the last time such events took place. Within months Rodríguez became embroiled in a dispute with both Governor Enríquez and President Obregón over the disposition of funds from the city's gambling concessions. Caught in the cross fire, Rodríguez succeeded in alienating not only the governor but powerful gambling interests as well. After his removal from office, four mayors followed in quick succession over the next two years, only one of whom, Antonio Corona, left office with his reputation untarnished.[48]

New governor Jesús Antonio Almeida and his family attempted to extend their influence to Ciudad Juárez in 1926. Alberto B.

Almeida, the governor's brother, ran against Marcos Flores for the municipal presidency. The Almeidas counted as allies two other influential *juarense* families, the Cuaróns and the Azcarates, whose ranks included several former mayors. With his brother as governor, Almeida was preordained the winner. The Flores faction refused to acknowledge defeat and held their own swearing-in ceremonies in January 1926. Flores was subsequently arrested for sedition.[49]

Almeida was reputedly a respected, honest administrator. His support of gambling allowed the municipality to regain its solvency. The U.S. consul attributed the city's strong fiscal condition to the fact that the mayor was "independent of the customary graft."[50] Of course, Alberto lost power as a result of the Caraveo-led coup against his brother in 1927. Agustin Gallo, a saloon-keeper and close ally of Caraveo, won the mayorship in 1928.[51] But when Caraveo joined the Escobar rebellion, Gallo's administration fell. The Escobarista rebels occupied Ciudad Juárez during March and April 1929.[52]

From 1929 until 1932 Chihuahuan politics were in chaos. Since Ciudad Juárez was the potential generator of enormous revenues, its control was crucial. In the aftermath of Obregón's assassination and Caraveo's ill-fated adherence to the Escobar rebellion, factional disputes erupted. The intense rivalry between the followers of Luis León and his ally Francisco R. Almada and another group led by Manuel Prieto and Manuel Jesús Estrada, and also between León and his successor as governor and former protégé, Andrés Ortiz, inevitably spilled over into *juarense* politics.

Arturo N. Flores, a strong supporter of León, was elected *presidente municipal,* and his brother Gustavo succeeded him in 1930. These elections marked the entry of the new Partido Nacional Revolucionario into city politics. Organized to bring harmony to Mexican politics, the PNR was initially unable to accomplish this in Ciudad Juárez. Two groups vied for control over the local PNR. Gustavo Flores ran as the candidate of the Partido Revolucionario del Norte. The rival Liga Resistencia del Norte backed former mayor Antonio Corona. At the party nominating convention held at the Juárez racetrack, a riot erupted. Although Corona got more votes, many were disallowed because they were allegedly cast by non-Mexican citizens imported from across the border.[53]

During the June 1930 coup against Governor Almada and its

aftermath, municipal governments came and went. Substitute governor Rómulo Escobar in August 1930 jailed Gustavo Flores and his entire administration because of charges of corruption and graft. Prominent citizens formed a *junta civil,* with Alberto B. Almeida (the very same man ousted in the 1927 coup) as president, to govern the city.[54] When Almada was restored to the governorship, he removed the *junta* and reinstated Gustavo Flores's administration, but Jesús Quevedo, the alternate, took over as mayor.[55] The state legislature named Arturo N. Flores, but Governor Ortiz pushed him out. Balthazar Adame took over with the support of Ortiz and Jesús Quevedo.[56] When Ortiz lost control of the state later in 1931, Alberto Almeida once again became mayor of Juárez.[57] Federal troops oversaw the 1932 elections, which resulted in the victory of Jesús Quevedo.[58] His brother Rodrigo subsequently won the gubernatorial election in July 1932, effecting the family's takeover of the state.

Factional strife broke out again in 1933, when the Quevedos sought to impose a successor. Eventually Dr. Daniel Quiroz Reyes, a pharmacist whose father was a former city councillor, was selected as a compromise. Relative peace reigned in 1934 and much of 1935 under Quiroz Reyes. But by late 1935, Quiroz Reyes's position was untenable and he gave way to Ricardo Espinosa Ramírez, the local leader of the CROM, and a well-known orator. In October 1935, José Quevedo, brother of Jesús and Rodrigo, won an especially violent election against an opposing faction led by Margarito Herrera, former president of the Chamber of Commerce.[59]

The bitter dispute between Rodrigo Quevedo, who completed his term as governor in 1936, and his successor, Gustavo L. Talamantes, also affected *juarense* politics. Talamantes, seeking to strengthen his base in Juárez, ousted Quevedo from the mayoralty in March 1937.[60] But the Quevedos did not give up easily. For a time, the new members of the city council could not meet because the Quevedista police chief would not permit them to enter the council chambers.[61] The Quevedo-Talamantes feud inevitably exploded into violence. A series of shootings in March preceded the murder of newly elected mayor José Borunda, once a political ally and business partner of the Quevedos but more recently an ally of Talamantes, who was blown to pieces by a bomb in his office.[62]

The other members of the Borunda family were not deterred

from politics. The dead mayor's nephew Teófilo ran for and won the mayoralty in 1939, serving two consecutive terms, 1940–41. He later became governor of Chihuahua. Ironically, his opponent in 1939 was Demetrio Ponce, the brother-in-law of Gustavo Talamantes.[63] Alliances changed quickly in Ciudad Juárez politics.

The successive elections of Espinosa Ramírez and the Borundas marked an important change in the political alignment of the city. Espinosa Ramírez's ascendance indicated the rising importance of labor unions. The foundation of the Borundas' power was the Bloque Izquierdista del Norte, which replaced the Partido Revolucionario del Norte as the official party in Juárez.[64] Through the party, they established a strong base among the city's organized labor unions, especially the powerful bartenders', musicians', and waiters' union. The last organization had been a pillar of the Quevedo regime.

No matter who ruled Ciudad Juárez, the method of rule was the same. Violence and corruption were ever present. Juárez was a border town, with all its predictable vices. To these, for much of the era, were added legalized gambling and bootlegging. None of these enterprises could exist without some form of official, legal or illegal, sanction. Revolutionary politicians were, first and foremost, entrepreneurs. There was money to be made, be it through extortion, bribery, or partnership.

For all of the turnover in municipal presidents, there was an underlying stability, as four families dominated local politics—the Flores, the Almeidas, the Quevedos, and the Borundas—the former two during the 1920s and the latter two during the 1930s. (And a fifth, the Bermúdez, wielded considerable influence. Antonio J. Bermúdez later presided over Juárez and Chihuahua politics.)

Change took place over this bedrock. The balance of power among the different political levels was altered because the national regime, through the revolutionary party, grew ever stronger. After the 1930s the party was the arena for all political disputes and rivalries. Nonetheless, Chihuahuan and *juarense* politicians, in particular, showed ornery independence. The PNR incorporated into its make-up the predominant characteristics of *juarense* (and Mexican) politics: personalism, family *camarillas,* violence, and corruption.

Old and New Elites

Juárez was, until after World War II, a small city. Its political and economic elites were not numerous and are thus easily identifiable. Under the rule of Porfirio Díaz and Luis Terrazas, there was a distinction between economic and political elites, because local government officials were often imported agents of either leader. The three most important *jefes políticos* of Juarez between 1897 and 1910 were Valentin Onate, Silvano Montemayor, and Francisco Mateus. Only Mateus was a native of the city. They were, respectively, a career soldier and two merchants. Onate was a close ally of Governor Miguel Ahumada and President Porfirio Díaz, then in opposition to Luis Terrazas. Montemayor and Mateus were agents of the Terrazas family, which regained its power in 1903.[65]

Of the native *juarenses,* the Samaniegos were the most prominent. Of all the prerevolutionary elite families, they were perhaps the most successful at perpetuating themselves through intermarriage to the new elite. Dr. Mariano Samaniego was the political boss of the city from the 1860s until his death in 1905, serving as *jefe político* of Bravos district (of which Juárez was part), state legislator, and acting governor. He was the chief ally of Luis Terrazas. The family owned a large hacienda, Samalayuca, on the outskirts of the city and had interests in banking and urban transit. Samaniego's brothers and sisters and his eight children married into several of the state's and city's most important families: Siquieros, Velarde, Daguerre, Ochoa, Castillo. Son-in-law Inocente Ochoa, in his time, was reputed to be the richest man on the border. The Revolution battered the family's holdings: Samalayuca was lost. Nonetheless, the Samaniegos' extensive family ties assured them a place in post-revolutionary Juárez. No fewer than six revolutionary municipal presidents after 1910 were related: Benjamín Castillo, José Velarde Romero, José J. Flores, Arturo N. Flores Daguerre, Gustavo Flores Daguerre, and Teófilo Borunda.[66]

The Revolution permitted no political ascendency, for Chihuahua was in arms, at war, during the decade from 1910 until Pancho Villa laid down his guns in 1920. Juárez was a major battleground. Thirty different men held the post of municipal president during these years. Of these, three deserve note. José J. Flores (1913) was the first of his family to hold the office. Nephews Arturo and Gustavo would follow in his steps in the 1920s. Manuel M. Prieto (1915–16) later became administrator of customs on the border, federal senator, and a losing gubernatorial candidate in 1931. The third, Melchor Herrera (1916–17), was notable more for what "might have been" than for what was. The eight revolutionary Herrera brothers, originally Villistas, came the closest to establishing a dynasty in wartime Chihuahua. However, they fell victim to a bloody vendetta by Villa. The Villistas shot Melchor in 1919.[67]

At first glance, political power for much of the next two decades continued to be fragmented. As we have seen, the turnover of elected officials was high. This was true not only for the office of municipal president but for the *ayuntamiento* as well. It was rare for a *regidor* to gain reelection. Public officials came from no particular common background. Municipal presidents continued to be outsiders. Of the twenty-one (there were forty-two in all) for whom I have information, only six were native *juarenses,* although eleven others came from the state of Chihuahua (four of whom came from neighboring communities). They had at least twelve different occupations (four merchants, three politicians, three industrialists, one each of landowner, union leader, barber, jeweler, railroad agent, physician, soldier, gambler, and saloon-keeper). Only Almeida, Borunda, and Quevedo were or became large land and cattle owners, the traditional base of economic power.

The Cámara Nacional de Comercio de Ciudad Juárez (Chamber of Commerce) emerged during the 1920s as an important center of power outside the government. Men like Raymundo García, José Velarde, Antonio J. Bermúdez, and Margarito Herrera exercised considerable influence as presidents of the chamber. In the upheaval of 1930 a group of distinguished businessmen from the chamber actually ran the municipal government for a short time. But even among the officers and boards of directors of the chamber there was high turnover.[68] The extent of the turnover in both the *ayuntamiento* and the Cámara may be misleading, for although reelection was infrequent, the same family names appear repeatedly. But lacking family trees for these men, we can only surmise connections.

Even more pertinent, the 1920s saw the start of the emergence of the five families mentioned earlier: the Flores, Almeidas, Quevedos, Bermúdez, and Borundas. In alliance or in conflict they dominated politics in Ciudad Juárez in the postrevolutionary era. With the exception of the Flores, each acquired state and, in the case of the Quevedos and Bermúdez, national power.

The families married strategically into both old and new elite. Arturo N. Flores and Gustavo Flores Daguerre, who served as municipal presidents successively in 1929 and 1930, for example, were connected by marriage to Daguerre, Martínez, Borunda, Canales, Medina, and Samaniego. The Quevedos married into old-line *juarense* families like the Cuaróns, Abuds, and Martínez, to legitimize themselves. The Borundas were kin of the Flores.

All five groups constantly sought alliances at the state and national levels. The Flores cooperated closely with Luis León during the late 1920s and early 1930s. The Flores lost out when León succumbed to the Quevedos, but, allied with the Talamantes wing of the party, staged a comeback in the late 1930s.[69] Arturo N. Flores's son-in-law Teófilo R. Borunda became mayor of Juárez in 1940. The Quevedos, of course, were part of the original revolutionary party, organized by Calles as a coalition of regional, usually military, bosses. They were central figures in the transition in Chihuahua from strictly personalist, regionally and locally based rule to the "institutionalized" revolution that emerged after 1940. The Borundas' rise, based on their association with the national political party, signaled the ascendance of the national regime.

A solid economic foundation was crucial to competing for political power. The Flores' economic base was flour milling. Two of the three dominant families, the Flores and the Quevedos, were reputedly connected to criminal activities. The Quevedos were also associated closely with gambling interests. Enrique Fernández, the gambling and drug boss, was supposedly an ally and perhaps a partner of Governor Rodrigo Quevedo in his casino. According to the U.S. consul, echoing charges made by the political opposition, José Quevedo either catered to or ran the underworld in the city. Undesirable elements, particularly the chauffeurs' union, were said to have provided crucial support for Rodrigo's campaign for governor in 1932. The family's access to large amounts of money generated by gambling and illicit trade may very well have made possible its ascendancy in Chihuahuan politics.[70] As delineated in Chapter 6, the Quevedos also had substantial landholdings, as did the Borundas and Almeidas. The Almeidas, Bermúdez, Borundas, and Quevedos were among the state's business leaders.

The Quevedos and Borundas had much in common and their respective rises illustrate much about *juarense,* Chihuahuan, and Mexican politics of the era. Both came from western Chihuahua—the Quevedos from Casas Grandes and the Borundas from Satevo. Both areas had strong traditions of small independent landholding amid the enormous estates of the Terrazas and Zuloagas. As we have seen, the Quevedos had fought in the Revolution, sometimes as bandits. Both families had moved east to Juárez, realizing that the center of political power had shifted. The Quevedos gravitated toward the potential riches of the border city, and they were not especially fastidious about how they acquired their fortune. The Borundas adapted to the new populism under Cárdenas, incorporating the expectations of the peasants and labor into the political arena. The Quevedos resisted violently and lost out.

The New Elite: Methods of Rule

As in other municipalities, the method of rule changed little from the Díaz-Terrazas era, with the exception of a distinct lack of order after 1911. Fraud and violence continued to be accepted practices. Increasingly over time, though, local politics lost its independence. Even in the 1920s, when independent, raucous political parties vied, state-level politics were crucial. Leaders or factions could not survive for long in Juárez without benefactors in Ciudad Chihuahua, the state capital. Municipal administrations at times, as in 1930, changed as if on the end of a chain yanked from 250 kilometers south.

After the founding of the revolutionary party in 1929, political competition shifted from independent parties to party primaries, and then caucuses. Riots, mayhem, stuffed ballot boxes, and purchased votes remained staples of the system. Although, as Evelyn Stevens has remarked, "the new paths to power required the exercise of new political skills, including the distribution of patronage, the manipulation of organizational rules, informal alliances. . . ." The Borundas epitomized these new skills.[71]

Until the mid-1930s, when the Quevedos, in conjunction with Mexico City, curtailed Chihuahuan and *juarense* political autonomy, local factions had had some leeway when turmoil prevailed at the state or federal level. The advent of the Bloque Izquierdista and the Borundas completed the transition to centralization.

Corruption was at the heart of the system, old or new. In the freewheeling atmosphere of the border—and all the towns on the United States–Mexican border were alike in this respect—there was money to be made and few compunctions about how. The Revolution, with its smuggling and intrigue, exacerbated these conditions. The importance of gambling, bootlegging, drugs, and contraband to the Juárez economy from 1920 to 1940 and the crucial role government authority played in their profitability made corruption an integral part of the city's politics.

Much has been written about corruption in United States politics in urban machines and somewhat less about it in developing nations. The emphasis has been on the transitional nature of the economic and political environment—rapid economic growth, urbanization, and influx of immigrants. According to James Scott, for example, corruption was the means by which out-of-power groups exerted influence during the transition from old to new structures.[72] To a certain extent this was true of Juárez in the postrevolutionary era. Since the rule of government was uncertain and laws were enacted without popular representation and enforced erratically, the only way to influence the system—or better, to protect oneself from it—was through corruption of the enforcement process.

More important, however, was the fact that Juárez's economy was depressed virtually throughout the era. With the cattle trade in ruins, commerce in decline, and mining cyclical, the city's traditional role as a commercial broker eroded. Landholding in the barren north was not an important economic pursuit. Corruption and other illegal activities therefore became the mainstays of the economy. They became the fuel of politics as well. The combination of unstable politics and minute regulation made corruption inevitable.

The makeup of the city's economy encouraged corruption. Of the four largest categories of economic activity in 1927 three were based on liquor sales or tourism. Cantinas (66), variety stores (22), restaurants (16), and hotels (14) were the largest categories of enterprise.

There were other examples of this occurring in Mexico during the same period. Abelardo Rodríguez, for example, as governor of Baja California, compiled a fortune from similar border activities.[73] He later became president of Mexico. All of Mexico was in transition; in most of it, political turmoil, not order, prevailed. If, as John Womack cynically has remarked, the business of the Revolution became business, throughout the 1920s and 1930s one of the most lucrative businesses in Ciudad Juárez was corruption.[74]

Conclusion

Neither Ciudad Juárez, as a small northern city on the United States border, nor the other Chihuahuan municipalities completely reflect Mexican politics during the era under study. The picture we get is not a complete one, for documentation is only now forthcoming. Nonetheless by studying them we can still learn much about the evolution of postrevolutionary Mexico.

To begin with, Mexican municipal politics, as other studies have amply revealed, cannot be examined in isolation. Chihuahuan local politics were intimately entwined with politics at the state and national levels.[75] What is valuable about looking at Ciudad Juárez and other Chihuahuan municipalities in the two decades after the Revolution is that we can see that the process of centralization—city to state and state to national—was halting, difficult, onerous, inevitable perhaps, but not easy and confronted enormous resistance. Moreover, centralism, even as it grew stronger, was of necessity a flexible process.

Crucial characteristics of earlier politics, like the importance of personal and familial loyalties, the use of violence, and factionalism, remained incorporated, although somewhat modified, in the official party structure.[76] Despite the considerable turnover of political offices, there was an underlying stability, for often the same families (although different branches) competed for political power.

The municipalities, moreover, present a microcosm of the evolution of pre- and postrevolutionary local notables. Particularly well drawn are the extraordinary persistence of the old notables and their stratcgics for survival, especially their propensity for intermarriage with new notables. Outlined, too, is the emergence of new notables, primarily from the merchant class in the smaller communities. Ciudad Juárez furnishes a partial exception, because as a result of the monetary resources at stake, the most important notable families were members of the state elite as well. The local notables were not a large group in any of the communities.

Unlike in the larger cities researchers have studied, the business community of Ciudad Juárez was very active and influential in politics.[77] This seems to have remained true even after the organization of the official party, which pointedly excluded businessmen from its membership. Size of the population was one factor, but composition of the economy was more important. Since Juárez lived in part on its image and at times almost entirely on activities very closely regulated by the government (gambling and tourism), it became critical for the business elite, through its agent the Chamber of Commerce, to exert influence and actively participate in politics. Evidence from the smaller municipalities in Chihuahua indicates that the demarcation between economic and political elites was, perhaps, not as great as is generally believed. It is most probable that the strict separation of business and political elite was prevalent in only the largest cities and the national arena, and then only after 1940.

Whether the old elite retained its influence or whether a new elite arose, the methods employed to maintain elite rule changed little. All of the antidemocratic attributes of the Porfiriato reappeared to some extent in the postrevolutionary era: nepotism, abuse of office, imposition, and fraud. Corruption and other illegal (or borderline legal) activities were a central factor in the struggle for political hegemony. Lacking other sources in a time of instability and depression, illicit enterprise assumed disproportionate importance. Unchanging, too, was the adaptability of the local notables. The postrevolutionary notables accustomed themselves to party organization and populism. Thus, by 1940, the landowning Borundas led an agrarian-oriented political party. Finally, Ciudad Juárez, in particular, provides us with a clear outline of the final revolutionary arrangement among the competing interests that had fought for hegemony since 1920. How this adaptation fits into an overall interpretation of the Revolution will be analyzed in the following chapter.

8 Comparative
Perspectives

Its historical peculiarities, not the least of which was the presence of the Terrazas family, preclude Chihuahua as a model of the Mexican Revolution, but its evolution reveals possible interpretations and tendencies. Taken with others, the Chihuahuan case enables us to make an overall assessment. The Mexican Revolution was regionally based and, as a consequence, comparisons of the various regional versions of the upheaval allow us to formulate hypotheses not effectively derived from a national viewpoint. Understanding why one region (state) developed one way and another in a different one between 1910 and 1940 will explain much about the Revolution. Whatever happened in this era did not occur uniformly either in substance or chronology. In essence, what we are doing is breaking the Revolution into its component geographic parts, comparing and contrasting the political development of these parts, and then using these results to construct a composite.

The central issue—whether the Mexican Revolution was, in fact, a "real" revolution—breaks down into five elements: (1) the survival of the old elite; (2) the emergence of a new elite; (3) the interaction of old and new elites; (4) the methods of rule of the new regime; and (5) the participation of the popular classes in the Revolution. By exploring these phenomena in a number of different regions, we can compile enough of a data base to formulate some general conclusions.

The Old Elite

Comparisons of Chihuahua with other states provide us with a reasonably clear outline of which of the old elite survived, why they survived, and what place their members took in the new order. The old elite that was the most diversified economically, especially those least dependent on landholding, most easily endured. The most visible Porfirian elites, such as the Terrazas or the Escandóns, often suffered the most extensive damage to their properties. But that did not mean that they were the least likely to persist. Families like the Terrazas had wide kinship ties, diversified holdings, and enough resources to see them through.

Local or village notables, some of whom competed for power at the regional level, but most of whom did not, seem to have survived at a higher rate than state elites. Geographic isolation contributed to their ability to carry on. In some cases, local notables left their homes during the violent years, then returned, some as much as a decade later, to resume their role as political bosses. Local notables were not as rich and, having less to lose, not as conspicuous. It took a long time, moreover, for the national regime to reach the municipalities in many states. Even if and when the Revolution arrived in the form of the PNR or PRM, and the municipalities confronted a national state that was powerful and consolidated, it was more likely that the interests of local notables would merge with those of the party. It was sometimes easier for postrevolutionary factions competing for state or national power to ally themselves with entrenched, local notables than risk messy defeat (or messy victory). Powerful as they were, caudillos like Saturnino Cedillo and Felipe Carrillo Puerto controlled their states through local bosses.[1] Of course, in some areas the Revolution never arrived.

Two other crucial factors shaped the Revolution in the municipalities. The first has to do with what Alan Knight calls the "logic of the revolution." He points out that the original *serrano* revolutionaries fought for goals that were strictly related to local autonomy.[2] The locally oriented rebels were perfectly willing to deal with any outsiders, it did not matter which side, to accomplish their aims. The second factor, according to Knight, was the "classlessness" of the *serrano* movements. Local notables and poor campesinos joined together in Bachíniva, Temósachic, Guerrero, and elsewhere. The *serranos* fought for themselves; their leaders had fought against the French and Porfirio Díaz at the side of Luis Terrazas during the nineteenth century. Their sons led them to rebel in 1910 and would lead these pueblos through the thicket of postrevolutionary alliances.[3] Although not all municipalities were *serrano* regions, the predominance of local priorities was almost universal.

The chronological pattern of the survival of the Porfirian elite for the areas most affected by the Revolution followed discernible cycles. Under Madero, with the exception of the Terrazas, few elite families suffered loss of their property. Often there were only superficial changes in politics. In Mascota, Jalisco, the Maderistas arrived in 1913 and appointed a *presidente municipal* from a family that had always been "the political arbiters and social and economic pacesetters of the district."[4] In Sonora, José María Maytorena, a hacendado, took the reins. Coahuila's Maderistas were also large landowners. One prominent elite family, the Braniffs, even purchased haciendas and started up a factory in the early 1910s.[5]

During the "war of the winners," between 1914 and 1917, the old elite endured considerable economic damage. Carranza, however, restored much of the Porfirians' land and, in many cases, their political influence as well.[6] The Sonorans, who ruled from 1920 to 1934, represented the entrepreneurial middle class, who aspired to riches and were thoroughly pragmatic in their relations with the old elite. They sought their economic and political alliance when needed but also expropriated their property when the pressures from the popular classes necessitated concessions. This pragmatism sometimes led to strange bedfellows. In Chiapas, large landowners, the so-called Mapaches, backed Obregón against Carranza, and as a result controlled the state during the early 1920s. But after Obregón won the allegiance of state agrarians, politics took an ironic twist, when the latter rebelled against the Obregonista, conservative state government in 1923.[7] The depression years, 1929 to 1932, further weakened the old elite—again, as during the years 1914 to 1917, not so much because of revolutionary actions as the economic environment. Even after the near death blows of the Cárdenas presidency, the old elite persisted. The greatest changes came because large landowners lost political power. They often maintained at least the core of their properties and economic influence. In the state of Hidalgo, for example, rancheros displaced hacendados as the regional political elite, but the hacendados regained their economic power by the late 1920s.[8]

The most successful survivors were the elite of Monterrey, the *regiomontanos*. The least dependent on landholding of any regional elite, they followed a simple rule: "to participate in direct, conspicuous political activity only when necessary and profitable." From 1911 to 1920 the businessmen of the city swayed with the political and military winds. Economically, they endured extortion, confiscation, loans, and taxes. They paid, because they had little choice. Some resisted by force, but with mixed results. In 1914 the Garza-Sada family, owners of the Cervecería Cuauhtemoc, fortified their brewery and armed their employees against the invading Constitutionalists, but they soon surrendered and fled to the United States. Carranza invited them to return from exile less than two years later, in order to resume operations of the brewery.[9]

According to Alex Saragoza, the Monterrey elite took an aggressive stance during the 1920s in order to "reestablish their local hegemony and to protect their national economic interests."[10] Obregón, no less than Carranza, needed the *regiomontano* expertise and capital to help in the nation's economic reconstruction. Eventually the Monterrey elite proved strong enough to defy Lázaro Cárdenas at the height of his power, during the late 1930s.

Not everywhere was the old elite treated well by any means. In Jalisco by 1936, "conservative elements not only have withdrawn from politics, but . . . have been more and more castigated by the triumphant revolutionaries and politicians who have come in with the Revolution." The latter were of the poor and middle class.[11] Sometimes it took a while, but the Revolution had its vengeance. Avelino Montes, the son-in-law of Olegario Molina, who ranked only slightly behind Luis Terrazas among the regional elite of the Porfiriato, fled Mexico only in early 1932.[12]

Aguascalientes provides insight into how the transfer of property from old to rising elite occurred. Beatriz Rojas observed repeated cases in which the owner of an estate left it in the hands of a resident administrator, who proceeded to "subtract his profit" and later purchased the almost bankrupt estate with these funds. It also often happened that the absentee owner leased his property with the aim of returning, but could not because he could not obtain sufficient capital. The threat of expropriation made land a bad risk. Eventually the owner sold to the lessor.[13]

The New Elite

The Revolution produced a new political elite that displaced the old at the state level—if not immediately, certainly by 1940. Its members came from the middle and lower classes. But the composition of the new elite changed over time. The transitional presidency of Francisco Madero included a preponderance of dissident elites in important political posts; they gave way by 1914. The most upwardly mobile period took place from 1914 to 1917, when Villa, Zapata, and their popular class followers held center stage. Thereafter, with crucial exceptions from above and below, the middle class (which included small landowners) dominated Mexican politics. In Sonora, "small farmers, relatively unimportant managers, tradesmen, school-masters, and rancheros" reached power by disposing of the original Maderistas, who were hacienda owners.[14] Since Carranza did not restore the *científicos* in Sonora as he had elsewhere, including Chihuahua, there were ample economic opportunities for those like Obregón and Benjamín Hill who were willing to use political influence to advance their economic interests. Consequently, there emerged a "nascent agricultural and industrial bourgeoisie, created by state patronage," which employed the "often clumsy and primitive means of gaining social eminence exemplified by so many of the revolutionary family: seizing a hacienda, marrying a daughter of the Porfirian aristocracy, taking irredeemable loans from state banks, selling their influence in government circles, embezzling government funds or dealing in the food of their soldiers."[15]

The emergence of the new elite elsewhere followed much the same pattern it did in Chihuahua. The freebooters came to dominate the 1920s and early 1930s, to be supplanted by the bureaucrats (later *técnicos*) and professional politicians by the 1940s. Rural people rose to public office, although less commonly as the 1930s wore on. The governor of San Luis Potosí during the early 1920s, Ildefonso Turrubiate, for example, was an illiterate ranchero. His contemporary, governor of Durango Enrique Najera, was a peasant.[16] In some cases agrarian leaders with military backgrounds attained high office. General Pedro Rodríguez Triana, a leader of the Coahuilan state Liga de Campesinos Agraristas, was elected its governor in 1937.[17] Local agrarian leader and former undersecretary of agriculture Melchor Ortega was elected governor of Guanajuato with PNR backing in 1931.[18] Labor officials not uncommonly held important local posts throughout the period. A leader of the musicians' union became municipal president of Monterrey in 1939. Manuel Flores, a violin teacher and bandleader, was first a workers' representative to the Junta Central de Conciliación y Arbitraje and then a federal deputy before rising to the governorship.[19] The municipal elections in Nuevo Laredo in 1938 produced a mayor and council all of whom were labor leaders, mostly from the CTM.[20] The less educated among them were pushed aside as time went on. Many lower-class leaders, as Dudley Ankerson maintains, were liquidated or absorbed by the bourgeoisie by the 1930s.

The entrepreneurial middle class, typified by the northerners, especially the Sonorans, led the way. Freebooters, like Almeida, Quevedo, Obregón, Calles, Rogríguez, Almazán, and Avila Camacho, acquired power and riches. Modest though their origins may have been, wealth and power turned them conservative.

In the Chihuahuan case, the middle class was particularly successful, for its antireelectionists in 1910 had fought to break the economic hold of the Terrazas and to open the system to themselves. The expropriation of the Terrazas estates, the destruction of the family's banking empire, and the dissolution of its various monopolies paved the way for the rise of a significant number of modest and great fortunes. The *latifundio* of Luis Terrazas furnished the basis for almost every major cattle enterprise in Chihuahua.

Chihuahua may have had more turnover of political leadership than other states. This, if true, probably resulted from the major disruptions caused by the de la Huerta and Escobar rebellions. In San Luis Potosí, where the Cedillos maintained a high degree of stability, for example, legislators were reelected more often.[21]

The Interaction of Old and New Elite

The bases of the relationship between the Porfirian and revolutionary elites were: (1) the need to rebuild the economy of the country; (2) the shared values of private ownership and entrepreneurship; (3) political expediency; and (4) a similar view of regional autonomy.

Reconstruction was the most important priority of the national regime under both Carranza and Obregón. The vast destruction wrought by the decade of civil wars was almost universal in Mexico. Capital and technical and managerial expertise were in short supply. It was not surprising that new elites would look to the Porfirians for both. In regions where export agriculture was predominant, latifundists often quickly regained and then held onto their property. Land reform did not strike the Laguna region until the mid-1930s. The government ignored the petitions of *ejidos* in an effort to maintain cotton production that required large-scale operations. Cárdenas finally ordered the reform in 1935 and 1936 in response to widespread agitation.[22] It was not until 1937 that the national government redistributed the land of the henequen plantations of Yucatán.[23] Until Cárdenas, the production of commercial crops like cotton and henequen were more important than agrarian reform. The downturn in market prices decreased the importance of these crops, at least to the extent that landowners who produced them were no longer protected from expropriation.

As the lower- and middle-class revolutionaries acquired the spoils of victory, they became more conservative and protective of private property rights. Many, of course, had never opposed them in the first place. The small businessmen and rancheros who had led the Maderista rebellion and subsequently joined Carranza and the Sonorans had never had much stomach for land and labor reform. They had fought for equal opportunity for themselves. As Hans Werner Tobler has documented, the revolutionary military leadership became the prime protector of landholding interests.[24] Quevedo, Almeida, and the other Chihuahuan generals were not the only ones who obtained great estates. Obregón, Calles, Cedillo, and Villa, to name just four, became substantial landholders.

Tobler points to a "growing fusion, at least in the second generation, between old and new elites."[25] Intermarriage was often an excellent economic and political instrument. The Vallinas' partnership with the Terrazas was duplicated all over Mexico. In a political sense, pragmatism was inherent in both revolutionary and Porfirian elites. The freebooters had changed sides in order to survive. The old elite, too, learned well. Isidro Rabasa, the grandnephew of a Porfirian governor, for example, was a conservative Mapache during the 1910s but became a Cardenista in the 1930s.[26]

In Sonora old and new elite collaboration took an interesting turn. Several of the revolutionaries were "poor relations" of the "elite network" (Obregón, Elías Calles, and Hill). As such, they acted as "mediators" through which the network "adjusted to revolutionary realities."[27]

Above all, the Porfirians and revolutionaries found common ground in political expediency. Simply put, they needed each other. We discussed above the pragmatic alliance in the municipalities. Independent factions and official parties alike sought collaborators on the local level. Winning and maintaining power were paramount. In the violent and chaotic environment of the era, allies were taken where and when they were available, no matter what their ideology. The old elite often, but of course not always, held the balance of power among revolutionary factions. Their not inconsiderable resources made them even more attractive comrades.

When we examine why many of the middle-class revolutionaries took to arms in the first place, the last basis of old and elite collaboration is clarified: in many instances, they had fought to restore local or regional autonomy. The appointment of *jefes políticos* by state governments and state governors by dictator Díaz were inarguable sources of the discontent of local notables and regional elites before 1910. The new revolutionary chiefs "disliked and distrusted the intrusion of the federal government."[28] This agreement between old and new elites on regional autonomy was strong enough to drive the national regime to join with popular class organizations in order to outweigh their alliance.

Methods of Rule

The fourth central issue, that of method of rule, in great part revolves around the evolution of the modern Mexican state. Nora Hamilton posits that the basis for the autonomy of the Mexican state was threefold: those who controlled the state came from a different pool and followed different career patterns than the private sector;

state control over crucial sectors of the economy allowed it to act above the interests of any one class; and the state had capital resources independent of the private sector.[29] But it would be a serious mistake to transfer this finding, which is reasonable for post-1950 Mexico, to an earlier period when the state was much weaker (and did not fulfill any of the three criteria above). Furthermore, these criteria do not apply at the state and local levels. There is only incomplete evidence on the background of state and local officeholders, but what we do know indicates a less defined separation between political and economic elites before 1940. During the 1920s and 1930s, local governments still had considerable control over access to land, taxes, and other patronage. They also had crucial regulatory authority over business. Gradually, in the 1930s, centralization through the formation of the PNR-PRM-PRI brought the federal government into matters formerly only of local concern. The party took over patronage. Federal agencies assumed regulatory authority over all aspects of the economy. Shut out of the national party, businesspeople looked to "informal mechanisms," such as chambers of commerce and other pressure groups, rather than direct political participation.[30]

The Mexican state developed only gradually as an independent entity. The model of the corporate or authoritarian state (if it is even appropriate for recent times) certainly did not apply to the national government from 1920 to 1940. According to Hamilton, during the first years of the Sonoran dynasty, 1920 to 1926, the state was still weak and the "structures of domination of the pre-revolutionary period continued to exist although the dominant Porfirian classes and groups—traditional and commerical landowners, the commercial, financial and industrial bourgeoisie—had been considerably weakened." Foreign capital remained in control of crucial sectors of the economy. The Sonorans sought allies in the popular classes through unions and agrarian leagues. In return for their support, the popular classes demanded satisfaction of their demand for reforms. The regime was prepared to allow land reform based on private smallholdings. However, once the government was secure, it sought to abandon its old allies and seek rapprochement with "dominant groups."[31]

Hamilton characterizes Obregón's presidency as "an uneasy

truce with regional generals who had been his allies in the conflict with Carranza." They were a dual threat, because they sought not only to strengthen their own region bases, but also because they would use these bases to challenge for national power. Obregón used the support of organized labor and the peasantry to defeat one such challenge in the de la Huerta rebellion. After the sobering loss of 1923–24, the generals and regional bosses turned to self-enrichment.[32]

The main challenges thereafter came from regionally based leaders who employed Obregón's strategy of allying with the organized popular classes in more sophisticated ways. Francisco Múgica, Felipe Carillo Puerto, and Adalberto Tejeda were examples. They used their connections with powerful mentors to gain governorships in the early 1920s. They obtained the support of popular class organizations to form an independent regional base.[33] Múgica became governor of Michoacán in 1920 by virtue of the support of military-zone commander Lázaro Cárdenas. In the face of opposition from the powerful Ortiz Rubio faction and the national regime, Múgica gained support from the CROM and fostered the first peasant leagues. Múgica, like Enríquez and Almeida, had his strongest backing in the *defensas sociales*.[34] Tejeda was governor of Veracruz from 1920 to 1924 as a loyal Obregonista. He, too, associated closely with worker and peasant organizations. Like Múgica, he came into conflict with a conservative military-zone commander, in this case Guadalupe Sánchez, who opposed agrarian reform and arming the peasantry. Obregón objected to an independent, armed peasantry, but Tejeda's solid support in 1923 closed much of the breach.[35]

In the instances of Michoacán and Veracruz, middle-class military officers with close connections to the national regime sought to build their own regional political base. Obregón left them alone so long as they supported his regime. Tejeda, like Chihuahuan governor Enríquez, came through in 1923, rallying the popular classes to the defense of the regime. But two outstanding issues remained—economic independence and local armed forces. Obregón quarreled with Tejeda over the disposition of revenues from oil taxes. As in the case of gambling revenues from Ciudad Juárez, at stake was financial independence. He objected to the *defensas sociales,* but had to reverse his stand when they supported him against de la Huerta.

Because of the national government's weakness in the regions, Obregón's only recourse was to play off the bosses.[36] Civilian caudillos challenged military caudillos, as in Veracruz, with Tejeda the civilian against Sánchez the general.

Aurelio Manrique in San Luis Potosí, José G. Zuno in Jalisco, and Emilio Portes Gil in Tamaulipas organized new regional movements and promulgated new reforms. They established "bureaucratic institutions" to stimulate "state populism and state capitalism."[37] These state governments played an important transitional role in the centralization process, for it was through the popular organizational base pioneered by these caudillos that the national revolutionary regime became centralized.[38]

Obregón, for the most part, let the regional bosses alone: conservatives like Amado Azuara of Hidalgo, César López de Lara in Tamaulipas, Tiburcio Fernández Ruiz in Chiapas, and Angel Flores in Sinaloa. He also tolerated radicals like Carrillo Puerto.[39] The federal government, however, though generally cautious about removing governors, had periods when it did so regularly. One such period was 1925 to 1927. Another was 1931, when the governors of Nayarit, Colima, and Durango were ousted. The meddling was most overt in Tamaulipas in 1931, when the federal government made abrupt changes in local personnel, sometimes by telegram.[40]

The political economy of the era in Chihuahua duplicated itself all over Mexico. The struggle between national, state, and local governments and elites dominated, but the balance between reconstruction and reform shaped these struggles. Agrarian reform was at the heart of Mexico's postrevolutionary political economy. As Arturo Warman has remarked: "Agrarian reform was not going to legitimize the historic right of the villages to the land nor strengthen their autonomy; it was not going to carry out acts of justice, although the legislation allowed the government to do so. On the contrary, it was going to distribute the land as a unilateral concession from the State. . . ."[41] Thus it was, inarguably, a political tool.

Conflict between state and local governments was commonplace. Often the municipalities displayed considerable independence. The state government of Tamaulipas had a very difficult time during the 1930s bringing the municipalities under control. At one point the city council ousted the chief of police, a state appointee, while he was out of town. The more isolated communities in the central part of Tamaulipas were often beyond the reach of the state government.[42]

The actual day-to-day operations of the new elite changed little from those of its predecessors. Corruption, the use of public office to further one's own economic interests, nepotism, voting fraud, arbitrary and capricious actions, and violence persisted as integral aspects of politics and government.

Many governors acted as though state treasuries were personal bank accounts. We have seen earlier how almost every Chihuahuan governor stood accused at the end of his term of one form or another of peculation. Saturnino Cedillo left the coffers in San Luis Potosí bare when his term expired.[43]

Feathering one's own and one's family's nest was an entrenched tradition, unbreakable in revolution. Cedillo, however modest in ambition, nevertheless saw to it that his sister obtained a concession for the city slaughterhouse. He himself had part of a monopoly in the sale of *ixtle*. José G. Zuno, governor of Jalisco, confiscated the property of many wealthy residents of Guadalajara who had sympathized with the de la Huerta revolt and took the proceeds for himself. He was said to have obtained three million pesos of "lucre" while in office.[44]

Nepotism was a crucial aspect of politics. Its use by Almeida and Quevedo we have documented earlier. Luis Castillo Ledón, the governor of Nayarit, in 1931 employed eighteen relatives, including his wife, on the state payroll.[45] Perhaps the most blatant case of nepotism was in Sonora, where the Calles extended family held sway. In 1930, for example, Francisco Elías was provisional governor, his brother-in-law, Alejandro Villaseñor, was municipal president of Nogales, and the ex-president's eldest son, Rudolfo Elías Calles, was elected governor.[46]

The emergence of the new elite was no assurance that conditions for other classes would improve. In Morelos the hacendados returned in the 1930s. "Little by little a number of agricultural enterprises reared their heads, some in the hands of new, enterprising owners." The recovery of commercial agriculture also brought the return of what Arturo Warman labels "peonage." Ernest Gruening shrewdly observed in the late 1920s that "politics is the great impediment in carrying out the agrarian program." It was not so much the hacendados as the agrarian bureaucrats who stood in the way.[47]

Case Studies

Important elements of the Chihuahuan pattern were universal, particularly in the other northern states. The closest parallel to the Chihuahuan case occurred in Durango. Agrarianism flourished under Governor General Jesús A. Castro (1920–24) during the early 1920s, as it had under Enríquez. But his successor, Enrique Najera, like Almeida, was less enthusiastic about reform and allowed large landowners to reassert their influence despite the fact that *agraristas* had provided the base of his support in the 1924 election. The third *duranquense* governor of the decade, General Amaya, like Caraveo, revolted with Escobar. The next, Alberto Terrones Benitez, like León, had to defend the regime with the help of agrarians.[48] As in Chihuahua, governors during the years 1929 to 1931 were caught between the turmoil in Mexico City, especially Calles's move to consolidate under the auspices of the PNR, and the demands for reform from below. At first Terrones's reforms were extensive, but with his main supporter, Portes Gil, ousted and Ortiz Rubio president, he had to rein in or eliminate independent agrarian leaders.[49] Moreover, it was his task, as it was for León, to combine competing political parties into the PNR in 1930.[50] His successor, José Ramón Valdez, also attempted to constrain newly influential agrarian organizations. State politics were torn apart by the conflicting pressures. In September 1930, Durango had two legislatures and three governors at one time.[51] Over the next year and a half, the legislature was dissolved twice, as various deals between factions collapsed. It was not until General Carlos Real won the governorship in September 1932 that the PNR emerged in control of the state.[52] Whereas in Chihuahua Quevedo had established a semblance of order in 1932, peace in Durango did not last long, for by late 1934 a Cristero movement erupted in southern Durango.[53] In 1935 and 1936 the Cárdenas government intervened to maintain order and install Enrique Calderón as governor. He served out his term to 1940.[54]

Tamaulipas, another northern border state, exhibited several similar tendencies to Chihuahua and Durango but differed in that a populist leader, Emilio Portes Gil, arose. The state's conservative era came sooner than in Chihuahua. General César López de Lara obtained the governorship by backing Obregón against Carranza in 1920. Like Almeida (and to some extent Enríquez), López de Lara sought the support of landowner and commercial groups. Rather than proffer land reform, López de Lara organized colonization schemes; the state government bought private land and resold it. As in Chihuahua, gambling became an important source of funds in Tamaulipas. López de Lara brought about his own demise when he backed de la Huerta in 1923.[55]

Emilio Portes Gil dominated Tamaulipas for years thereafter.[56] He, too, had gained prominence initially by joining Obregón in 1920. After a short period as governor of Tamaulipas, he became head of the National Cooperatist Party, but subsequently split with it when he went over to Calles. A stint in the national congress preceded his election as governor of his home state in 1925, as a "loyal and faithful lieutenant."[57] Although a self-proclaimed radical, agrarian reform, for him as for Enríquez and other bosses of the time, was a political tool. Portes Gil did not intend to ruin the hacienda or landowning class. Like Obregón, he believed in large-scale commercial agriculture. Consequently, Portes Gil distributed a modest amount of land. Despite his growing conservatism (his position was similar to that of Luis León), he began the League of Peasant Communities, which proved the forerunner of subsequent peasant organizations in the state.

Typical of the political bosses of the era, José Guadalupe Zuno, a "bohemian" portrait painter, established a record for corruption in Jalisco during the 1920s. One critic wrote of him and his followers that "they were stricken with insanity for power."[58] Zuno was governor from 1922 to 1926 and his protégés presided over the state from 1926 until 1932, when Calles wrested control of the state in alliance with Sebastián Allende. The Zunistas were persistent, however, and their candidate, Silvano Barba González, captured the governorship in 1938.[59]

The conflicts interwoven among regional factions and the national regime were no more in evidence than in Nuevo León. There a group led by Aaron Sáenz, who had nearly become president of

Mexico in 1928, dominated the state during the early 1930s. In 1933 Sáenz and his son-in-law, Plutarco Elías Calles, Jr., the municipal president of Monterrey, took on Governor Francisco A. Cárdenas, formerly his protégé, and the Monterrey Chamber of Commerce, which represented the city's powerful industrialists, and eventually forced him out.[60] Calles Jr.'s attempt to take over the governorship, however, was thwarted in a hectic, violent period in 1935.[61] In the midst of the struggle between President Lázaro Cárdenas (no relation to the governor) and Plutarco Elías Calles, Sr., there was no room for the latter's son in the governorship of a crucial state. Although the power of the national regime prevented Calles from becoming governor, it nonetheless was not sufficient to impose its will on the state's elite, which continued its open and bitter opposition to Cardenismo.

Portes Gil, Sáenz, and León were contemporaries who shared a more national viewpoint than many of the state bosses of the period. But they discovered, to their chagrin, that one could not have feet in two places at one time. None of the three could hold together simultaneously both a regional and national political base.

At times national rivalries created political space for state factions. Governor Román Yocupicio of Sonora was a hard-liner against labor unions at the time of their greatest triumphs.[62] A Mayo Indian, he had fought in the Revolution since 1910. A staunch Obregonista, he split with Calles in 1929, siding with Escobar. Calles, however, asked him to return to the fold. Yocupicio refused, asking only protection for the Yaqui army that had rebelled with him. He farmed for a number of years before he was elected governor in 1936, defeating the official PNR candidate.[63] Yocupicio succeeded without official party endorsement only through Cárdenas's intervention.[64] At first glance this is curious, given the governor's negative attitude toward agrarianism and labor.[65] But Cárdenas sought to break the Calles family's control of the state. This, of course, was a reversal of his common practice of allying with state radicals in the form of peasant and worker organizations to defeat state elites. In the Sonoran case, Cárdenas joined with a conservative for the same ends.

The politics of Chiapas, another state at the periphery, illustrate the interaction of competing regional elites and the national regime.

Conservatives (the so-called Mapaches), allied with Obregón, grabbed power in the early 1920s.[66] The Mapache governor, Tiburcio Fernández Ruiz, aimed at reconstruction and political consolidation. Unlike Enríquez in Chihuahua, however, Fernández Ruiz did not include the popular classes and their aspirations in his formula. With the state in ruins, the Mapaches sought to restore the Porfirian order, reinstituting such abuses as debt servitude and company stores. Nonetheless, they could not reconstitute the "absolute power" of the large landowners (*finqueros*).

Despite the Porfirian hacendados' initial victory, politics in Chiapas quickly evolved into a struggle much like that elsewhere between local, state, and national elites for control, and between elites and the popular classes over issues of land and labor reform. The Revolution, by replacing strong Porfirian district leaders with numerous municipalities, fractionalized politics. *Finqueros,* agrarian committees, and labor unions vied for power.[67] Matters came to a head in 1924, when, in the confusion after the election, the garrison commander of the state capital arrested the entire Mapache legislature. The opposition invaded and took over the legislative chambers, giving the state two legislatures and two governors. The union-agrarian party, with strong support from national popular organizations, won out in 1925. The new Callista governor, Carlos Vidal, presided over an extensive land reform, although much of the land distributed was either idle or national land.[68] He pursued a strategy of preemptive reform, in order to prevent future unrest. Vidal joined a rebellion against Obregón's reelection in 1927, after which the federal government executed him, took over the state, eliminated all local governments, and replaced them with loyal agents.

Despite the fall of Vidal, the alliance among the agrarians, unions, and the state government solidified. But there soon ensued a struggle between official and dissident popular organizations. Some popular class leaders refused to sell out. Tiburcio Fernández Ruiz of the Gran Partido Obregonista de Chiapas wrangled control of the state in 1927. In the elections of 1928 three gubernatorial candidates and three slates for the legislature all claimed victory and all installed themselves. With federal support, Callista Raymundo Enríquez took over. A year later he organized the defense forces against the Escobar rebellion. Enríquez, however, eventually crossed swords with Calles, when in 1930 he refused to end agrarian reform, which had barely begun in Chiapas. Despite the upsurge under Enríquez, the 200,000 hectares distributed hardly put a dent in the problem. Coffee plantations, like the cotton producers of the Laguna, were protected from expropriation through 1936.

Victorio Grajales, a wealthy *finquero,* was the new governor in 1932. Cattlemen ran the state government, deemphasizing reform and favoring large landowners. Grajales met his downfall in 1936, when he sent a twenty-five-man assassination squad against the new governor-elect. The federal army went in to restore order. Grajales, like Quevedo, was willing to use violence to sustain his power. Similarly, his fundamental lack of responsiveness to agrarian demands led to his ouster.

Chihuahua's state political bosses in the era between 1920 and 1940 exerted influence for relatively short periods. Elsewhere, bosses like Tomás Garrido Canabal, Adalberto Tejeda, and Saturnino Cedillo dominated for more than a decade.

The regional caudillo with the longest tenure was Saturnino Cedillo, who ruled San Luis Potosí until 1938.[69] In the beginning, the unpretentious general did not want "to establish himself in politics or business. He wanted to enjoy the untroubled use of Palomas and to reward his followers with land."[70] Small landholders, who owed their proprietorship to their chief, formed the base of his support. He took the same principle employed by Enríquez and Almeida in organizing the *defensas sociales* and went one step beyond it: he secured land for them. Like the *defensas,* his military colonists were a reserve army that would prove a crucial ally for the Sonoran regime.

Nowhere was the political economy of Mexico during the 1920s more evident than in San Luis Potosí. The quid pro quo for peasants was clear: land in return for fighting for the government (under Cedillista leadership). Moreover, these agrarians were clients of the state (at first, solely of Cedillo).[71] In his two years as governor of San Luis Potosí (1923–25)—years that coincided with the eruption and defeat of the de la Huerta rebellion—Aurelio Manrique, Jr., organized the first peasant leagues and distributed a considerable amount of land to 12,000 *ejidatarios.*[72] But his "model of socialism" outlived its usefulness to both Cedillo and Calles. "Manrique had sought to create a revolution in San Luis Potosí, without the power base that any revolutionary needs. . . ."[73] He reformed only with the concurrence of his leaders' pragmatism. In return for their help against the Cristeros and Escobaristas, Cedillo's agrarian veterans received 100,000 hectares. San Luis Potosí distributed the third largest amount of land through 1930, ranked only behind Chihuahua and Yucatán. It had the highest total of *ejidatarios* in the north. Almost one-fourth of the agrarian work force, 32,732 *ejidatarios*, got 811,800 hectares.[74]

As Ankerson points out, Obregón, Calles, and Portes Gil instituted agrarian reform as a payoff for agrarian support, which saved the regime on three occasions during the 1920s. In a disorganized manner, they thus established links between the national regime and the rural population. Initially these ties were forged primarily through intermediaries, some of them regional caudillos like Cedillo.[75] They would later be forged, through the PNR-PRM, to the national regime. The national government would eliminate the intermediaries.[76]

Cedillo's position was stronger than that of Tejeda and Garrido Canabal, who organized political machines, based on patronage, whose clientele were labor and peasant organizations. But they also relied heavily on patrons in the army and federal government.[77] Cedillo's support rested on agricultural colonies and *ejidatarios*. He did not establish a political machine, but rather a patriarchal system founded on kinship and friendship, which the general ruled through local bosses.[78]

Despite his iron-clad support in his home state, Cedillo fell victim to the Cardenista push to eliminate regional bosses and incorporate the popular classes directly into the national revolutionary regime. After Cárdenas forced Calles into retreat in Sonora in 1935, he deposed three powerful Callista state bosses, Rafael Villarreal in Tamaulipas, Saturnino Osornio in Querétaro, and Tomás Garrido Canabal in Tabasco. By mid-1936, Cárdenas had eliminated another rival, Portes Gil, as party president. Only two major figures remained: Juan Andreu Almazán in Nuevo León and Cedillo. Cedillo foolishly rebelled in 1938 and was killed.

Cedillo came from the same ranchero stock as had Almeida and

Quevedo. But, unlike the Chihuahuans, he took care of his troops and never abandoned them. He also established patronage ties that endured until wrested from him by Cárdenas. As a result, neither Almeida nor Quevedo had as fervently loyal a following. Nor did Chihuahua have the strategic importance of San Luis Potosí. Cedillo's veteran army, situated as it was in the nation's heartland, was a crucial element in the national balance of power. It was this loyal army, too, that enabled him to hold off the central regime as long as he did. Cedillo, unlike Quevedo and Garrido Canabal, sided with Cárdenas in his split with Calles, only, as it turned out, postponing the inevitable. Cedillo, like the Chihuahuan rancheros, was conservative, but unlike Quevedo he was not anticlerical.

As Cárdenas abolished the caudillos' fiefdoms in Tabasco, San Luis Potosí, and Veracruz, new bosses arose. But these men, like Maximino Avila Camacho in Puebla, were firmly attached to the national regime. The Avila Camacho family established its political empire in the aftermath of nearly two decades of chaotic politics. The 1920s were particularly tumultuous because the state government backed the losers in the revolts of Agua Prieta in 1920 and de la Huerta in 1923. Popular class organizations that sided with Obregón squandered an opportunity to compete for power when they split into agrarian and labor-union groups. The "commercial, industrial, and landholding bourgeoisie" remained firmly opposed.[79] There were nineteen governors between 1920 and 1930. Six held the office in 1925 and 1926. The PNR did not unify Pueblan politics any more than it had in Ciudad Juárez. Two factions, one led by Callista José Mijares Palencia and another by Leonidas Andrew Almazán, vied for control. They succeeded each other as governor. Almazán distributed 210,000 hectares of land between 1929 and 1933, a figure not surpassed even in the Cárdenas era. Mijares was governor from 1933 to 1937.

The Avila Camachos were originally muleteers. Like many of the state political bosses of the postrevolutionary era, Maximino had had an undistinguished military career during the Revolution. After the Calles-Cárdenas showdown, Cárdenas placed Maximino Avila Camacho in Puebla as military-zone commander. He created his own private army in the form of new *guardias blancas* and restructured the *defensas sociales*. Pushing aside Almazán in 1937, Avila

Camacho installed his family and henchmen in crucial political posts.
One brother headed the PNR and later was *presidente municipal* of
Puebla; another was chief of police. The Avila Camacho *camarilla*
was probably the most successful of the regional elites at competing
at the national level, for it produced two presidents, Manuel Avila
Camacho and Gustavo Díaz Ordaz, in addition to controlling the
governorship through the 1970s.[80]

In state after state the federal government and the national party
gained control by 1940. The warring state factions did not end their
conflicts but subsumed them within the PRM. In some states, like
Puebla, new satrapies appeared. However imperfect the dominance
of the national regime, everyone in the political arena had to play
within the rules.

Perhaps the best case for examining the tactics used by the national regime to undermine strong state elites was Guerrero. "For
Guerrero the years of Obregón, Calles, and Cárdenas were a painful,
chaotic experience."[81] As in Chihuahua, factions bitterly fought
among themselves and with the central government for control. As
in Chihuahua, many of the Revolution's leaders had perished by
1920. The Figueroa family attained dominance by the end of 1919
and kept it when they backed Obregón in 1920. One brother, Rómulo, was zone commander and another, Francisco, governor. A
new generation, which was willing to ally with the national regime,
soon challenged the Figueroas. Obregón saw an opportunity to curtail the Figueroas by supporting the younger generation's candidate
for governor, Rodolfo Neri. The Figueroas' power base, like that of
Enríquez, Almeida, Caraveo, and Quevedo, was the military (federal or local). Like Tejeda and Portes Gil, the challengers had no
independent military power base, relying on the central government. Neri had the backing of *agrarista* and labor groups against the
more conservative Figueroas. Neri distributed substantial lands in
his first two years, but after the defeat of the de la Huerta rebellion,
reform slackened. The Figueroas joined de la Huerta, and their defeat pushed them out of the limelight for more than a decade. The
slowdown of land redistribution led to rebellion. An uprising in the
Costa Grande lasted for three years between 1926 and 1929. The
Escobar revolt spurred a new burst of reform during the governorship of General Adrián Castrejón (1928–32). As in the case of the
León-Almada administration in Chihuahua, *agraristas* were Castre-

jón's power base. Continuing the Chihuahuan pattern, this period of reform was succeeded by a hard-nosed conservative, landowner General Gabriel R. Guevara, in 1933, who, like his contemporary Quevedo, brought an anti-*agrarista* view, backed up with gun battles and murders.[82] Guevara was one of the governors deposed in the 1935 struggle between Calles and Cárdenas. The decade ended with Alberto F. Berber as governor and the national regime in full control.

Other parallels in chaos and violence abound. Political factions set up rival legislatures and each recognized its own governor in Aguascalientes in 1924. Shortly after the federal government recognized him as the legitimate governor, José María Elizalde imprisoned the entire state supreme court.[83] In Coahuila federal troops surrounded the state legislature in 1922 to restore order. But factions established rival legislatures nonetheless. This dispute was further complicated by wrangling between Obregón and the national senate over jurisdiction. Not long after the national regime recognized the "rebel" faction, the legislature divided again, when Obregón attempted to impose his chief of staff, Manuel Pérez Treviño, as governor in 1925.[84] Two rival legislatures set themselves up in the State of Mexico in 1921, on the doorstep of the Obregón regime. Each elected a governor. The federal government finally imposed its candidate, General Abundio Gómez.[85] José de la Pena, the governor of Nayarit, was overthrown in 1927 by a *camarazo* similar to the one that ousted Jesús Antonio Almeida in Chihuahua. General Alejandro Monge led a subsequent reign of terror.[86]

On the municipal level, the rough and tumble of Ciudad Juárez politics was duplicated elsewhere in the north. Torreón in 1937 had three different groups claiming to be the city's administration after a disputed election. After a few days, the federal ministry of government installed a new municipal president. In San Pedro, Coahuila, the same year, the local Liga de Comunidades Agrarias refused to recognize election results and took over city hall. The state government stepped in to settle this dispute.[87] A dissident group in Monterrey in 1935 took over city hall and proclaimed itself the city council. Two groups claimed to be the city government.[88] Two factions constituted two councils and two mayors and functioned as the city government of Nuevo Laredo in 1935.[89]

Nor was the violence confined to Chihuahua. In Veracruz a PNR candidate for governor was killed in June 1936. A year later a state deputy was murdered. And later on, in 1937, the state attorney general was killed in a shootout between factions.[90] During the 1930s, four factors provoked the violence that was always simmering beneath the surface of Mexican politics: the confrontation between Calles and Cárdenas; the incorporation of sometimes reluctant popular class organizations under the PNR-PRM umbrella; the division between old and new agrarians; and the split within the labor movement between the CROM and the CTM.

In the north the violence had an added dimension: the rise of legal and illegal gambling and the narcotics trade. The destruction of the economic infrastructure, repeated revolts, and the depression of 1929–32 left every Mexican state in financial crisis. As in Ciudad Juárez and Chihuahua, state elites looked for alternative sources of revenues. Consequently, gambling became an issue all along the northern border. The controversy was, as in Chihuahua, often formulated in moral terms but in actuality was a problem of fiscal independence from the national government. In Nuevo Laredo, Tamaulipas, in 1930, municipal officials allegedly promoted the installation of slot machines in local bars. None other than Juan Garza García, the father-in-law of President Emilio Portes Gil, was said to be personally involved.[91] The tourist industry in Matamoros depended on gambling.[92] There, too, gambling resorts opened and closed according to whomever had the upper hand at the moment. As in Juárez, nongambling merchants (even saloon-keepers) objected to the gambling. As in the case of Chihuahua, revenue was to be used to improve highways. Interestingly, state officials in Tamaulipas claimed that it was pressure from the federal government that led to open gambling on the frontier and in Tampico. Gambling became an important issue in Sonora in 1931. Francisco Elías, the provisional governor, protected it in Hermosillo, while zone commander General Jaime Carrillo, following federal dictates, sought to discourage it.[93]

Drugs were a problem elsewhere on the border as well. The assistant chief of immigration in Matamoros was charged with smuggling narcotics in late 1931.[94] In Nuevo Laredo in 1938 prominent local officials were rumored to be part of a drug "mafia." There were a series of drug-related murders at the time.[95] Late in his term, there were charges that Governor Yocupicio of Sonora was getting a cut of the narcotics-trade profits in that state.[96]

Popular Participation

Of our five central issues, we know the least about popular participation in the period after 1920, both in Chihuahua and the other regions of Mexico, although the importance of the popular classes is evident both in defending the regime against periodic rebellions and in forming the PRM. Individual case studies, such as those by Ronfeld and Friedrich, give us some clues about how certain aspects of popular organizations operated. But we still know little about how peasant organizations and labor unions were established locally and regionally, how their relations with the national regime evolved, how much autonomy they had (after 1929 in particular), who their leaders were, or what the leaders' relations were with local authorities.

The general outline of the evolution of popular class involvement is clear. In the initial stages of the Revolution it took place through military, often guerrilla, activities. There was some participation of unions in the precursor movements at Cananea and Puebla and by the Casa de Obrero Mundial and Partido Liberal Mexicano. In the early 1920s there were incipient peasant leagues in a number of states. The CROM led the workers' movement. This was a transitional decade, for there was no formal tie between the regime and the leagues, often opposed vehemently by Obregonista allies, or unions. Luis Morones, who headed the CROM, was a crucial ally of the Sonorans, but had all too evident ambitions of his own and thus maintained his independence. The most important popularly based organizations were the local militias of *defensas sociales* (*guardias minicipales,* and so on). Variants of these groups played vital roles in politics in Chihuahua and elsewhere and in defending the regime against the de la Huerta revolt. In the 1920s, too, the so-called laboratories of the Revolution relied on popular organizations, fostered by regional bosses like Tejeda, Carrillo Puerto, Garrido Canabal, and Portes Gil. Personalist caudillos such as Saturnino Cedillo also brokered less formal popular participation under their leadership.

The national regime, of course, realized all along that maintaining these armed and potentially armed groups was dangerous; they could just as easily side against it as ally with it. The Cristero Rebellion was proof enough. The peasant leagues and unions would have to be incorporated. The PNR was a start, but local groups, especially in the countryside, were not yet disarmed. (It is unlikely that they were ever totally disarmed.) Much of the unrest of the early 1930s erupted because of the efforts of federal zone commanders to rein in the militias. (As I mentioned earlier, the campaign against the *defensas* was not just against peasant autonomy but local elite independence as well, for the local militias often were used by the latter for their own ends.) But the popular groups—and this included the unions, which grew stronger in the mid-1930s—had to receive something in return for putting down their arms and, in effect, surrendering all or part of their autonomy. Lázaro Cárdenas was willing and able to provide the material gains for the exchange. At the same time, the regime divided the popular groups, setting unions off against peasants, workers against workers, and peasants against peasants. The unions experienced jurisdictional disputes between the faltering CROM and the burgeoning CTM. More important was the split within peasant ranks after the 1934 modification of the reform laws that enlarged the number eligible for land distribution. This turned new agrarians against previous recipients.

The broadening of the agrarian reform laws created tremendous strife in the countryside between earlier recipients of redistributed lands and new seekers. In Chihuahua this was probably at the heart of Talamantes's problems in the latter part of his term. In Tamaulipas there were clashes between military colonists (among the earlier recipients) and agrarians in 1936. The colonists were revolutionary veterans to whom the government had given land in 1921 and who owned individual plots of varied size, maintaining themselves in a quasi-military system. Cárdenas disarmed and disbanded most of them.[97] But the conflict between small landowners and agrarians erupted elsewhere. In Mexicali in May 1937, three thousand small farmers protested against expropriations of their land. In the previous March, Cárdenas had to publicly assure thirty thousand smallholders in Jalisco, Michoacán, and Zacatecas that they would not lose their land.[98]

During the 1920s, regional bosses acted as intermediaries between the popular classes and the Sonoran-led national regime. The weak national regime, torn as it was between Obregón and Calles, and then disrupted by the assassination of Obregón, was unable to topple the more powerful of the caudillos. Calles's strategy incorporated rather than confronted the bosses. Cárdenas finally eliminated the strongest, like Cedillo and Garrido Canabal. His reorganization of the official party into the P R M in 1937 brought the popular classes directly into the sphere of the national regime. Thereafter there would be intermediaries, but not so powerful as before.

The French Revolution

The French Revolution provides an extraordinary basis for comparison from which we can gain insight into the Mexican one. For our purposes, we can focus our discussion on the general plight of the elite of the ancien régime and the debate over its role in the aftermath of the revolution.[99]

Economically, the revolution had considerable impact, but not necessarily an adverse one, over the long run. In fact, by almost all accounts, the French Revolution had relatively little effect on property ownership and the ways in which property was exploited. Through the middle of the nineteenth century, landowners (noble and non-noble) were the dominant social group.[100] Before the revolution nobles owned 20 to 33 percent of the land. They suffered some losses: the land of émigrés was auctioned off and the new regime ended many of the exactions imposed on tenants. But the nobles were not "spoliated"; instead they fought back, setting off a "whole network of complicities to defend their patrimonies."[101] The nobles were also fortunate in that in 1825 they were indemnified by the government for much of their revolutionary losses.[102] Most noble families managed to survive the most difficult period and even repurchase confiscated property. In the Sarthe region, for example, nobles lost 40,500 hectares, all of which they had regained by 1830.[103] This high percentage of recovery was not duplicated in Mexico, but a similar pattern did exist in some regions, such as Chihuahua.

French nobles used a whole range of strategies to survive and maintain their wealth. They used "every procedural device to stave off confiscation and exactions on family property."[104] In one instance, the Marquise du Hardas de Hauteville actually obtained a legal separation from her émigré husband in order to retain her dowry (which included a chateau and estate that had been in her family for two hundred years). She later managed to repurchase some of her husband's land. By 1825 her properties had regained half their prerevolutionary value.[105] Higgs claims that a majority of noble families kept most of their wealth, although a minority suffered enormously. The main losers were the lesser nobles, many of whom were military officers called to duty against the revolution. Nobles "knew they were no longer the rulers of France," but they learned quickly the ins and outs of private influence. Their most important "weapon to ensure collective survival was the determination to resist absorption into the mass of the nation by maintaining a sense of 'stigma and otherness.'"[106] The French Revolution brought a few advantages to some nobles. The abolition of the tithe made up for the loss of revenues from seigneurial dues. There were a number of business opportunities for those who had capital and were willing to take risks.[107]

As in Mexico, the plight of the old elite varied over the course of the revolution. Like the Porfirians, some French nobles underwent considerable suffering during the early years of the revolution (in Mexico, of course, not for the most part until 1914–17). War and the Reign of Terror thinned the noble ranks, but not greatly. Only 1,158 nobles of approximately 400,000 perished in the terror.[108] As in Mexico, too, many of the nobility fought on the side of the revolutionaries—in the French case, as Republicans. (Thirty percent of the Republic's officers were nobles.) The nobility received an important boost when Napoleon created a new set of hereditary dignitaries. The emperor, like Carranza, sought to recruit members of the old elite.[109] Old elites in both Mexico and France possessed considerable expertise that was needed by revolutionary regimes; revolutionary principles quickly gave way to pragmatism.

Unlike the discredited Porfirian elite, however, the French nobility remained a vibrant political force throughout almost every revolutionary and postrevolutionary regime. They were able to participate far more openly than the old Porfirians in politics and government at the national level. As in Mexico, the old elite showed exceptional flexibility, some shifting from monarchist to republican to imperialist.[110] Thirty percent of the bureaucracy of the First Empire were retainers from the monarchy. The nobility was a powerful influence in politics through the fall of Louis-Napoléon in 1870; even when the electorate expanded 275 percent between 1831 and 1848, their influence did not decline markedly. Nobles were overrepresented proportionately in every political assembly and in the bureaucracy. In 1869, 34.6 percent of the deputies in the national legislature were nobles. Surprisingly, the ethos of public service continued to be observed among the nobility, although there was some withdrawal after 1830. Its members were drawn to the military, the courts, and administration. As it had in Chihuahua, local influence in particular remained at a high level.[111]

One clear difference between the French and Mexican cases is that after the revolution "the nobility remained an identifiably separate and self-conscious element of French society," while in Mexico the old Porfirians faded into, and sometimes merged with, the new rising elite. The French nobility entered into alliances, but always maintained its separateness.[112] The old Mexican elite wanted nothing more than to blend in, to be left alone to grow even richer. In France common misfortune created closer ties among the nobility and fostered family traditions. This, in part, enabled the nobility to "survive the revolution as a status group." Perhaps more importantly, nobles continued to set the tone of how to rule.[113]

Upward mobility was possible in both revolutions, especially during the most fluid and tumultuous periods. The French Revolution and Empire enabled a relatively large number of people, mostly from the middle class, to acquire wealth and status rapidly. As in Mexico, many opportunities for entrepreneurship presented themselves in wartime. The postrevolutionary nineteenth century, however, was not fertile ground for upward mobility in France.[114] The most open path to class mobility was through the military, as it was in Mexico. Officers were the largest group ennobled; the French officer corps became increasingly lower-class.[115] But the process of upward mobility in France in postrevolutionary society should not be overestimated, for the middle and upper classes had gained access to the nobility in an ongoing process that began long before the revolution. Businessmen and professionals were even able to purchase noble status.[116]

Battered, sometimes poorer, the old elite in both Mexico and France struggled successfully for a place in the new, postrevolutionary order. Their material and human resources were badly needed to rebuild what the violent stages of the revolutions had destroyed.

Conclusion

Finally, we should address the question of whether or not the Mexican Revolution really was a revolution. This book is about continuity and change. We should assess how much of the change that occurred after 1920 resulted from the Revolution, how much would have come anyway given shifts in the construction of world markets and the Mexican economy, and how much would have stayed the same. This is what the argument over revisionism now turns on. Enrique Semo, borrowing from the French case, has offered the concept of successive blows against the old regime—in 1911, 1913 (for Chihuahua), 1915 (Law of January 6), 1920, and 1934, for example. This does not imply that revolutions are actually evolutionary, but rather that they do not follow a steady line. Societies have to "rest" and absorb sudden change before another blow can effectively be struck.[117]

The structure of Chihuahuan (and Mexican) politics and economy remained similar to that which existed during the Porfiriato. The final equation of Chihuahuan politics—the alliance between the national political regime, through the revolutionary party, and the popular classes, through campesino organizations and labor unions—was nothing new in the state's history. The popular classes, most especially the small landholders who populated the sierras and northern desert, had often held the balance of power in Chihuahua: the French and Maximilian had failed to win them over and lost the state to Luis Terrazas. Terrazas himself had allied with the rancheros in resistance to Porfirio Díaz in the 1870s. Díaz had then temporarily won them over and pushed the Terrazas aside for a bit more than a decade. The same small landholder groups helped overthrow the dictatorship and continued to play a major role throughout the Revolution. Madero's inability to satisfy their demands (ironically, Abraham González, whose roots were among them, lost their support) led to his downfall. Campesinos formed the basis of the important *defensas sociales* of the 1920s, which produced two governors and probably held the balance in state politics. Almeida and Caraveo came from this group.

The difference in the end was that the new additions to the popular classes' alliance with the elite—the formerly landless peasants, now owners (members) of *ejidos,* and the labor unions—were less attached to local and regional autonomy than their predecessors, the rancheros, had been. Often it was the local power structures (sometimes associated with the small landowners and merchants) which impeded their efforts to acquire land. The national regime offered an alliance of opportunity. Higher wages and access to land superseded local autonomy as an objective.

The pattern of old elite alliance with new, too, was of a piece with the rest of Chihuahuan history. Discredited conservatives, barred from open political participation because of collaboration with the French, had allied with the Terrazas during the end of the nineteenth century, providing the latter with enough financial and political support to tip the balance in their favor, even against Porfirio Díaz. The overwhelming economic power of the Terrazas-conservative alliance was too great for other groups to overcome. In the postrevolutionary era no group could muster the same kind of economic clout (although the Vallina-Terrazas alliance may have rivaled it after 1950). But the pattern became clearer in the formation of the Banco Comercial in 1934. Neither in the aftermath of the French intervention nor that of the Revolution did all the old elite survive.

There was nothing new, either, in the three-way struggle among municipal, state, and national elites. Perhaps more than in the Porfiriato, the 1920s and 1930s were an era of regional strongmen. What the Mexican Revolution changed was the balance of power between region and center. It took the revolutionary regime more than two decades to achieve its national control. As Roger Hansen has astutely pointed out, over time, the regime came ever more to resemble the Porfiriato.[118]

But, as Gilbert Joseph concluded, "it would be incorrect to minimize the major accomplishments of the Mexican Revolution." In Yucatán it ended slave peonage and developed a "political and social consciousness among the working classes, created thousands of new schools, and dramatically increased health, sanitation, and other social welfare benefits for the region's population."[119] In their judgments, historians must consider the millions of acres of land that were redistributed, not infrequently remedying long-term injustices, to millions of landless rural dwellers. Undoubtedly, the reform was flawed and insufficient, but it was nonetheless extensive.

Although popular participation continues to be, for historians, the most elusive part of the interpretive and evaluative puzzle of the Mexican Revolution, there is much to be said for concluding that the known crucial and widespread popular involvement was in itself sufficient to allow us to consider the Mexican Revolution a true revolution. Peasants and workers played major roles in each critical stage of the Revolution. They were the soldiers for the overthrow of Díaz and Huerta. They held center stage briefly from 1914 to 1917. Eventually they tipped the balance to the Constitutionalists, and then against Carranza. The popular classes defended the revolutionary regime from violent challenges during the 1920s. Without organized labor and rural militias, neither Obregón nor Calles would have survived. Finally, they were the critical counterweight to regional elites for the national regime in the 1930s and enabled the revolutionary party to triumph. Peasants and workers did not always acquire immediate rewards for their efforts. Centuries of oppression had taught them great patience. But they did demand a price for their support. Given the strength of the forces that opposed them, it is remarkable they succeeded as well as they did.

There were, as Joseph points out, powerful external and internal limitations that placed restraints upon change. Some were overcome (albeit only temporarily) by a second great wave of revolution during the Cárdenas era, but others remain to the present day.[120] Not least among them were the persistent oligarchs of the Porfiriato.

Appendix

Statistical Tables

Table 1 Staple Crop Production in Chihuahua, 1923–1942

Year	Corn (tons)	Wheat (tons)	Beans (tons)
1910–22	—	—	—
1923	25,166[d]	13,096[d]	2,585[d]
1924	40,926[d]/ 36,923[g]/ 37,345[e]	24,451[d]	8,127[d]
1925	60,613[c]/ 27,000[e]	21,098[f]/ 24,963[h]	7,848[a]
1926	71,493[c]/ 26,000[e]	22,313[c]	7,254[a]
1927	63,627[c]	26,314[c]	5,887[a]
1928	72,049[h]	20,339[h]	7,008[h]
1929	47,268[h]	20,051[h]	3,452[h]
1930	43,546[h]	22,681[h]	2,676[a]
1931	52,105[h]	30,366[h]	4,717[h]
1932	69,977[h]	17,879[h]	5,403[h]
1933	69,689[h]	22,924[h]	11,873[h]
1934	27,267[a]	21,400[h]	3,688[a]
1935	54,967[a]/ 55,371[h]	17,261[a]	6,571[a]
1936	54,690[h]	19,475[h]	5,712[h]
1937	44,872[h]	23,468[h]	4,971[h]
1938	57,091[h]	23,910[h]	4,556[a]
1939	56,326[h]	27,294[b]	8,277[h]
1940	64,436[h]	27,541[b]	12,485[a]
1941	82,436[h]	26,250[b]	12,397[a]
1942	60,434[a]	26,556[b]	6,109[a]

Sources:
[a] Moisés T. de la Peña, *Chihuahua económico* (1948), 2:75, 78, 101–2.
[b] de la Peña, *Chihuahua económico*, 3:15.

Table 1 (*Continued*)

c *Directorio Nacional de Agricultura y Ganadería.*

d Chihuahua, Secretaría General de Gobierno, Sección Estadística, *Boletín Estadístico del Estado de Chihuahua, 1923–1924* (1926), 75.

e Thomas McEnelly, American consul, to Julio Ornelas, Feb. 2, 1927, USNARG 84, ACCC, 1927.

f Chihuahua, Secretaría General de Gobierno, Sección Estadística, *Boletín Estadístico del Estado de Chihuahua, 1925,* No. 4, Pt. 2 (1927), 33.

g Manuel Aguilar Sáenz to McEnelly, American consul, April 8, 1925, USNARG 84, ACCC, 1925.

h Ulises Irogoyen, *Chihuahua en cifras* (1943), 107–9.

Note: In 1925–44 the average production of corn in Chihuahua was 58,000 tons; in 1925–43 the average production of beans, 6,110 tons.

Table 2 Prices for Staples in Chihuahua, 1917–1941
(Pesos per Kilogram)

Year	Corn (Wholesale/Retail)	Wheat Flour (Wholesale/Retail)	Beans (Wholesale/Retail)
1917	.1933/.2150	.2700/.3216	.2000/.2233
1918	.2400/.2600	.4800/.5533	.2970/.3233
1919	.1025/.1142	.2983/.3292	.2892/.3200
1920	.0800/.0925	.3083/.3492	.1642/.1883
1921	.0975/.1100	.2375/.2900	.1483/.1750
1922	.0925/.1100	.2050/.2600	.0800/.1000
1923	.1000/.1142	.2300/.2700	.1525/.1775
1924	.0850/.0950	.2233/.2658	.1216/.1433
1925	.1000/.1100	.2600/.3000	.2500/.2900
1926[a]	.07	.10[b]	.08
1927	.07	.10	.08
1928	.07	.09	.10
1929	.08	.11	.14
1930	.07	.11	.23
1931	.04	.06	.11
1932	.04	.09	.09
1933	.04	.12	.04
1934	.07	.14	.06
1935	.07	.13	.06
1936	.08	.13	.10
1937	.11	.18	.17
1938	.09	.18	.20
1939	.11	.18	.19

Table 2   (*Continued*)

Year	Corn (*Wholesale/Retail*)	Wheat Flour (*Wholesale/Retail*)	Beans (*Wholesale/Retail*)
1940	.09	.18	.17
1941	.09	—	.16

Sources: Chihuahua, Secretaría General de Gobierno, Sección Estadística, *Boletín Estadística del Estado de Chihuahua, 1925* (1927), 202–3; Ulises Irigoyen, *Chihuahua en cifras* (1943), 109.

[a] From 1926 to 1941 the figures represent *precio medio rural*.
[b] From 1926 to 1941 the figures represent the price per kilogram for wheat.

Table 3   Cattle in Chihuahua

Year	Number
1902	396,023[h,1]
1906	947,167[j]
1910	1,500,000[a]/1,000,000
1921	60,000[f]
1923	176,191[b]/100,000[i]
1924	120,230[c]/125,000[i]
1925	296,230[d]
1926	397,975[h,1]/150,000[k]/100,000[g]
1930	685,280[h,1]/300,000[g]
1931	300,000[e]
1940	907,332[l]

Sources:
[a] de la Peña, 2:251–52.
[b] Chihuahua, Secretaría General de Gobierno, Sección Estadística, *Boletín Estadístico del Estado de Chihuahua, 1923–1924.*
[c] *Censo producía, 1924,* 35.
[d] Chihuahua, Secretaría General de Gobierno, Sección Estadística, *Boletín Estadístico del Estado de Chihuahua, 1925,* 66.
[e] Robert M. Ott, "Agricultural Resources of the State of Chihuahua," July 24, 1931, USNARG 84, ACCJ, 1931:7.
[f] J. B. Stewart to secretary of state, Feb. 17, 1922, USNARG 59, Decimal Files, 812.52T2/6.
[g] Manuel A. Machado, Jr., *The North Mexican Cattle Industry, 1910–1975: Ideology, Conflict, and Change* (College Station, Tex., 1981), 31–32.
[h] Pedro Saucedo Montemayor, *Historia Ganadería en México* (Mexico City, 1984), 94.

Table 3 (*Continued*)

[i] Oscar C. Harper, American consul, "Cattle Industry in Ciudad Juárez," Aug. 1, 1924, USNARG 84, ACCJ, 1924:5. These figures are for the Ciudad Juárez consular district only.
[j] Chihuahua, *Anuario Estadístico del Estado de Chihuahua, 1906*, 171–81.
[k] McEnelly, "Review of Commerce and Industry, First Six Months 1926," July 8, 1926, USNARG 84, ACCC, 1926. This is an estimate for the Chihuahua consular district and includes 50,000 head grazed in Chihuahua by the United States War Finance Corporation on the Hacienda de Santa Clara.
[l] Ulises Irigoyen, *Chihuahua en cifras* (1943), 81.

Table 4 Chihuahua Mineral Production, 1905–1940

Year	Value
	US$
1905	7,916,025
1906	8,453,459
1907	11,927,155
1908	11,504,274
1909	10,288,425
1910	8,735,548
1911	9,069,189
1912	8,576,433
1913	4,861,378
1914	5,678,229
1915	4,541,152[a]
1916	1,056,123[b]
1917	2,943,263[c]
1918	9,420,019[c]
1919	10,483,137[a]
1920	11,508,500
1921	11,092,679
1922	12,970,313
	M$
1923	31,567,270
1924	30,232,630
1925	85,240,556
1926	103,809,520
1927	102,769,655
1928	104,490,371
1929	106,686,249
1930	94,685,149

Table 4   (*Continued*)

Year	Value
1931	88,671,779
1932	53,058,260
1933	78,897,276
1934	131,314,978
1935	156,322,323
1936	166,035,181
1937	219,528,693
1938	234,874,108
1939	205,771,250
1940	267,483,492

Sources: Chihuahua, Secretaría General de Gobierno, Sección Estadística, *Boletín Estadístico, 1923–1924,* no. 3 (Chihuahua, 1926), 86. Comité Directivo para la Investigación de los Recursos de México, *La Industria Minera en el estado de Chihuahua,* Boletín no. 7 (Mexico City, 1946), 8; "Report on the Mineral Deposits and Industries in Chihuahua for the Year Ending Dec. 31, 1921," USNARG 59, Decimal Files, 812.63/637; "Report on Mineral Deposits and Industries in the Year Ending Dec. 31, 1922," USNARG 84, ACCC, 1922.

aFigures for 1915, 1919, 1920, and 1921 represent exports declared at consulate plus US$150,000.
b1916 does not include Parral, where only one mine operated.
cTotal declared exports in Chihuahua and Ciudad Juárez plus US$150,000 for 1917 and 1918.

Table 5   Chihuahua Municipal Government Revenues and Expenditures, 1909–1940

Year	Revenues ($)	Expenditures ($)
1909	1,219,640	
1910	—	—
1911	—	—
1912	—	—
1913	—	—
1914	—	—
1915	—	—
1916	—	—
1917	—	—
1918	—	—

Table 5   (*Continued*)

Year	Revenues ($)	Expenditures ($)
1919	—	—
1920	—	—
1921	—	—
1922	—	—
1923	1,416,095	1,404,357
1924	—	—
1925	1,598,507	1,591,810
1926	—	—
1927	—	—
1928	—	—
1929	—	—
1930	1,592,653	1,517,132
1931	1,492,891	1,461,341
1932	1,361,993	1,394,054
1933	1,264,260	1,241,973
1934	3,641,480/	1,411,726
	1,564,008	
1935	1,713,103	1,840,535
1936	1,741,536	1,720,417
1937	1,843,128	1,839,434
1938	2,080,831	2,032,437
1939	2,112,892	2,148,921
1940	2,256,292/	2,228,142/
	2,222,541	2,183,328

Sources: Moíses T. de la Peña, *Chihuahua económico,* 1:154–71; Chihuahua, Secretaría General de Gobierno, Sección Estadística, *Boletín Estadístico del Estado de Chihuahua, 1923–1924;* Chihuahua, Secretaría General de Gobierno, Sección Estadística, *Boletín Estadístico del Estado de Chihuahua, 1925;* Ulises Irigoyen, *Chihuahua en cifras,* 31.

Table 6   Chihuahua State Government Budgets, 1910–1938

Year	Amount (M$)
1910	1,243,481
1911	1,299,506
1912	925,586
1913	—

Table 6   *(Continued)*

Year	Amount (M$)
1914	838,816
1915	4,343,242
1916	—
1917	2,393,506
1918	—
1919	—
1920	1,206,891
1921	—
1922	—
1923	—
1924	—
1925	2,430,070
1926	2,393,576
1927	2,573,082
1928	2,828,850
1929	3,135,124
1930	—
1931	—
1932	2,660,000
1933	2,807,972
1934	3,492,486
1935	4,750,857
1936	4,972,980
1937	6,781,980
1938	7,642,445

Sources: USNARG 59, 812.00 Chihuahua/24, Chihuahua/41, Chihuahua/186; *El Heraldo,* Sept. 7, 1929, and Jan. 1, 1938, 3; AGN, Ortiz Rubio, 24 (1932), 2037, Legajo 6; AGN, Cárdenas, 568.2/13.

Table 7   Chihuahua State Government Revenues and Expenditures, 1908–1942

Year	Revenues (M$)	Expenditures (M$)
1908	1,307,489	1,439,439
1909	1,321,317	1,189,672
1910	1,501,766	1,291,816
1911	1,127,631	1,147,371

Table 7 (*Continued*)

Year	Revenues (M$)	Expenditures (M$)
1912	1,038,378	1,280,394
1913	492,203	575,275
1914	431,286	777,349
1915	733,610	878,589
1916	—	—
1917	1,087,549	1,141,255
1918	1,374,469	1,368,349
1919	1,048,065	937,829
1920	1,494,857	1,307,131
1921	2,079,394/ 1,196,216	2,059,675
1922	—	—
1923	2,603,416/ 2,648,809	2,618,100
1924	2,892,960/ 3,014,793	2,822,976/ 2,645,315
1925	2,887,962/ 2,903,445	2,676,092/ 2,669,891
1926	3,037,359	2,817,482
1927	2,862,112	2,878,799
1928	—	—
1929	—	—
1930	2,855,674/ 2,367,457	2,784,132
1931	3,116,645	3,250,080
1932	2,618,084	2,569,657
1933	3,327,238	3,434,639
1934	4,829,609/ 4,928,282	4,796,120
1935	5,624,447	5,688,486
1936	5,466,464/ 6,407,442/ 7,119,548	5,299,961/ 6,196,256
1937	6,111,461/ 6,526,285	6,598,841
1938	7,081,414/ 7,584,440/ 7,990,663	6,846,869/ 6,835,783

Table 7   (*Continued*)

Year	Revenues (M$)	Expenditures (M$)
1939	6,873,105/ 7,455,196	6,750,512
1940	10,684,002/ 7,653,897/ 8,198,819	8,415,022 — 7,833,584
1941	8,442,367	8,728,250/ 8,440,125
1942	10,509,507	10,559,135/ 9,425,123
1943	12,319,192/ 13,455,063	12,237,572

Sources:
1908–21: *Boletín Estadístico, 1910–1921,* 59.

1921–42: Moíses T. de la Peña, *Chihuahua económico,* 1:145–51, 164–69; Chihuahua, Secretaría General de Gobierno, Sección Estadística, *Boletín Estadístico del Estado de Chihuahua, 1923–1924;* Ulises Irigoyen, *Chihuahua en cifras,* 24; Chihuahua, Secretaría General de Gobierno, Sección Estadística, *Boletín Estadístico del Estado de Chihuahua, 1925,* 154–59; J. D. Myers, American consul, "Report on Financing of Cost of Water Works in Chihuahua," Dec. 7, 1928, usnarg 84, 1928:5.
Note: From 1934 to 1941 Chihuahua ranked third in state government expenditures; from 1935 to 1941 it ranked third in revenues as well.

Table 8   Cattle Exports from Mexico, 1910–1942

Year	N
1910–14	339,616
1916	197,738
1917	183,828
1918	105,410
1919	90,541
1920	58,926
1921	13,874
1922	22,076
1923	20,301
1924	12,853
1925	13,326
1926–27	99,000

Table 8   (*Continued*)

Year	N
1927–28	204,000
1928–29	309,000
1929–30	226,000
1930–31	56,000
1931–32	79,000
1933	60,000
1934	59,000
1935	245,636
1936	171,774
1937	204,916
1938	264,744
1939	489,557
1940	428,285
1941	542,899
1942	512,704

Source: Ulises Irigoyen, *Chihuahua en cifras* (1943).
Note: Chihuahua accounted for 40 to 45 percent of cattle exports to the United States.

Table 9   Petitions for Land Initiated between 1915 and 1935 in Chihuahua

Year	N	Governor	Affirmed	Denied	Executed	Extent	Beneficiaries
1915	0		0	0	0	0	0
1916	0		0	0	0	0	0
1917	4		0	0	0	0	0
1918	14		0	0	0	0	0
1919	14		4	0	0	0	0
1920	16	Enríquez	2	0	0	0	0
1921	85		10	0	7	57,974	1,828
1922	34		12	0	11	60,817	2,178
1923	26		25	0	22	226,556	4,526
1924	25	Almeida	17	0	14	150,776	2,404
1925	8		15	7	7	122,870	1,966
1926	7		22	10	20	65,960	2,137
1927	15		7	5	2	5,724	313
1928	14	Caraveo	15	7	10	41,060	986

Table 9   (*Continued*)

Year	N	Governor	Affirmed	Denied	Executed	Extent	Beneficiaries
1929	53	León/Almada	32	4	27	98,002	3,412
1930	36	Ortiz	23	1	22	40,356	1,779
1931	31	Fierro	29	12	24	54,153	2,203
1932	58	Quevedo	27	9	16	33,703	11,454
1933	40		25	4	29	68,659	2,736
1934	95		16	0	17	57,041	222
1935	125		21	7	16	53,679	1,152
Totals	700		302	66	244	1,137,338	39,296

Year	President	Affirmed	Denied	Executed	Extent	Beneficiaries
1915	Carranza	0	0	0	0	0
1916		0	0	0	0	0
1917		0	0	0	0	0
1918		0	0	0	0	0
1919		0	1	0	0	0
1920	Obregón	3	1	2	5,501	305
1921		1	0	2	4,453	324
1922		3	0	0	0	0
1923		9	0	6	56,594	1,767
1924	Calles	5	0	6	36,665	1,092
1925		13	3	13	68,171	2,440
1926		26	3	26	245,310	6,009
1927		11	1	15	395,375	4,424
1928		16	11	13	80,481	1,741
1929	Portes Gil	16	1	11	51,134	1,480
1930		3	1	7	66,182	1,105
1931	Ortiz Rubio	19	5	10	17,015	825
1932	Rodríguez	11	7	6	81,575	1,064
1933		16	7	6	31,019	476
1934		49	0	29	92,266	2,647
1935	Cárdenas	25	0	55	548,106	6,481
Totals		226	42	207	1,789,857	32,180

Sources: Hans Werner Tobler, "Peasants and the Shaping of the Revolutionary State," in Katz, ed., *Riot, Rebellion, and Revolution: Rural Social Conflict in Mexico*, 501–2. Mexico, Departamento Agrario, *Memoria, 1936–1937*, Appendice estadística, 55.

Table 10 Federal Government Agrarian Actions: Restitutions, Dotations, and Amplifications

Year	No. of Actions	Total Land	Public	Private	Beneficiaries
Obregón					
1920–24	22	116,160	101,656	14,504	5,066
Calles					
1924–28	32	173,497	96,775	76,722	8,169
Portes Gil					
1928–30	19	403,117	—	—	2,329
Ortiz Rubio					
1930–32	27	86,375	—	—	2,055
Rodríguez					
1932–34	70	295,088	—	—	7,329
Cardenas					
1935	15	93,633	93,633	0	1,304
1936	31	192,654	148,138	44,516	2,410
1937	90	607,128	342,138	264,990	9,333
1938	35	126,897	112,834	14,063	3,103
1939	27	106,226	61,073	45,153	1,576
1940	31	113,234	101,286	11,948	1,327
Totals	229	1,239,772	859,102	380,670	19,053

Sources: Everardo Escarcega López, "El principio de le reforma agraria," *Historia de la cuestión agraria mexicana: El cardenismo, un parteaguas histórico en el proceso agrario,* vol. 5, pt. 1 (Mexico City: Siglo Veintiuno, 1990), 125–38, 250–51, 65–68; Mexico, Departamento Agrario, *Memoria, 1936–1937* (Mexico City, n.d.), 45.

Table 11 Estimates of Agrarian Reform, 1916–1940

Source	Year	Estimate
De la Peña	To 1944	467 *ejidos;* 54,665 *ejidatarios;* 3,553,689 hectares
Escarcega	1934–40	229 actions; 1,239,772 hectares; 19,053 beneficiaries
	1924–28	32 actions; 173,497 hectares; 8,169 beneficiaries

Table 11   (*Continued*)

Source	Year	Estimate
	1920–24	22 actions; 116,160 hectares; 5,068 beneficiaries
Hall	1921–24	16 cases; 80,165 hectares
Simpson	1915–33	123 actions; 1,149,484 hectares; 23,052 affected
Departamento Agrario	1915–35	207 actions; 1,789,857 hectares; 32,180 affected
Chihuahua en cifras	To 1940	2,737,448 hectares; 47,054 beneficiaries

Table 12   Land Grants in Chihuahua, 1920–1937

Year	N
1920	6,034
1921	1,744
1922	42,658
1923	55,352
1924	16,512
1925	48,287
1926	297,679
1930	108,715
1931	44,513
1932	53,161
1933	21,554
1934	66,539
1935 (Jan.–July)	41,331
1936–37 (Oct. 3–July 31)	74,066

Sources: 1920–26: Gruening, *Mexico and Its Heritage,* 167. This figure includes restitutions and grants. Gruening's numbers conflict rather sharply with those of Escarcega. 1930–37: Blohm, "Agrarianism in Chihuahua 2 March 1938," USNARG 59.

Table 13 Privately Held Farms in Chihuahua, 1930

Size (hectares)	Number	Total Hectares	% of Total Farms/Hectares
1–50	9,458	100,300	69.6/0.5
51–100	780	59,500	5.7/0.3
101–200	798	120,500	5.9/0.6
201–500	824	304,300	6.1/1.6
501–1,000	432	323,000	3.2/1.7
1,001–5,000	814	1,871,700	6.0/9.6
5,001–10,000	172	1,163,200	1.3/6.0
Over 10,000[a]	316	15,544,300	2.2/79.7
Totals	13,594	19,486,800	

Source: Eyler N. Simpson, *The Ejido: Mexico's Way Out* (Chapel Hill: University of North Carolina Press, 1937), 640–43.

[a] In percentage of land concentrated in private holdings larger than 10,000 hectares Chihuahua ranked third among the states, behind Queretaro and Coahuila. The concentration of land in such holdings was over 70 percent in both Durango and Campeche as well. The national percentage of land in private holdings over 10,000 hectares was 55.

Notes

Abbreviations

AC	American Consul
ACCC	U.S. National Archives, Record Group 84, Records of the American Consular Post in Chihuahua City, Mexico, 1918–35
ACCJ	U.S. National Archives, Record Group 84, Records of the American Consular Post in Ciudad Juárez, Mexico, 1918–35
AACC	Archivo del Ayuntamiento de Ciudad Chihuahua
AGN	Mexico, Archivo General de la Nación
APEC	Fideicomiso Archivos Plutarco Elías Calles y Fernando Torreblanca, Archivo Plutarco Elías Calles
DS	U.S. Department of State
EMJ	*Engineering and Mining Journal*
EPMT	*El Paso Morning Times*
EPT	*El Paso Times*
HAHR	*Hispanic American Historical Review*
POC	*Periódico Oficial del Estado de Chihuahua*
PSP	Private Secretary of President (Mexico)
SS	U.S. Secretary of State
STC	Silvestre Terrazas Papers and Correspondence
USNARG	U.S. National Archives, Record Group
UTEP	University of Texas at El Paso
TVC	Condúmex, Venustiano Carranza Telegramas

1 Introduction

1. Mark Wasserman, "Provinces of the Revolution: An Introduction," in Thomas Benjamin and Mark Wasserman, eds., *Provinces of the Revolution: Essays on Regional Mexican History, 1910–1929,* 1–14; Alan Knight, "The Mexican Revolution: Bourgeois? Nationalist? Or Just a 'Great Rebellion'?" and "The Political Economy of Revolutionary Mexico, 1900–1940."

2. Linda Hall, "Alvaro Obregón and the Politics of Mexican Land Reform, 1920–1924," *HAHR* 60:2 (May 1980): 213–38.

3. Jean Meyer, *Historia de la Revolución Mexicana, Periódo 1924–1928: Estado y sociedad con Calles,* 175–98.

4. Stuart F. Voss, "Nationalizing the Revolution: Culmination and Circumstance," 273–317.

5. For far fuller and more learned analyses, see Robert D. Putnam, *The Comparative Study of Political Elites,* 1–17, passim; Geraint Perry, *Political Elites;* and Peter H. Smith, *Labyrinths of Power: Political Recruitment in Twentieth-Century Mexico,* chap. 1.

6. *El Correo de Chihuahua* (Ciudad Chihuahua), Oct. 6, 1925, 1, and Oct. 7, 1925, 1 (hereafter *El Correo*).

7. *El Periódico Oficial del Estado de Chihuahua,* Nov. 14, 1925, 13 (hereafter *POC*). The land was in Guapalaina, Urique.

2 The Age of the Centaur

1. There are two important biographies of González: Francisco R. Almada, *Vida, proceso y muerte de Abraham González,* and William H. Beezley, *Insurgent Governor: Abraham González and the Mexican Revolution in Chihuahua.*

2. The Orozquistas were comprised of smallholders impatient with the slow pace of reform under Madero, middle class dissatisfied with the lack of opportunities presented by the revolutionary regime, and members of the Orozco family network in western Chihuahua. Orozco's rebellion was in part a movement of western Chihuahua against Ciudad Chihuahua, in part a movement of Chihuahuans against the central government, and in part a personalist rebellion by an ambitious caudillo. The Terrazas financed Orozco, in keeping with their long practice of underwriting opponents of a national regime they opposed. Chihuahuan politics, as we shall see, often made strange bedfellows.

3. Beezley, *Insurgent Governor,* 94–95.

4. Ibid., 109. The *jefes políticos* were district political bosses who, after the 1890s, were appointed directly by Díaz or state governors. They symbolized lost local autonomy. Since many *jefes* came from outside the districts they ruled, they were despised by local residents.

5. *POC,* April 14, 1912, 2.

6. Beezley, *Insurgent Governor,* 141–42, 150–51.

7. *POC,* June 3, 1913, 3, "Informe del Gobernador Interino Constitucional de Estado General Antonio Rábago"; *POC,* June 15, 1913, 2.

8. *POC,* June 3, 1913, 3–4. Rábago appointed municipal officials in several municipalities where there were none and where *ayuntamientos* did

not meet their quorums. There was also difficulty in administering the judicial system.

9. Francisco R. Almada, *Gobernadores del estado de Chihuahua,* 525–31. Andrés Ortiz was the other figure who played an important role in politics.

10. Francisco Murguía to Primer Jefe, July 3, July 10, July 14, July 17, and Oct. 1, 1918; Enríquez to Carranza, July 15, 1918, Condúmex, Fondo XX-4, Carpeta de Chihuahua, Telegramas de Venustiano Carranza, 1916– (hereafter TVC). Murguía objected to the organization of the Cuerpos Rurales o Regionales on two counts: they were not under his jurisdiction and Enríquez used them to organize his gubernatorial aspirations.

11. Almada, *Gobernadores,* 532, 534–35; Sen. A. S. Rodríguez to Carranza, April 1919, TVC; Almada, *Gobernadores,* 539–40.

12. He defeated federal troops at Cañon Bachimba in January, occupied the important mining town of Santa Eulalia in February. Villistas raided Santa Bárbara and San Francisco del Oro in March and took Parral in April. He captured Ciudad Juárez in June and was defeated only when three thousand U.S. troops crossed the border. *La Patria,* Jan. 29, 1919, 1; Feb. 24, 1919, 1. *EPMT,* March 26, 1919, 1, April 25, 1919, 1, May 13, 1919, 3, June 15, 16, 17, 1919, and June 4, 1919, 1.

13. *EPMT,* Dec. 2, 1919, 1. The federals claimed victory. *EPMT,* Dec. 5, 1919, 1; *EPMT,* May 10, 1920, 1.

14. See, for example, *Mexican Mining Journal* 15 (Oct. 1912): 47.

15. *Engineering and Mining Journal* 95 (Feb. 15, 1913): 394 (hereafter *EMJ*).

16. *El Pobre Diablo,* June 9, 1913, 1.

17. *EMJ* 97 (Jan. 31, 1914): 293. "Mining in Mexico, 1914," *EMJ* 99 (Jan. 9, 1915): 422, and (April 3, 1915): 632. "Mining in Mexico in 1915," *EMJ* 101 (Jan. 8, 1916): 116–18.

18. *EMJ* 101 (Jan. 15, 1916): 164. S. W. Eccles, "AS and R Co.'s Mines," *EMJ* 101 (Jan. 8, 1916): 58. *EMJ* 101 (June 24, 1916): 1123.

19. *EPMT,* Nov. 29, 1919, 10.

20. U.S. Department of Commerce, Bureau of Foreign and Domestic Commerce, *Supplement to Commerce Reports,* No. 32a (April 28, 1919), 2.

21. Herbert A. McGraw, "Metallurgy of Gold and Silver," *EMJ* 105 (Jan. 12, 1918): 103.

22. *El Monitor* (Mexico City), Dec. 22, 1919, Nettie Lee Benson Collection, University of Texas at Austin, William F. Buckley Collection, 153.5.

23. *EPMT,* Oct. 10, 1919, 3. This despite the fact that bandits had ransacked it a few months before (a reference to Villa's raid).

24. *POC,* March 12, 1911, 12.

25. J. O. Crockett to H. I. Miller, July 17, 1913, Ferrocarriles Noroeste de México (hereafter FNM), Box 4.

26. J. L. Treviño to Primer Jefe, July 10, 1916, Condúmex, Fondo XX-4, Carpeta de Chihuahua, TVC.

27. Col. Carlos Carranza to Primer Jefe, Aug. 16, 1916, TVC.

28. "Corn Committee Reports," Ciudad Juárez, Oct. 5, 1917, and Chihuahua City, Oct. 5, 1917, USNARG 59, 812.50/46. A hectoliter equals ten cubic decimeters.

29. *POC*, June 16, 1917, 5. Enríquez to Carranza, Jan. 4, 1917, TVC; F. A. Espinosa, Camargo, to Primer Jefe, March 25, 1917, TVC. There was some improvement in climatological conditions. Cobb to Alexander Bullock, War Trade Board, Oct. 26, 1917, USNARG 59, 812.50/51, and "Corn Reports," USNARG 59, 812.50/49, reported abundant rains everywhere except in Casas Grandes.

30. *EPT*, Jan. 1, 1918, 1 (Spanish edition).

31. Arnulfo González to Primer Jefe, May 4, 1918, TVC.

32. *EPMT*, Feb. 27, 1918, 12. Reports for 1918 were mixed. There were reports of improved harvests (*Boletín Comercial* [Ciudad Chihuahua], Nov. 15, 1918, 6). Another reported drought with one-half the normal planting. Still another related loss of half the bean crop to locusts. William Blocker, AVC, Piedras Negras, Coahuila, March 12, 1918, USNARG 59, 812.50/65.

33. Wasserman, "Strategies for Survival," 94.

34. *EPMT*, Sept. 14, 1919, 5.

35. *EPMT*, May 2, 1911, cited in Beezley, *Insurgent Governor*, 64.

36. *EMJ* 92 (July 22, 1911): 180 (July 29, 1911): 227, and (Aug. 5, 1911): 280.

37. Beezley, *Insurgent Governor*, 99–102.

38. *El Monitor*, Feb. 21, 1912. The bill authorized the executive to obtain a loan of six million pesos: 2 million to be spent on irrigation works; 2 million to buy land for redistribution; 1 million to found the Banco Agrícola; and 500,000 to build new schools.

39. Letcher, Chihuahua, Sept. 5, 1913, USNARG 59, 812.00/5051, cited in Alan Knight, *The Mexican Revolution*, 2:98.

40. Francisco R. Almada, *La revolución en el estado de Chihuahua*, 2:21.

41. Friedrich Katz, "Pancho Villa: Reform Governor of Chihuahua," in Wolfskill and Richmond, eds., *Essays on the Mexican Revolution*, 34–35.

42. Ibid., 35; *POC*, Dec. 21, 1913, 1.

43. *POC*, Dec. 21, 1913, 1. There were other decrees in 1915: *La Nueva Era*, June 8, 1915, 1, and June 11, 1915, 1, 3.

44. *POC*, March 8, 1914. The Municipal Land Law of 1905 opened

communal lands to private owners. It led to an enormous onslaught of claims for these lands, and widespread discontent followed. See Mark Wasserman, *Capitalists, Caciques, and Revolution,* 110.

45. *La Vida Nueva,* Feb. 1, 1915, 1, and Feb. 14, 1915, 1.

46. Letcher to Secretary of State (hereafter SS), Aug. 1, 1915, USNARG 59, 812.00/5607, and July 30, 1915, 812.00/15610.

47. *POC,* Dec. 21, 1913, 1; Sept. 22, 1914, 1.

48. *POC,* Aug. 2, 1914, 1–2. Governor Avila called a meeting with the mining companies in August 1914 to urge them to resume operations. *POC,* Aug. 9, 1914, 1–2.

49. *EMJ* 98 (Oct. 3, 1914): 632.

50. Knight, *Mexican Revolution,* 2:456–66.

51. J. L. Treviño to Primer Jefe, July 13, 1916, and July 15, 1916, TVC. The governor found it difficult to comply with the order because of the need to sustain his troops.

52. *EMJ* 107 (May 3, 1919): 779.

53. *POC,* Feb. 1, 1916, 10–11.

54. Friedrich Katz, *The Secret War in Mexico,* 290.

55. Ibid., 536; AGN, Ramo de Gobernación, Revolución, Box 83, exp. 32.

56. *POC,* May 20, 1916, 2.

57. *POC,* June 23, 1916, 5.

58. *POC,* Nov. 18, 1916, 3.

59. *La Patria,* Jan. 15, 1919, 3.

60. Cobb to SS, July 20, 1916, USNARG 59, 812.50/17.

61. Charles Blainer to SS, Sept. 19, 1916, USNARG 59, 812.63/209.

62. Miguel Angel Giner Rey, *Uruachic: 250 años de historia,* 65.

63. *El Monitor,* March 21, 1912, 4. Giner Rey, *Uruachic,* 46. Almada, *La revolución,* 2:85.

64. *La Patria,* Feb. 24, 1914, 2.

65. *POC,* Dec. 28, 1918, 2–5.

66. Edwards, U.S. consul, Ciudad Juárez, Dec. 31, 1913, USNARG 59, 812.00/10021, cited in Knight, *Mexican Revolution,* 2:178.

67. West to DS, Feb. 1915, USNARG 59, 812.00/14622; cited in Knight, *Mexican Revolution,* 2:178.

68. Knight, *Mexican Revolution,* 2:282, 358, 454–55.

69. Beezley, *Insurgent Governor,* 90.

70. Luis Terrazas to Enrique C. Creel, Jan. 20, 1911, cited in José Fuentes Mares, *Y México se refugió en el desierto: Luis Terrazas, historia y destino,* 244 (hereafter *Luis Terrazas*). Fuentes Mares conveys the sense that the old general was totally disillusioned by the events of 1910–11. Knight,

Mexican Revolution, 2:87, concludes from a passage in Edith O'Shaughnessy, *A Diplomat's Wife in Mexico,* 112, that Creel was a "broken man." Surely this is an exaggeration.

71. Alberto Terrazas to Juan Creel, Dec. 22, 1910, Silvestre Terrazas Papers, Box 84; cited in Knight, *Mexican Revolution,* 2:86, 546.

72. Fuentes Mares, *Luis Terrazas,* 248.

73. *El Correo,* June 20, 1911. Rodolfo A. Ugalde was an employee of the Compañía de Tranvías Eléctricas, managed by Martín Falomir. The Terrazas were large stockholders in the company.

74. *El Monitor. Diario Católico-Social de Información* (Chihuahua), Oct. 27, 1911, listed advertisements for the professional and commercial services of Dr. Miguel Márquez, Jesús L. Terrazas, and Carlos Cuilty. *POC,* Nov. 24, 1912, 17, records that Luis Terrazas, Jr., and two partners claimed mining properties, for example.

75. Letcher to SS, Feb. 21, 1914, USNARG 59, 812.00/11043. Letcher also maintained that the first anti-González rally was sponsored by family member Antonio Horcasitas, the brother of Enrique Creel's son-in-law. Letcher to SS, March 20, 1912, USNARG 59, 812.00/3424.

76. *El Monitor,* June 19, 1912, 1.

77. *El Monitor,* June 30, 1914, 4.

78. *POC,* Dec. 29, 1912, 23.

79. *POC,* Oct. 27, 1912, 20.

80. *POC,* Jan. 5, 1913, 23.

81. Francisca M. Viuda de Prieto to President Obregón, April 30, 1923, AGN, Obregón-Calles, 802-P-28.

82. Grandson Federico Sisniega was reported to be conspicuously active in this support. Letcher to SS, Dec. 17, 1913, USNARG 59, 812.00/11043.

83. Almada, *La revolución,* 2:48–49. Michael C. Meyer, *Mexican Rebel,* 56–57.

84. Almada, *La revolución,* 2:37.

85. *POC,* Nov. 16, 1913, 4.

86. Almada, *La revolución,* 2:42–43.

87. *La Patria,* Dec. 24, 1913, 1. Bryan to G. C. Carothers, U.S. consul, El Paso, Jan. 14, 1914, de la Garza Archives, W9A.

88. See Wasserman, "Strategies for Survival," p. 96, n. 40. Letter to H. I. Miller, Aug. 19, 1913, McNeely, Box 10. Almada, *La revolución,* 2:69. *La Patria,* June 6, 1914, 1. Villista authorities questioned whether or not Luis Jr. was still plotting.

89. *EPMT,* Oct. 20, 1914, 2.

90. Wasserman, "Strategies for Survival," p. 96, n. 42.

91. *La Patria,* Dec. 23, 1913.

92. Shepherd, *Silver Magnet*, 283. Manuel A. Machado, Jr., "The Mexican Revolution and the Destruction of the North Mexican Cattle Industry," 13, maintains that Carranza sold Terrazas cattle, too.

93. *La Vida Nueva*, Feb. 24, 1915, 1.

94. *POC*, Feb. 15, 1914, 7. This decree did not single out the Terrazas banks, but included the Banco de Sonora and the Banco Nacional de México's branch in Chihuahua.

95. McEnelly, "Review of Commerce and Industry for the Quarter Ending September 30, 1923," Oct. 19, 1923, USNARG 84, ACCC; Myers, American consul, to Juan A. Creel, manager of the Banco Minero, Jan. 8, 1929, USNARG 84, ACCC. The Banco Minero suspended operations in March 1911 (*El Monitor*, June 25, 1912, 4). In June 1912, Banco Minero opened a branch in El Paso where it conducted all its business (*Chihuahua Enterprise*, Oct. 5, 1912). It reopened for business in the state capital a few months later (*POC*, Feb. 15, 1912, 32). The bank paid out loans to the Orozco and Huerta governments. Villa imposed a loan of M$50,000 on its branch in Parral in June 1912. *El Monitor*, June 27, 1912, 4.

96. *EPMT*, July 29, 1919, 3.

97. AGN, Gobernación, Revolución, Box 221, exp. 45.

98. They were Juan Terrazas, Teresa Bobadilla Viuda de Luis Terrazas, Jr., and granddaughter Adele Creel de Cortazar. AGN, Gobernación, Revolución, Box 245, exp. 16; Box 255, exp. 58.

99. *EPMT*, April 16, 1919, 8. The first rumors of the impending restoration started in January. *EPMT*, Jan. 23, 1919, 5; *EPMT*, July 29, 1919, 3. Neither had to pay delinquent taxes.

100. Katz, *The Secret War in Mexico*, 536; AGN, Gobernación, Revolución, Box 83, exp. 32.

101. *POC*, March 2, 1918, 9, Sept. 8, 1918, 16; Feb. 8, 1919, 24.

102. *Excelsior* (Mexico City), Dec. 28, 1919.

103. Contract signed by Francisco C. Terrazas, Alfonso Galindo, and Celestino Velázquez, Sept. 9, 1924, as an agreement between the Caja de Préstamos and Creel. AGN, Caja de Préstamos, exp. 64. The *El Paso Morning Times*, June 2, 1919, 8, reported that Creel recovered four million, stolen during the Revolution, which had been stored in two wooden boxes in a room in a public building in Mexico City. The boxes contained "gilt-edged" negotiable securities, stocks, and bonds of American railroads, banks, and mines.

104. *EPMT*, Jan. 23, 1919, 8; Feb. 20, 1919, 6B; March 20, 1919, 1; July 29, 1919, 3; March 20, 1919, 5. His wife died in 1919.

105. *La Nueva Era*, Sept. 20, 1914, 1; *POC*, Feb.16, 1913; Nov. 23, 1913, 1.

106. Knight, *Mexican Revolution*, 2:87.

3 Chihuahua during the 1920s

1. J. B. Stewart to SS, Feb. 17, 1922, USNARG 59, 812.52T2/6; Manuel A. Machado, Jr., *The North Mexican Cattle Industry, 1910–1975*, 31–32; Lorenzo Meyer, *Historia de la Revolución Mexicana, 1928–1934*, 288; Pedro Saucedo Montemayor, *Historia de la ganadería en México*, 94.

2. *POC*, July 8, 1922, 5; C. Harper, American vice-consul, "Crop Conditions in Ciudad Juárez, 1923," Dec. 29, 1923, USNARG 84, ACCJ, 1923:5; Robert M. Ott, American vice-consul, Chihuahua City, "Agricultural Resources of the State of Chihuahua," July 24, 1931, USNARG 84, ACCC, 1931:7; Thomas McEnelly, American consul, "Review of Commerce and Industry for the Quarter Ending September 30, 1927," Nov. 7, 1927, USNARG 84, ACCC, 1927; Manuel Aguilar Sáenz to McEnelly, April 8, 1925, USNARG 84, ACCC, 1925; McEnelly to Julio Ornelas, Feb. 17, 1927, USNARG 84, ACCC, 1927, "Review of Commerce and Industry for the Quarter Ending September 30, 1924," Oct. 18, 1924, USNARG 84, ACCC, 1924. Unofficial estimates, J. B. Stewart to SS, Feb. 17, 1922, USNARG 59, 812.52T52/6; *Boletín Comercial* (Ciudad Chihuahua), July 15, 1924, 24.

3. "Review of Commerce and Industry for the Quarter Ending March 31, 1927," April 27, 1927, USNARG 84, ACCC, 1927.

4. "Review of Commerce and Industry for the Quarter Ending September 30, 1924," Oct. 18, 1924, USNARG 84, ACCC, 1924; McEnelly to Department of State (DS), Jan. 7, 1925, USNARG 84, ACCC, 1925; Dye, "Economic Report for Ciudad Juárez for the Quarter Ending June 30, 1926," USNARG 84, ACCJ, 1926:3; "General Economic Report, April–July, 1928," USNARG 165, U.S. Military Intelligence Reports: Mexico, 1919–41, no. 2231, Reel 9.

5. McEnelly, "Review of Commerce and Industry for the Quarter Ending December 31, 1924," Jan. 27, 1925, USNARG 84, ACCC, 1925.

6. Governor Ignacio C. Enríquez to Torreblanca, Private Secretary to the President (PSP), July 9, 1923, AGN, Ramo de Presidentes, Obregón-Calles, 101-P-10; David J. D. Myers, American consul, "Report on the Financing of Construction of Water Works in Chihuahua," Dec. 7, 1928, USNARG 84, ACCC, 1926:5.

7. Chihuahua, Secretaría General de Gobierno, Sección Estadística, *Boletín Estadística del Estado de Chihuahua*, No. 3, Años de 1923–24 (Chihuahua, 1926), 86; Comité Directivo para la Investigación de los Recursos de México, *La industria minera en el estado de Chihuahua*, Boletín No. 7 (Mexico City: n.p., 1946), 8; McEnelly, "Review of Commerce and Industry for

the Quarter Ending December 31, 1924," Jan. 27, 1925, USNARG 84, ACCC.

8. R. F. Manahan, "Historical Sketch of the Mining Operations of the American Smelting and Refining Company in Mexico" (unpublished MS, 1948), provides an excellent summary of ASARCO's acquisitions during this period.

9. The first three centers were dominated by ASARCO.

10. *Informe* of the Presidente Municipal of Batopilas, J. M. Morales, March 26, 1921.

11. Early in 1922, a rebel band led by Nicolas Rodríguez in the north was dispersed by federal troops. Rosalio Hernandez led another group in Santa Rosalía. Later, yet another rebel, Captain Valverde, with 150 men, briefly took Ciudad Juárez. *El Paso Times,* Feb. 11, 1922, 3, and Feb. 17, 1922, 12; Letter to R. H. Smith, Feb. 10, 1922, Mexican Northwestern Railway Papers, John H. McNeely Collection, Box 11, University of Texas at El Paso. Letter to R. Home Smith, President, Oct. 2, 1922, Mexican Northwestern Railway Papers; *El Paso Times,* Sept. 30, 1922, 1, and Oct. 1, 1922, 1.

12. G-2 Report, "Stability of Government and Revolutionary Activities," Dec. 29, 1923, USNARG 165, 4367, Reel 1; Obregón to Enríquez, Jan. 30, 1924, AGN, Obregón-Calles, 101-R2-P; *El Paso Times,* Jan. 3, 1924, 1; *La Patria* (El Paso), Feb. 11, 1924, 1, and March 18, 1924, 1. It is clear from the accounts in *La Patria* and the *El Paso Times* that neither Villa nor Chao fared very well, suffering defeat after defeat.

13. "Review of Commerce and Industry for the Quarter Ending 30 June 1924," USNARG 84, ACCC, 1924.

14. *El Correo,* July 11, 1925; *El Paso Times,* Nov. 14, 1926, 1; Dye, "Political Report for Ciudad Juárez for January 1927," Feb. 7, 1927, USNARG 84, ACCJ, 1927:3.

15. *El Continental* (El Paso), June 18, 1927, 2.

16. G-2 Report, "Mexico Politics: Stability of Government, Armed Revolutionary Movements throughout the Republic from January 1 to February 1928," Feb. 16, 1928, USNARG 165, 1942, Reel 2; G-2 Report, "Armed Revolutionary Movements from February 1 to March 1928," March 23, 1928, USNARG 165, 1996, Reel 2.

17. *La Voz de Parral,* March 5, 1929, March 6, 1929, and March 7, 1929; G-2, "Armed Revolutionary Movements," May 14, 1929, USNARG 165, 2392, Reel 2; Enrique Leikens, Consul General of Mexico, El Paso, to John W. Dye, American consul, Ciudad Juárez, March 26, 1929; Mexico, Archivo General de la Nación, Portes Gil, 3/343, 5613; General José Luis Amezcua, Jefe del Estado Mayor de la Jefetura de Operaciones Militares de

Chihuahua to Secretario A. Roldán, June 22, 1929, AGN, Portes Gil, 617, 11180.

18. Linda B. Hall, "Alvaro Obregón and the Politics of Mexican Land Reform, 1920–1924," *Hispanic American Historical Review* 60 (May 1980): 226.

19. "Cuarta Soberina Convención de Obreros y Campesinos del Estado de Chihuahua," AGN, Obregón-Calles, 818-Ch-26, cited in Rivera Castro, "Política agraria," 119. Only 25 of 170 *solicitudes* were resolved.

20. Octavio Santibañez, Secretario Interno, Partido Nacional Agrarista, to Obregón, July 14, 1923, AGN, Obregón-Calles, 701-Ch-3. One instance of the use of force was at the Bosque de Aldama. See Confederación de Obreros y Campesinos del Estado de Chihuahua to Calles, May 20, 1922, AGN, Obregón-Calles, 818-A-3; another was at Páramo. See Pablo González Sánchez to Calles, Feb. 23, 1923, AGN, Obregón-Calles, 805-Ch-23.

21. Files 812.52T27/1-40, USNARG 59, 1910–1929, and Expediente 806-T, AGN, Obregón-Calles, deal with the Terrazas-McQuatters transaction. Machado, *Cattle Industry,* 40–48, summarizes the affair.

22. *El Paso Times,* Sept. 11, 1923, 2.

23. E. Martínez to General of Division F. R. Serrano, May 6, 1922; Governor Enríquez to President, June 27, 1922; Enríquez to Obregón, July 7, 1922, AGN, Obregón-Calles, 818-C-66. There were at least three haciendas controlled by Villista generals. Informe respeto de la Hacienda de San Isidro, March 30, 1922, AGN, Obregón-Calles, 423-S-12. Obregón to Secretario de Hacienda y Crédito Público, AGN, Obregón-Calles, 423-S-12.

24. *POC,* July 28, 1923, 2 (Chuvíscar), Aug. 11, 1923, 1 (San Andrés), June 16, 1923, 4 (Bachíniva), Dec. 16, 1922, 2–3 (Namiquipa).

25. Acuerdo de la Secretaría de Hacienda y Crédito Público, June 4, 1923, Agustín Moye to Obregón, Oct. 3, 1923, Moye to Obregón, Nov. 23, 1923, and Serafín Legarreta to Obregón, July 27, 1926, AGN, Obregón-Calles, 818-P-13.

26. Vargas Torres, president of the Gran Unión de Campesinos y Obreros del Norte, to President, May 9, 1924, AGN, Obregón-Calles, 408-Ch-7.

27. G-2, "Mexican Rebellion Daily Information Sheet," Jan. 14, 1924, USNARG 165, U.S. Military Intelligence Reports: Mexico, 1919–41, Reel 1. There were limits to their loyalty, however. The American consul reported that many of the militia refused to fight outside their municipalities, maintaining that they were defensive organizations only. McEnelly to Alexander W. Wedell, American consul-general, Aug. 20, 1926, USNARG 84, ACCC, 1924.

28. McEnelly to Alexander Wedell, American consul-general, Dec. 3, 1924, USNARG 84, ACCC, 1924.

29. ASARCO to Obregón, Sept. 19, 1923, Ignacio Enríquez to Obregón, Sept. 19, 1923, and Enríquez to President, Oct. 1, 1923, AGN, Obregón-Calles, 407-A-12; William Parker Mitchell, American consul, to SS, Sept. 19, 1923, and Mitchell to SS, Oct. 3, 1923, USNARG 84, ACCC; Harry B. Ott, American vice-consul, Chihuahua, "Economic Report, January to April 1923," USNARG 84, ACCC, 1923. The miners struck for higher pay, improvement of sanitary conditions, elimination of contract labor, an end to unjust firings, and removal of abusive supervisors.

30. *El Paso Times,* Jan. 15, 1924, 2; *La Patria* (El Paso), Jan. 15, 1924, 2. Alvelais was formerly secretary of state and later became manager of the Caja de Préstamos, which oversaw the Terrazas estate for the federal government.

31. Ariosto G. Castellano to Calles, Dec. 24, 1923, APEC, Gaveta 10, exp. 63. Almada, *Gobernadores,* 557. Talavera was a ranch owner from Aldama, a former city council member from Ciudad Chihuahua, and state legislator.

32. Guadelupe Gómez to President, July 11, 1924, AGN, Obregón-Calles, 818-S-301.

33. Reinaldo Talavera to President, May 19, 1924, E. Cervantes to Obregón, Aug. 20, 1924, Ricardo Ruiz to President, Dec. 5, 1924, Letter to Calles, Dec. 12, 1924, AGN, Obregón-Calles, 407-S-28; McEnelly to SS, "Labor Troubles at Santa Eulalia Mining District," May 13, 1924, USNARG 84, ACCC, 1924.

34. *EMJ* 114 (Oct. 14, 1922): 695.

35. *EMJ* 120 (Nov. 21, 1925): 831.

36. David A. Brush, "The de la Huerta Rebellion in Mexico, 1923–1924" (Ph.D. diss., Syracuse University, 1975), 5.

37. Ibid., 21.

38. Ibid., 49–52.

39. Almada, *Gobernadores,* 559–61; Armando B. Chávez M., "Hombres de la revolución en Chihuahua" (unpublished MS), 9.

40. *El Correo,* Oct. 6, 1925, 1, and Aug. 21, 1925, 4.

41. *POC,* May 29, 1926, 7; June 12, 1928, 8; July 10, 1926, 8. They were, respectively, Hilario Ramos Baeza y Socios, the Corralitos Company, and the Palomas Land and Cattle Company.

42. Ian Benton to Juan F. Treviño, May 3, 1925, Benton Collection, UTEP, Folder 4.

43. "Extracto del Informe General del Estado que guardan los terrenos que comprenden el latifundio Terrazas propiedad de la Caja de Préstamos

para Obras de Irrigación y Fomento de la Agricultura, S.A.," enclosure to Ing. Manuel Romero González, Banco Nacional de Crédito Agrícola, S.A., to President Pascual Ortiz Rubio, Nov. 7, 1930, AGN, Ortiz Rubio, 24 (1930) 13564.

44. *El Correo*, April 4 and 10, 1928.

45. *POC*, July 9, 1927, supplement.

46. McEnelly to Michael Brady, Nov. 24, 1926, USNARG 84, ACCC.

47. *POC*, Sept. 25, 1926, 3.

48. *POC*, Oct. 9, 1926, 1.

49. "Review of Commerce and Industry for the Quarter Ending 31 December 1924," Jan. 27, 1925, and McEnelly to SS, Nov. 26, 1924, USNARG 84, ACCC. See also Barry Carr, *El movimiento obrero y la política en México, 1910–1929*, 2:89.

50. "Review of Commerce and Industry for the Quarter Ending 31 December 1924," Jan. 27, 1925, USNARG 84, ACCC; McEnelly to SS, Nov. 26, 1924, USNARG 84, ACCC; Lázaro Canares, Secretario Exterior, Confederación Obrera de Chihuahua, to Calles, Jan. 21, 1925, AGN, Obregón-Calles, 707-Ch-5.

51. William Drury, "Mexico," *EMJ* 119 (Jan. 17, 1925): 123.

52. McEnelly, "Report on Commerce and Industry, Quarter Ending 31 December 1924," Jan. 17, 1925, USNARG 84, ACCC.

53. McEnelly to SS, June 29, 1926, USNARG 84, ACCC.

54. *POC*, Jan. 16, 1926, 3. He voided elections in Villa Matamoros, Coyamé, and Dolores (Guerrero) in 1926.

55. Almeida to Diputado Francisco García Carranza, Nov. 12, 1925, AGN, Obregón-Calles, 428-Ch-12. The governor complained as early as November 1925 that his opponents were trying to undermine his relations with the central government.

56. McEnelly, "Report on Commerce and Industry for the Quarter Ending September 30, 1927," Nov. 7, 1927, USNARG 84, ACCC; *El Paso Times*, April 16, 17, 19, 20, 21, 1927; Ernest Gruening, *Mexico and Its Heritage*, 410–12; Jean Meyer, *Historia de la Revolución Mexicana, Periódo 1924–1928*, 184 (hereafter *Estado y sociedad con Calles*).

57. Dudley Ankerson, *Agrarian Warlord: Saturnino Cedillo and the Mexican Revolution in San Luis Potosí;* Heather Fowler Salamini, *Agrarian Radicalism in Veracruz, 1920–38.*

58. Lázaro Canales, Secretario Exterior, Confederación Obrera de Chihuahua, to President, Jan. 21, 1925, AGN, Obregón-Calles, 707-Ch-5.

59. *El Correo*, Sept. 8, 1925, 1.

60. "Annual Report on Commerce and Industry for 1926," USNARG

84, Confidential Files, 1922–28; Armando B. Chávez M., *Sesenta años de gobierno municipal,* 221–31.

61. There is considerable debate over Calles's role in the coup. Some observers thought that the president had not instigated or even condoned it. The U.S. Embassy believed that Calles opposed the coup. Ernest Gruening reported that the president found it "extremely distressing." Mexico City newspapers considered the ouster a defeat for Calles, perhaps, the first blow of an anti-Obregón campaign. A few days after the coup, the president publicly declared that he believed Almeida was a personal friend. The *El Paso Times* maintained that the ouster resulted from the feud between Almeida and Chief of Military Operations Caraveo, and thus was a purely local matter. To add credibility to this view, Calles refused to recognize the rebels' choice for governor, Manuel Mascareñas, Jr. Nonetheless, the day before the coup a close associate of Calles, federal Senator Nicolás Pérez, had flown into Chihuahua, allegedly to give the go-ahead. Almeida himself blamed Pérez for his demise. If the incident is placed in national context, the hand of Calles may be seen more clearly, for in 1925, 1926, and 1927 he deposed no fewer than twenty-five governors. Whatever the case, however, the central government could not or did not reinstate Almeida. The state legislature installed Mascareñas as governor, but the national government refused to recognize him because, as customs collector at Ciudad Juárez, he was a federal employee and, as such, not eligible to hold state office. The legislature named Fernando Orozco E. to the office in May. H. F. Arthur Schoenfeld, Counselor, U.S. Embassy, to McEnelly, April 26, 1927, USNARG 84, Confidential Files, 1922–28; Gruening, *Mexico and Its Heritage,* 411; Jean Meyer, *Estado y sociedad con Calles,* 184; *El Paso Times,* April 17, 1927, 1, April 19, 1927, 8, April 20, 1927, 8, and May 9, 1927, 1; *El Continental,* April 17, 1927, 1; McEnelly to James R. Sheffield, U.S. Ambassador, May 6, 1927, USNARG 84, Confidential Files, 1922–28.

62. Enclosure to David J. D. Myers to SS, Dec. 7, 1927, USNARG 84, ACCC, 1928, 5; McEnelly, "Report on Commerce and Industry for the Quarter Ending September 30, 1927," Nov. 7, 1927, USNARG 84, ACCC, 1927. There was some question regarding the misappropriation of 200,000 pesos during his term.

63. Confidential Enclosure to Myers to SS, Dec. 7, 1927, USNARG 84, ACCC, 1927.

64. Marcelo Caraveo, "Memorias" (memoir, 1931), 210–63.

65. Almada, *Gobernadores,* 571–73; W. J. McCafferty, American consul, Chihuahua City, "Political Conditions in Chihuahua during Months of May, June, and July 1929," July 30, 1929, USNARG 59, 812.00 Chihuahua/32.

66. León to President, April 25, 1929, AGN, Portes Gil, 3/340, 7038.

67. McCafferty, "Political Conditions in Chihuahua during August 1929," Aug. 31, 1929, 812.00 Chihuahua/34, USNARG 59.

68. León to Pascual Ortiz Rubio, May 17, 1929, APEC, 39: 121: 7, and Luis León to President, April 25, 1929, AGN, Portes Gil, 3/340, 7038.

69. Portes Gil, 3/340, 7038; Ing. Luis L. León to President, April 25, 1929, AGN, Portes Gil, 3/340, 7038; McCafferty, "Political Conditions in Chihuahua during August 1929," Aug. 31, 1929, USNARG 59, 812.00 Chihuahua/34.

70. León to Pascual Ortiz Rubio, May 17, 1929, APEC, 39: 121: 7.

71. 812.00 Chihuahua/32, USNARG 59.

72. Lorenzo Meyer, *Historia de la Revolución Mexicana, 1928–1934: El conflicto social*, 294.

73. León purchased a part of the Terrazas estate. See correspondence in AGN, Ortiz Rubio, 24 (1930) 13564 and 24 (1930) 13187; León to President, Nov. 10, 1930, AGN, Ortiz Rubio, 24 (1930) 13681; Luis León, *La doctrina, la táctica, y la política agraria de la Revolución Mexicana* (Mexico City, 1931), 4–11; cited in Albert L. Michaels, "Mexican Politics and Nationalism from Calles to Cárdenas" (Ph.D. diss., University of Pennsylvania, 1966).

74. *El Continental* (El Paso), Dec. 6, 1929, 1.

75. Almada, *Gobernadores*, 572.

76. "Political Conditions in Chihuahua, September 1929," Oct. 4, 1929, USNARG 59, 812.00 Chihuahua/41; *El Continental*, Dec. 27, 1929, 6.

77. *Informes del Gobernador del Estado Dip. Francisco R. Almada . . .* (Chihuahua, 1929), enclosed in 812.00 Chihuahua/41, USNARG 59. The governor claimed that the amount of land under cultivation rose dramatically as a consequence of his reforms.

78. McCafferty, "Political Conditions in Chihuahua, October 1929," Oct. 31, 1929, USNARG 59, 812.00 Chihuahua/42; Memorandum dated Oct. 1929, AGN, Portes Gil, 6/500; *El Paso Times*, June 26–29, 1930.

79. "Extracto del Informe General del Estado que guardan los terrenos que comprenden el latifundio Terrazas propiedad de la Caja de Préstamos para Obras de Irrigación y Fomento de la Agricultura, S.A.," enclosure to Ing. Manuel Romero González, Banco Nacional de Crédito Agrícola, S.A., to President Ortiz Rubio, Nov. 7, 1930, AGN, Ortiz Rubio, 24 (1930), 13564. See Chapter 5 for the plight of the Terrazas.

80. Eyler N. Simpson, *The Ejido: Mexico's Way Out*, 610–11.

81. Moisés T. de la Peña, *Chihuahua económico*, 2:252.

82. *EPMT*, Feb. 14, 1921, 5. "Review of Mining and Industry in the Quarter Ending 31 December 1924," Jan. 27, 1925, USNARG 84, ACCJ. John W. Dye, "Political Conditions in Ciudad Juárez during February 1928," March 8, 1928, 812.00 Chihuahua/7, USNARG 59.

83. Thomas Benjamin, "Laboratories of the New State, 1920–1929: Regional Social Reform and Experiments in Mass Politics," in Benjamin and Wasserman, eds., *Provinces of the Revolution*, 71–90.

84. Almada, *Diccionario*, 188–89; Almada, *Gobernadores*, 525–31; Chavez M., "Hombres de la revolución en Chihuahua" (unpublished MS), 84–85.

85. *EPMT*, March 13, 1922, 10, claimed that some agrarians had filed charges of treason against Enríquez for his role in the McQuatters deal.

86. Heather Fowler Salamini, "Revolutionary Caudillos in the 1920s," 169–72.

87. For a more detailed discussion of the Becerras, Rascóns, and Samaniegos, see Wasserman, "Strategies for Survival," and Wasserman, *Capitalists, Caciques, and Revolution*, 39, 137, 24, 35, 38, and 53.

88. *POC*, Feb. 15, 1906, 6–7, Jan. 15, 1908, 7, Jan. 23, 1910, 10, Oct. 26, 1919, 9, and Nov. 30, 1929, 6; Chihuahua, *Directorio General de Municipios* (Chihuahua: n.p., 1927), 340; Chihuahua, Secretaría de Gobierno, Sección Estadística, *Chihuahua 1934*, 93; *El Correo*, March 17, 1904, 2.

89. *POC*, Jan. 9, 1908, 5, Sept. 21, 1929, 12, Dec. 21, 1929, 5, Nov. 23, 1929, 12, Oct. 12, 1929, 12–13; *Chihuahua 1934*, 116; José María Ponce de León, *Directorio Industrial, etc. del Estado de Chihuahua* (Chihuahua: n.p., 1907), 119; Chihuahua, *Directorio General de Municipios*, 359–61; *El Correo*, Nov. 28, 1923, 2, and Dec. 8, 1925, 3.

90. *POC*, Jan. 12, 1908, 6, Jan. 23, 1910, 8–9, Nov. 30, 1929, 5; *Chihuahua 1934*, 113–14; Chihuahua, *Directorio General de Municipios*, 353–57, 359; *El Correo*, Dec. 15, 1925, 1.

4   Chihuahua during the 1930s

1. Eduardo Espinosa Romero to President, June 30, 1930, AGN, Ortiz Rubio, 230/1930/7857. Blocker to SS, June 25, 1930, USNARG 84, ACCJ, 1930:4. *EPT*, June 26, 1930, 1. It seems that Almada suspected his opposition was planning a *camarazo* and consequently fled to Ciudad Juárez earlier in the day.

2. Almada had evidently complained earlier about General Ortiz's meddling and in April elicited his promise to desist. Francisco R. Almada to President, April 28, 1930, and General Eulogio Ortiz to President, April 30, 1930, AGN, Ortiz Rubio, 230 (1930), 5761 and 5706.

3. *EPT*, June 27, 1930, 1.

4. *EPT*, June 28, 1930, 1–2.

5. Ibid.

6. *El Correo*, July 11, 1930, 1–2. The government ruled that the legislative action which deposed Almada was illegal because three of the deputies

who voted for impeachment were not legitimate members of the legislature.

7. *EPT,* July 15, 1930, 1, and July 16, 1930, 1; *El Correo,* July 30, 1930, 1. Estrada and five other legislators were impeached for inciting and participating in a riot. General Matías Romero replaced Eulogio Ortiz as Fifth Zone Commander. Two weeks later, the Supreme Court of Chihuahua upheld the appointment of Escobar and the dissolution of the legislature.

8. G-2, "General Economic Conditions, July–September 1930," Nov. 25, 1930, USNARG 165, no. 3019, Reel 9; G-2, "General Economic Situation 1931," no. 3890, Reel 9; G-2, "General Economic Conditions 1932," no. 4627, Reel 9.

9. Robert M. Ott, AVC, "Political Conditions in Chihuahua, Jan. 1930," USNARG 59, 812.00 Chihuahua/48; G-2, "General Economic Conditions, July–September 1930," Nov. 25, 1930, no. 3153, USNARG 165, Reel 9.

10. G-2, "General Economic Conditions, April–June 1930," July 29, 1930, no. 3019, USNARG 165, Reel 9; Francis H. Styles, "Notes on the Economic Condition of the Chihuahua Consular District," July 17, 1930, USNARG 59, 812.504/1116; M. Gallegos to Rodríguez, Aug. 17, 1933, AGN, Rodríguez, 525.3/288.

11. Julián Gardea, Presidente Municipal, Yepachic, to President, May 25, 1930, AGN, Ortiz Rubio 35 (1930), 8428.

12. Roberto Fierro to President, April 29, 1932, AGN, Ortiz Rubio 24 (1932), leg. 5, 1778.

13. W. C. Greene, vice-president, Compañía Ganadería Cananea, S.A., Memo on the United States Tariff on Mexican Cattle, Aug. 9, 1933, and Quevedo to Rodríguez, Oct. 7, 1932, AGN, Rodríguez, 571.4/1.

14. "Political Conditions in Ciudad Juárez, June 1932," USNARG 59, 812.00 Chihuahua/141; R. M. Quevedo to President, Feb. 20, 1935, AGN, Cárdenas, 565.4/27; "Political Conditions in Ciudad Juárez, May 1935," USNARG 59, 812.00 Chihuahua/219.

15. The two men openly disliked each other. At one point Ortiz had slapped León's face and challenged him to a duel. William P. Blocker, U.S. consul, Ciudad Juárez, "Political Conditions in Ciudad Juárez," April 23, 1930, USNARG 59, 812.00 Chihuahua/50.

16. Blocker, U.S. consul, Ciudad Juárez, "Political Conditions in Ciudad Juárez," April 23, 1930, USNARG 59, 812.00 Chihuahua/50.

17. Heather Fowler Salamini, "Revolutionary Caudillos in the 1920s: Francisco Múgica and Adalberto Tejeda," in Brading, ed., *Caudillo and Peasant in the Mexican Revolution,* 169–92.

18. F. H. Styles, "Political Conditions in Chihuahua, May 1930,"

812.00 Chihuahua/52; Robert M. Ott, "Political Conditions in Chihuahua, March 1930, April 3, 1930," 812.00 Chihuahua/53, USNARG 59.

19. *POC,* March 10, 1934, 3.

20. Sabás Aranda to Calles, July 27, 1930, General Matías Ramos, 56/55, APEC.

21. Andrés Mendoza to Calles, July 25, 1930, General Matías Ramos, 56/55, APEC.

22. "Political Conditions in Chihuahua, June 1930," 812.00 Chihuahua/64, USNARG 59.

23. "Political Conditions in Chihuahua, March 1930," 812.00 Chihuahua/53, USNARG 59.

24. *El Continental* (El Paso), Dec. 6, 1929, 1.

25. Ing. Luis L. León to President, April 25, 1929, AGN, Portes Gil, 3/340/7038; William J. McCarthy, "Political Conditions in Chihuahua during August 1929," Aug. 31, 1929, USNARG 59, 812.00 Chihuahua/34.

26. *EPT,* July 22, 1930, 1; Styles to Embassy, March 10, 1931, USNARG 84, ACCJ, 1931:5.

27. Lorenzo Meyer, *Historia de la Revolución Mexicana, 1928–1934: El conflicto social,* 298–99.

28. Blocker, AC, Ciudad Juárez, to SS, Dec. 26, 1930, USNARG 59, 812.00 Chihuahua/86.

29. *El Correo,* Dec. 15, 1930, 1, and Nov. 20, 1930, 1.

30. At one point, reportedly, he attemptd to flee the state but was stopped by General Matías Romero, the zone commander. Francis H. Styles to SS, March 11, 1931, USNARG 84, ACCJ, 1935:5.

31. William P. Blocker to SS, Sept. 25, 1931, USNARG 84, ACCJ, 1931. Blocker to SS, March 26, 1931, USNARG 84, ACCJ, 1931. Blocker to SS, March 17, 1931, USNARG 84, ACCJ, 1931:5. Blocker, "Political Conditions in Ciudad Juárez," March 17, 1931, USNARG 59, 812.00 Chihuahua/96. Blocker to SS, March 17, 1931, USNARG 84, ACCJ, 1931. G-2 Report, "Stability of Government: Conditions in the State of Chihuahua," March 17, 1931, no. 3276, USNARG 165, U. S. Military Intelligence Reports: Mexico, 1919–41, Reel 4. *El Correo,* April 1, 1931, 4; April 27, 1931, 3; Aug. 1, 1931, 1.

32. Blocker to SS, March 17, 1931, USNARG 84, ACCJ, 1931:5.

33. Blocker, "Political Conditions in Ciudad Juárez," March 17, 1931, USNARG 59, 812.00 Chihuahua/96; Blocker to SS, March 26, 1931, USNARG 84, ACCJ, 1931:5. J. Reuben Clark, Jr., to SS, March 26, 1931, USNARG 59, 1930–39, 812.00 Chihuahua/97. The conspirators allegedly were led by General José Ruiz, former head of the state's municipal guards (*defensas sociales*) and a friend of León, ex-governor Fernando Oroz-

co, Simon Puentes, and a group of legislators—Leonardo Revilla, Fernando García, Julián Aguilar, and Ramiro Valles. The latter was president of the state PNR, a post from which he resigned at Ortiz's insistence after the aborted plot. *El Correo,* May 27, 1931, 1; J. R. Clark to SS, March 26, 1931, 812.00/29582, USNARG 59. *EPT,* Oct. 31, 1931, 1; Blocker to SS, Nov. 2, 1931, USNARG 84, ACCJ, 1931:5; F. H. Styles, "Political Conditions in Chihuahua, June 1931," July 31, 1931, USNARG 59, 812.00 Chihuahua/108. The legislature accepted his resignation, praising his "high, patriotic spirit" and "acts of great honor." He, in turn, blamed his failure on the disillusioning acts of the agrarians and the Chihuahuan PNR, the latter of which had misunderstood its role, causing chaos in parts of the state. Ortiz claimed, too, that his repeated trips to Mexico City to defend his actions had distracted him from his work. Finally, he said that he preferred personal sacrifice to standing in the way of progress. *El Continental,* Nov. 4, 1931, 1.

34. Blocker to Reuben Clark, U.S. Ambassador, March 30, 1931, USNARG 84, ACCJ, 1931:5; *EPT,* Sept. 10, 1931, 1. In September the governor was ordered to Mexico City to face charges that he had misappropriated funds and persecuted agrarians. Enrique Fernández, the reputed narcotics and gambling tsar of Ciudad Juárez, reportedly wrote a letter accusing Andrés Ortiz of planning to kill him and of stealing funds meant for construction of a highway from Ciudad Juárez to Ciudad Chihuahua. *El Continental* (El Paso), Oct. 30, 1931, 1; Styles, "Political Conditions in Chihuahua, October 1931," Nov. 2, 1931, USNARG 59, 812.00 Chihuahua/120. Initially, the legislature refused to remove Ortiz. Eventually, Ortiz, Calles, and Ortiz Rubio worked out the resignation.

35. Simon Puentes to Calles, Aug. 10, 1931, Andrés Ortiz/17, APEC.

36. Blocker to SS, Nov. 2, 1930, USNARG 84, ACCJ, 1931:5. Fierro was the first cousin of Jesús Antonio Almeida. Roberto Fierro, *Esto es mi vida,* 277. Styles, "Political Conditions in Chihuahua, Nov. 1931," USNARG 59, 812.00 Chihuahua/126.

37. Styles to SS, July 5, 1932, USNARG 59, 812.00 Chihuahua/140 and 144; Blocker to SS, July 5, 1932, USNARG 84, ACCJ, 1932.

38. Fierro to President, March 17, 1932, AGN, Ortiz Rubio, 24 (1932), 1304.

39. William Nalle, Major, General Staff, AC of S, G-2, to Assistant Chief of Staff, 8th Corps, Fort Sam Houston, July 7, 1932, USNARG 59, 812.00 Chihuahua/145.

40. "Local Political Conditions, June 1932," G-2, 4033, July 15, 1932, USNARG 165, Reel 3.

41. Fierro to Calles, Nov. 3, 1931, Fierro/111, APEC.

42. Blocker to SS, July 31, 1935, USNARG 84, ACCJ, 1935:7. Vicente Anguiano A. to President, Oct. 7, 1935, AGN, Cárdenas, 544.5/469. Their support came through the chauffeurs' union. Blocker to SS, July 30, 1930, USNARG 84, ACCJ, 1930. The U.S. consul in Ciudad Juárez concurred that the Quevedos were involved in organized crime, maintaining that the city had experienced an unprecedented crime wave under the Quevedo regime. Blocker to SS, Oct. 31, 1932, USNARG 84, ACCJ, 1932:5.

43. Styles to SS, April 5, 1932, 812.00 Chihuahua/136, USNARG 59.

44. G-2, "Local Political Conditions, Feb. 1933," no. 4465, USNARG 165, Reel 3.

45. Quevedo to Rodríguez, Aug. 14, 1934, AGN, Cárdenas, 531.5/34; POC, June 30, 1934, 5, and Sept. 20, 1933, 1.

46. Memorandum, "Accomplishments of the Quevedo Administration," Jan. 18, 1934, Manuel M. Prieto 54/69, APEC.

47. "Political Conditions in Ciudad Juárez, Sept. 1933," 812.00 Chihuahua/180, USNARG 59.

48. Ortiz, in fact, had been ousted partly in a dispute with the Quevedos over the disposition of gambling monies. León and Ortiz had squabbled over these revenues in 1931: León had used the funds to further his own aims, but Ortiz wanted his share. The Quevedos, originally Leonistas, transferred their loyalties to Ortiz. Ortiz allegedly received a payment of 345,000 pesos in September 1931 from the new concessionaire, Manuel Llantada. G-2 Report, "Local Political Conditions, Present State Governments, Political Conditions in Chihuahua," April 24, 1931, no. 3329, USNARG 165, Reel 1; G-2 Report, "Resignation of Carlos Riva Palacio," June 16, 1931, no. 3401, USNARG 165; Col. Gordon Johnston to SS, June 23, 1931, 812.002/306, USNARG 59. "Resume of the Political Situation in Ciudad Juárez, Sept. 1931," USNARG 84, ACCJ, 1931. El Correo, Sept. 11, 1931, 1.

49. "Report of Treasurer-General of Chihuahua, March 23, 1932," AGN, Ortiz Rubio, 24 (1932), 1304. There is another copy of the report in Roberto Fierro/111, APEC.

50. The story of the Fernández assassination is best told by Edward L. Langston, "The Impact of Prohibition on the Mexican–United States Border: The El Paso–Ciudad Juárez Case" (Ph.D. diss., Texas Tech University, 1974), 159–77. The following derives from Langston's account, unless otherwise noted. See also Blocker to SS, Jan. 18, 1934, USNARG 84, ACCJ, 1934.

51. An agent of the *secretaría de gobernación* concluded that "the temptation of illicit profits produced by gambling have absorbed the attention of . . . men who are charged with directing public business" and "created

a worsened public morality and social order." *Informe que rinde el suscrito Secretario de Gobernación como resultando de su giro de inspección al Norte y Noroeste de la República,* March 15, 1932, AGN, Ortiz Rubio, 24 (1932), 2037, leg. 6. There is considerable circumstantial evidence linking Fernández's murderer, José Barragán Sánchez, to the Quevedos.

52. Blocker to SS, Dec. 19, 1934, USNARG 59, 812.40622/368.

53. William P. Blocker, AC, Ciudad Juárez, to SS, Oct. 15, 1934, USNARG 59, 812.404/1297; Blocker to SS, Oct. 25, 1934, 812.404/1299; Blocker to SS, Oct. 27, 1934, 812.404/1306.

54. George P. Shaw, AC, Ciudad Juárez, to SS, April 20, 1936, USNARG 59, 812.404/1875; "Present Religious Situation in Mexican States," May 8, 1936, 812.404/1880.

55. Memorandum, "Accomplishments of the Quevedo Administration," Jan. 18, 1934, APEC, Manuel M. Prieto, 54/69. He wrote to Calles in January 1934: "tengo en mi conciencia que trato de cumplir unicamente con mi deber y de que no me apartare de sus instrucciones para lograr el mayor beneficio al estado de Chihuahua." R. M. Quevedo to Calles, Jan. 18, 1934, APEC, R. M. Quevedo, 55/7.

56. "Political Conditions in Chihuahua, March 1934," USNARG 59, 812.00 Chihuahua/191.

57. Blocker to SS, USNARG 84, ACCJ, 1935:7.

58. Manuel Vazquez and others, Colonía Obregón, Cuauhtémoc to President, Oct. 7, 1935, AGN, Cárdenas 403/683.

59. Andrés Mendoza to Abelardo Rodríguez, July 21, 1934, AGN, Rodríguez, 515.5/75-1. Mendoza had to flee the state in fear of his life.

60. "Mexican Political and Revolutionary Movements," July 30, 1935, G-2, 6312, USNARG 165, U.S. Intelligence, Reel 1.

61. Blocker to SS, June 30, 1935, USNARG 84, ACCJ, 1935:7.

62. Alan M. Kirshner, *Tomás Garrido Canabal y el movimiento de las Camisas Rojas,* 165–90.

63. "Political Conditions in Chihuahua, August 1935," August 31, 1935, USNARG 84, ACCJ, 1935:4. To these were added another foe, Saturnino Cedillo, the boss of San Luis Potosí and a cabinet member, who began to slip opponents into strategic positions along the border.

64. "Political Conditions in Chihuahua, Dec. 1935," USNARG 59, 812.00 Chihuahua/237.

65. "Mexico: Political: State Elections," July 7, 1936, G-2, 7275, USNARG 165, Reel 2.

66. José María Aceitia to Cárdenas, no date, AGN, Cárdenas, 606.3/76. This is with another letter dated in December 1935.

67. "Resume of Conditions in Mexico, March 1936," USNARG 59,

812.00/30358; "Summary of Political Conditions in Ciudad Juárez, Mar. 1936," 812.00 Chihuahua/242; "Political Conditions in Chihuahua, Mar. 1936," 812.00 Chihuahua/243.

68. "Summary of Political Developments in Ciudad Juárez, Nov. 1936," USNARG 59, 812.00 Chihuahua/264; "Summary of Political Situation in Ciudad Juárez, Dec. 1936," 812.00 Chihuahua/266; "Summary of Political Developments in Chihuahua, April 1937," 812.00 Chihuahua/273; "Summary of Political Developments in Ciudad Juárez, April 1937," 812.00 Chihuahua/274.

69. "Summary of Political Developments in Chihuahua, May 1937," USNARG 59, 812.00 Chihuahua/275.

70. "Summary of Political Developments in Ciudad Juárez, July 1937," USNARG 59, 812.00 Chihuahua/280.

71. The narrative for both these occurrences comes from Charles E. Hershberger, "The Death of Borunda, Alcalde of Ciudad Juárez: Chihuahuan Politics during the 1930s," *Arizona and the West* 8 (Autumn 1966): 207–24, except where otherwise noted; *EPT,* March 13, 1938, 1. Also involved were Valentín Oñate, Jesús Chacón, Gilberto Martínez, and Felipe Aguila. Reportedly, General Quevedo barely escaped death when a bullet clipped off the tip of his necktie. Quevedo was eventually indicted for the murder, but nothing came of it (*EPT,* March 14, 1938, 1; March 15, 1938, 1–2; March 17, 1938, 1–2). Several Quevedistas were arrested on suspicion of the murder. Eventually two U.S. citizens, who owned mines in Chihuahua, were questioned. But the murder, in the end, went unsolved. *EPT,* April 4, 1938, 1; April 10, 1938, 4; April 13, 1938, 1; April 14, 1938, 1; April 26, 1938, 1.

72. Lee R. Blohm, "Labor Notes from Chihuahua, Mexico," March 15, 1938, USNARG 59, Confidential, 812.504/1724. Lee R. Blohm, "The Labor Set-Up in Chihuahua," Nov. 3, 1937, USNARG 59, 1930–39, Confidential, 812.504/1687. Historian Francisco R. Almada describes the Talamantes administration as "sustaining always its leftist tendencies with a frank and decided manner." Almada, *Diccionario,* 512.

73. Ibid.

74. Blohm, "Labor Notes from Chihuahua," March 15, 1938, 812.504/1724, USNARG 59. The consul bitterly complained that Talamantes favored the unions because he owed his political career to them. Labor's more advantageous position was reflected in the trend in wages over the decade. Agricultural wages increased only slightly. In 1937 most labor on cattle ranches and farms earned less than a peso and board for a day's work. Mine, smelter, and industrial wages increased 50 to 150 percent over the decade. (Industrial workers were paid 2–2.50 pesos and mine-

smelter 4–6 pesos per day.) To some extent the increases were eroded by the 50 percent rise in the cost of living from 1936 to 1938. Bad harvests pushed up staple prices. Blohm, "Labor Set-Up in Chihuahua" (see n. 72 above); "Summary of Political Situation in Ciudad Juárez, Oct. 1937," 812.00 Chihuahua/285; "Summary of Political Situation in Ciudad Juárez," June 1938, 812.00 Chihuahua/305, USNARG 59.

75. William Blocker, AC, to SS, Aug. 12, 1938, 812.00/30608, USNARG 59. There were some who believed that Talamantes was in office solely through the support of Vicente Lombardo Toledano, leader of the Confederación de Trabajadores Mexicanos (CTM).

76. "Political Conditions in Chihuahua, Jan. 1935," USNARG 59, 812.00 Chihuahua/212. There was a flurry of strikes in 1935, including a general strike called by the Sindicato Industrial de Trabajadores, Mineros . . . , Seccion 10 and another against ASARCO. Quevedo sent in the police against striking employees of the municipal water works but helped to settle a bakers' strike in 1936 by offering generous terms for the workers. Blocker to SS, June 11, 1935, USNARG 59, 812.5041/92; Consul to SS, Aug. 12, 1935, 812.5041/95; Blohm to SS, Sept. 20, 1935, 812.5045/241; Blohm to SS, Oct. 9, 1935, 812.5045/245. Blocker to SS, June 11, 1935, USNARG 59, 812.5041/92. "Summary of Political Situation in Ciudad Juárez, July 1936," USNARG 59, 812.00 Chihuahua/252.

77. "Local Political Conditions," March 1932, USNARG 59, 812.00/29707; "Labor Notes from Chihuahua," June 23, 1937, 812.504/1662.

78. "Labor Notes from Chihuahua," Aug. 25, 1936, USNARG 59, 812.504/1620.

79. "Labor Set-Up in Chihuahua," Nov. 3, 1937, 812.504/1687, USNARG 59.

80. Blohm, "Labor in Industry in Chihuahua," July 14, 1939, 812.504/1873, USNARG 59.

81. Nine local labor syndicates met in Delicias in November to organize an industrial and farm labor federation. Unions of municipal employees, bartenders, hotel and restaurant workers, chauffeurs, musicians, slaughterhouse employees, and baking and milling industrial workers met for "defensive and offensive resistance" in December. The following June a congress of state unions met, but delegates could not agree on consolidation with the CTM. "Labor Notes from Chihuahua, Mexico," Dec. 22, 1936, 812.504/1634, USNARG 59. Blohm, "Labor Notes from Chihuahua," June 23, 1937, 812.504/1662, USNARG 59.

82. Lee R. Blohm, "The Labor Set-Up in Chihuahua," Nov. 3, 1937, USNARG 59, 1930–39, Confidential, 812.504/1687.

83. Angel Valenzuela and others to the President, March 19, 1938, AGN, Cárdenas, 404.1/9225.

84. Justino Loya, Secretaria General, to the Directiva del V Pleno Nacional de la Confederación Campesina Mexicana, March 23, 1938, AGN, Cárdenas, 543.1/18, leg. 2.

85. Specific charges were that Talamantes ordered the killing of several important leaders: Agustín Mendoza, the former municipal president of Madera; Gabriel Chávez, a Parral businessman, former deputy, and candidate for municipal president against Gustavo Chávez, the brother of the inspector general of police and chief of rural forces in the state, Alfredo Chávez (elected governor in 1940); and Silverio Sierra, ex-secretary-general of the Síndicato de Mineros, Metallúrgicos y Similares. He jailed the former president of the Liga Regional Campesina de Satevó, Jesús Rodríguez Olivera, and José Simental, secretary-treasurer of the Liga de Comunidades Agrarias del Estado, in May 1937 and held them for two weeks without charges. Special police persecuted Cuauhtemoc Mendoza, secretary of organization and propaganda of the Liga de Comunidades Agrarias y Sindicatos Campesinos of Chihuahua, who had to flee to the sierras to save his life. Santos Caloca, Ricardo Espinosa Ramírez, and Carlos Enríquez Ch. to Comisión Parmanente del Congreso de la Union, July 16, 1937, AGN, Cárdenas, 543.1/18, leg. 1. José Simentel, Secretario-Tesorero de la Liga de Comunidades Agrarias de Chihuahua, to Cárdenas, July 19, 1937, AGN, Cárdenas, 534.1/18, leg. 2.

86. José Simentel y otros secretarios de La Liga de Comunidades Agrarias de Chihuahua to La Directiva del V Pleno de la Confederación Campesina Mexicana, March 23, 1938, AGN, Cárdenas, 543.1/18, leg. 2.

87. "Resume of Conditions in Mexico, March 1937," 812.00/30444, USNARG 59.

88. Ignacio Jaimes, Presidente de la Comité de Control Político de la Sección 45 del Sindicato de Trabajadores, Mineros, Metalúrgicos y . . . , Mina de Rincón, Dec. 16, 1939, AGN, Cárdenas, 544.5/563.

89. *EPT,* April 30, 1939, 4.

90. *EPT,* June 17, 1972.

91. "Summary of Political Developments in Chihuahua," Aug. 1939, 812.00 Chihuahua/374; "Resume of Political Situation in Ciudad Juárez," Sept. 1939, 812.00 Chihuahua/378; "Summary of Political Developments in Chihuahua," Sept. 1939, 812.00/379.

92. *POC,* Oct. 2, 1937, 798.

5   Persistent Oligarchs

1. Albert Saboul, *The French Revolution, 1787–1799: From the Storming of the Bastille to Napoleon,* 9, 15, 553–56.

2. Arno J. Mayer, *The Persistence of the Old Regime: Europe to the Great War,* 4.

3. See, for example, Frans J. Schryer, *The Rancheros of Pisaflores: The History of a Peasant Bourgeoisie in Mexico,* 3.

4. Arturo Warman, *We Come to Object: The Peasants of Morelos and the National State,* 134, 142, 152.

5. Roger D. Hansen, *The Politics of Mexican Development,* 37.

6. Beatriz Rojas, *La destrucción de la hacienda en Aguascalientes, 1910–1931;* Ian Jacobs, *Ranchero Revolt: The Mexican Revolution in Guerrero;* Schryer, *Pisaflores;* Paul Friedrich, *Agrarian Revolt in a Mexican Village;* Warman, *We Come to Object;* Alex M. Saragoza, *The Monterrey Elite and the Mexican State, 1880–1940;* Dudley Ankerson, "Saturnino Cedillo"; Alan M. Kirshner, *Tomás Garrido Canabal y el movimiento de las Camisas Rojas;* Gilbert M. Joseph, *Revolution from Without: Yucatán, Mexico, and the United States, 1880–1924.*

7. Warman, *We Come to Object,* 134.

8. Salamini, *Agrarian Radicalism in Veracruz, 1920–38,* 132. Hacendado Manuel Parra created a large force of gunmen that protected his property until his death in 1943, after which the government expropriated his land.

9. Nora Hamilton, *The Limits of State Autonomy: Post-Revolutionary Mexico,* 307–16.

10. Heather Fowler Salamini, "Caciquismo and the Mexican Revolution: The Case of Manuel Palaez," paper presented to the Sixth Conference of Mexican and United States Historians, Chicago, September 1980.

11. See, for example, William H. Beezley, "Madero: The Unknown President and His Failure to Organize Rural Mexico," in Wolfskill and Richmond, eds., *Essays on the Mexican Revolution,* 1–24.

12. Rojas, *Aguascalientes,* 122–23.

13. Katz, *The Secret War in Mexico,* 531–38.

14. Hans Werner Tobler, "Las paradojas del ejército revolucionario: Su papel social en la reforma agraria mexicana, 1920–1935," *Historia Mexicana* 21:1 (July–September 1971): 38–79.

15. Salamini, *Agrarian Radicalism,* 36.

16. Friedrich, *Agrarian Revolt,* 56.

17. Joseph, *Revolution from Without,* 265.

18. Hall, "Alvaro Obregón and the Politics of Mexican Land Reform," 213–38.

19. Gilbert M. Joseph, "The Fragile Revolution: Cacique Politics and the Revolutionary Process in Yucatán," *Latin American Research Review* 15:1 (1980): 41–64.

20. Salamini, *Agrarian Radicalism,* 36–37.

21. Simpson, *The Ejido,* 349.

22. Friedrich, *Agrarian Revolt,* 56.

23. Ibid., 103.

24. Jacobs, *Ranchero Revolt,* 116.

25. Salamini, *Agrarian Radicalism,* 96.

26. Edith B. Couturier, *La hacienda de Hueyapán, 1550–1936,* 177–78.

27. Rojas, *Aguascalientes,* 122.

28. Schryer, *Pisaflores,* 82.

29. Couturier, *La hacienda de Hueyapán,* 177.

30. Joseph, *Revolution from Without,* 255.

31. William P. Mitchell, U.S. consul, Chihuahua City, "Economic Report for the Chihuahua Consular District, January to April 1923," May 31, 1923; "Review of Commerce and Industry for the Quarter Ending Sept. 30, 1924," Oct. 18, 1924; "Report on Commerce and Industry for Quarter Ending Sept. 30, 1927," November 7, 1927—all in USNARG 84, ACCC, 1927.

32. Wasserman, *Capitalists, Caciques, and Revolution,* 43–70.

33. Lindley Garrison to SS, Dec. 17, 1913, USNARG 59, 812.00/10241; Letcher to SS, Dec. 21, 1913, USNARG 59, 812.00/10301.

34. McEnelly, "Review of Commerce and Industry for the Quarter Ending September 30, 1923," Oct. 19, 1923, USNARG 84, ACCC, 1923; Myers, U.S. consul, to Juan A. Creel, manager of the Banco Minero, Jan. 8, 1929, USNARG 84, ACCC, 1929.

35. Berta Ulloa, *Historia de la Revolución Mexicana, 1914–1917: La encrucijada de 1915,* 212–13; David P. Barrows to Benjamin I. Wheeler, July 25, 1915, USNARG 59, 812.00/15595; Friedrich Katz, "Agrarian Changes in Northern Mexico in the Period of *Villista* Rule, 1913–1915," in Wilkie, Meyer, and Monzón de Wilkie, *Contemporary Mexico,* 259–73.

36. The buyer was Francisca M. viuda de Prieto. The property was subject to considerable conflict thereafter between Señora Prieto and the Caja de Préstamos. Francisca M. viuda de Prieto to President Obregón, April 30, 1923, AGN, Obregón-Calles, 802-P-28.

37. *Excelsior,* Oct. 13, 1919, Buckley Collection, 123.1.

38. Katz, *The Secret War in Mexico,* 536; AGN, Gobernación, Revolución, Box 83, exp. 32.

39. For the quote, see Obregón to Arthur J. McQuatters, Franklin Remington, and James G. McNary, Dec. 10, 1921, enclosure to chargé d'affaires, Mexico City, to SS, Dec. 13, 1921, USNARG 59, 812.52T27. USNARG files 812.52T27/1–40 concern the McQuatters-Terrazas transaction. See also AGN, Obregón-Calles, 806-T. Machado, *The North Mexican Cattle Industry,* 40–48, has a summary of the affair.

40. James B. Stewart, U.S. consul, to SS, Feb. 7, 1922, USNARG 59, 812.52T27/1. Under the new agrarian law nearly all the estate was to be seized by the government. U.S. consul, Ciudad Juárez, to SS, Feb. 9, 1922, USNARG 59, 812.52T27/2.

41. Stewart to SS, Feb. 15, 1922, 812.52T27/4; Stewart to SS, Feb. 17, 1922, 812.52T27/5; Stewart to SS, Feb. 25, 1922, 812.52T27/8; Stewart to SS, April 8, 1922, 812.52T27/10—all in USNARG 59; Obregón to Enríquez, March 6, 1922, AGN, Obregón-Calles, 806-T-1.

42. Stewart to SS, April 10, 1922, USNARG 59, 812.52T27/13; Enríquez to Obregón, March 3, 1922, AGN, Obregón-Calles, 806-T-1.

43. Stewart to SS, April 18, 1922, USNARG 59, 812.52T27/14.

44. U.S. consul, Ciudad Juárez, to SS, April 28, 1922, USNARG 59, 812.52T27/16. Land under cultivation did not include that farmed by renters and sharecroppers. They were allowed to continue working the land and to be offered an opportunity to purchase it later. Claude I. Dawson, U.S. consul-general, to SS, May 4, 1922, USNARG 59, 812.52-T27/19.

45. U.S. consul, Ciudad Juárez, to SS, June 17, 1922, 812.52T27/25; Stewart to SS, July 7, 1922, 812.52T27/27, and July 11, 1922, 812.52T27/31; George T. Summerlin to SS, Feb. 23, 1923, 812.52T27/38—all in USNARG 59. As part of the government purchase, the estate agreed to forego damage claims that amounted to 400,000 cattle, 200,000 sheep, and 60,000 horses. AGN, Obregón-Calles, 806-T-1, contains all the correspondence about the purchase of the Terrazas estate.

46. Abdiel Oñate Villarreal, "Banca y agricultura en México: La Caja de Préstamos para Obras de Irrigación y Fomento de la Agricultura, 1908–1926" (Ph.D. diss., El Colegio de México, 1984).

47. George T. Summerlin to SS, March 2, 1923, USNARG 59, 812.52T27/40. The sale was finalized in June 1922. *EPT,* June 17, 1922, 1.

48. Hall, "Alvaro Obregón and the Politics of Mexican Land Reform."

49. Letter to the editor, *El Correo de Chihuahua,* June 25, 1930, 1.

50. *Boletín Comercial,* Dec. 15, 1926, 11.

51. Some were not mentioned in the decrees: Gallego (Villa Ahumada), Hinojos, La Luga (Chihuahua), La Nariz (San Buenaventura), Sacramento (Chihuahua), San Dionisio (Allende), Los Sauces (Chihuahua), Tabaloapa

(Chihuahua), and Virginia (Camargo). These may have been legally part of the expropriated lands.

52. "Extracto del Informe General del Estado que guardan los terrenos que comprenden el latifundio Terrazas propiedad de la Caja de Préstamos para Obras de Irrigación y Fomento de la Agricultura, S.A.," enclosure to Ing. Manuel Romero González, Banco Nacional de Crédito Agrícola, S.A., to President Ortiz Rubio, Nov. 7, 1930, AGN, Ortiz Rubio, 24 (1930), 13564. See also Ing. Luis L. León to President Ortiz Rubio, Oct. 27, 1930, AGN, Ortiz Rubio, 24 (1930), 13187.

53. Luisa Terrazas Viuda de Guerrero purchased lot 6 of Encinillas in 1932; Miguel Márquez, lots 30 and 31 of Encinillas and the Hacienda de San Lorenzo in San Buenaventura. They paid 2.34 pesos per hectare. Márquez paid 10 percent in cash and the remainder in bonds (the bonds used by the federal government to pay for the estate of Luis Terrazas in 1922). M. Romero González to Cástulo R. Chávez, July 16, 1932, AGN, Caja de Préstamos, Terrazas Latifundio, 160–14; Contract of Caja de Préstamos with Miguel Márquez, Jan. 13, 1932, AGN, Caja de Préstamos, Terrazas Latifundio, 189: 1 and 2.

54. *POC*, Dec. 8, 1923, 4; March 10, 1923. The haciendas involved were Las Orientales, Los Angeles, and San Eduardo.

55. *POC*, Feb. 27, 1932, 3; Nov. 17, 1934, 1; Aug. 11, 1934, 3; Sept. 25, 1937, 784; April 27, 1937, 346; Nov. 12, 1938, 896; March 2, 1940, 149.

56. *POC*, July 14, 1934, 6; Feb. 6, 1937, 99; Oct. 29, 1938, 739.

57. Anastasio Samaniego to Rodríguez, Oct. 21, 1932, and Juan F. Azcarate to private secretary to the President, Nov. 27, 1932, AGN, Rodríguez, 552.1/74.

58. *POC*, Jan. 16, 1937, 38.

59. *POC*, Oct. 9, 1926, 1, and Sept. 29, 1923, 1. Sisniega owned a textile factory on the property, which was the principal means of support of the pueblo of Valle de Zaragoza.

60. Enrique Creel Terrazas to President, March 31, 1938, AGN, Cárdenas, 404.1/2707.

61. *POC*, Feb. 3, 1940, 77. San Isidro had 136,549 hectares.

62. Ganadera "X" rented two lots with an option to buy. T. W. Duke to E. R. Stettinius, March 28, 1944, USNARG 59, 812.5211/38.

63. Teresa B. Vda. de Terrazas to Cárdenas, March 7, 1940, AGN, Cárdenas, 404.1/1193.

64. "Relación de las propriedades intervenidas que existen actualmente bajo el control de la Administración de Bienes Intervenidas en el estado de Chihuahua," March 31, 1919, Box 88, item 32, AGN, Gobernación, Revolución; Fernando Chávez to President Calles, March 25, 1925, AGN,

Obregón-Calles, 707-C-34; McEnelly, "Report on Commerce and Industry for the Quarter Ending 31 December 1924," Jan. 27, 1925, USNARG 84, ACCC, 1925; McEnelly, "Report on Commerce and Industry for the Quarter Ending 30 September 1927," Nov. 7, 1927, USNARG 84, ACCC, 1927 and McEnelly, "Report on Commerce and Industry for the First Six Months of 1926," July 8, 1926, USNARG 84, ACCC, 1926.

65. Fernando Chávez to Calles, March 25, 1925, AGN, Obregón-Calles, 707-C-34.

66. Francis H. Styles, U.S. consul, to SS, Sept. 6, 1933, and Styles to W. D. Duke, Feb. 29, 1932, USNARG 84, ACCC, 1932.

67. McEnelly to Thew J. Lovel Co., June 15, 1927, and Styles to Northwest Energy Co., Aug. 5, 1930, USNARG 84, ACCC, 1930.

68. Salvador Creel to director, Ferrocarriles Nacionales de México, Sept. 6, 1928, AGN, Obregón-Calles, 802-C-107; Ing. Manuel O'Reilly, director-general, Cía. Eléctrica y de Ferrocarriles de Chihuahua, to McEnelly, Aug. 24, 1924, and Oct. 3, 1924, USNARG 84, ACCC, 1924; O'Reilly to Styles, July 13, 1931, USNARG 84, ACCC, 1931.

69. List of prominent attorneys in Chihuahua, Sept. 21, 1928, USNARG 84, ACCC, 1928.

70. McEnelly, "Review of Commerce and Industry for the First Six Months of 1926," July 8, 1926, USNARG 84, ACCC, 1926; *El Correo*, July 24, 1925, 1, and July 28, 1925, 1. Allegedly, Juan A. Creel and Jesús J. Falomir had illegally combined three family banks, the Banco Minero, the Caja de Ahorros de la República Mexicana, and the Banco Comercial Refaccionario.

71. There were three federal decrees affecting old banks of emission: Jan. 21, 1921; July 9, 1924; and Jan. 25, 1929. Lic. Arturo H. Orci to President, April 9, 1929, AGN, Portes Gil, 3/627, 6410.

72. *POC*, April 1, 1922, 23. *Boletín Financiero y Minero de Mexico*, Feb. 21, 1925, 2; July 2, 1925, 5; July 24, 1925, 5; Aug. 5, 1925, 3; and Aug. 19, 1925, 5. AGN, Caja de Préstamos, Banco Minero 1931. See, for example, *POC*, Dec. 22, 1923, 19. The bank held the mortgage on the Hacienda de San Toribio, owned by Belem Terrazas de González as heir to Guadalupe E. González, in Carretas, Morelos. *POC*, Aug. 1, 1931, 6; June 27, 1931, 17.

73. *El Continental*, March 2, 1927, 5. *El Correo*, Nov. 5, 1927, 3. *POC*, Sept. 21, 1929, 5; Dec. 21, 1929, 32.

74. Fernando Chávez to Calles, March 25, 1925, AGN, Obregón-Calles, 707-C-34. In 1924 Governor Talavera accused it of extorting the people. *La Patria*, April 11, 1924, 1.

75. *El Correo*, July 24, 1925, 1, and July 28, 1925, 1.

76. *POC*, Dec. 9, 1933, 5; April 8, 1939, 266.

77. *El Continental,* June 17, 1922, 2; *POC,* July 2, 1927, 2.

78. *El Correo,* Nov. 25, 1928, 4.

79. Fuentes Mares, *Vallina,* 53–54.

80. *El Correo,* Nov. 14, 1925, 1, and Dec. 25, 1925, 1; Torreblanca (private secretary to the president) to governor of Chihuahua, Aug. 22, 1925, and J. A. Almeida to Fernando Torreblanca, Sept. 1, 1925, AGN, Obregón-Calles, 707-C-3; *El Correo,* Dec. 25, 1925. Martín Falomir, Jesús Falomir, Luis Creel, Manuel Prieto, Sr., and Joaquín Cortazar were all jailed. Juan Creel only escaped because he was in the United States. La Equidad went bankrupt in 1924 (*POC,* June 7, 1924, 20). The litigation was based on the investment in 1910 by the management of La Equidad of 39,000 pesos in the Banco Minero. Juan A. Creel was both a director of La Equidad and manager of the Banco Minero at the time. The company subsequently bought more shares of the bank without the approval of the board. Because of the Revolution, the bank's shares plunged in worth. *El Correo,* Dec. 25, 1925; *Boletín Comercial,* Aug. 15, 1926, 13; *Boletín Financiero y Minero,* Nov. 10, 1925, 1, and Nov. 18, 1926, 1, 5.

81. *El Correo,* July 18, 1925, 1, and July 19, 1925, 1. Zubarán to Torreblanca, July 28, 1921, AGN, Obregón-Calles, 814-R-37. *Boletín Comercial,* Oct. 15, 1926, 16.

82. Gregorio Rivera, Inspector de Trabajo, to Jefe de Departamento de Trabajo, Feb. 8, 1928, AGN, Trabajo, 1412/5. *Boletín Comercial,* Oct. 15, 1928, 14. *EC,* July 14, 1930, 1.

83. Ing. Pastor Roauaix, gobernador interino de Durango, to President Ortiz Rubio, Nov. 11, 1931, AGN, Ortiz Rubio, 8 (1931), 7515, leg. 21.

84. *POC,* March 15, 1924, 9.

85. Nov. 2, 1922, AGN, Trabajo, 396/2, 31.

86. *Boletín Comercial,* June 15, 1925, 13.

87. *POC,* Jan. 5, 1924, 21; July 26, 1924, 16.

88. Videl de la Graza to Lázaro de la Garza, Oct. 3, 1914, WIX, E. *POC,* June 25, 1921, 5; Aug. 8, 1931, 26; June 23, 1934, 4. J. A. Enríquez was manager of both companies. It is not clear if he was a front for the Terrazas or an independent.

89. Salvador Creel to Director de los Ferrocarriles de México and Creel to Torreblanca, Sept. 6, 1928, AGN, Obregón-Calles, 802-C-107.

90. *El Correo,* July 9, 1929, 1.

91. *POC,* May 21, 1921, 24; March 4, 1922, 24; June 18, 1927, 15; July 2, 1927, 2; Feb. 13, 1926, 32; June 23, 1934, 4; *Boletín Estadística 1925,* 88–112; *Anuario estadística minero 1932,* 76; AGN, Trabajo, 1311/4. The companies were the Cía. Minera La Unión, the Florencia Mining Company, Cía.

Mincra La Reina, Cía. San Francisco y Minas Aliadas, Cía. Minera de la Alianza, Cía. Minera Gibraltar Y Anexas.

92. *El Paso Herald,* May 2, 1924; Cía. Eléctrica y de Ferrocarriles de Chihuahua, S.A., to Secretaría de Industria, Comercio y Trabajo, Aug. 8, 1923, AGN, Trabajo, 690/7; *POC,* Sept. 1, 1923, 7, which includes the minutes of the Ayuntamiento de Ciudad Chihuahua, Aug. 14, 1923; *POC,* Oct. 4, 1924, 16; Oct. 17, 1925, 32; Nov. 9, 1929, 23; July 11, 1931, 15; *El Correo,* March 25, 1930, 1; Manuel O'Reilly to Styles, USNARG 84, ACCJ, 1931:7.

93. *POC,* Jan. 5, 1924, 20.

94. *El Correo,* April 6, 1928, and April 10, 1928, 3.

95. *El Correo,* Oct. 4, 1930, 1.

96. Carlos Helmus had embezzled US$62,000 from a bank in El Paso, Texas. President Obregón appealed to President Warren G. Harding and obtained his release from a five-year sentence. A. Obregón to W. G. Harding, April 4, 1922, June 9, 1922; Harding to Obregón, May 5, 1922, Sept. 30, 1922, AGN, Obregón-Calles, 104-H-16. Creel never ceased his opposition to the government's policies. Calles considered the National Chamber of Agriculture a group of "old hacendados," the most offensive of whom was Creel. Creel had remarked in a speech that "Agrarianism has led the country backward a thousand years. . . ." J. Reuben Clark Memo, Jan. 24, 1930, USNARG 59, 812.52/1592.

97. *POC,* Dec. 12, 1931, 7–10.

98. *Boletín Comercial* (Ciudad Chihuahua), June 15, 1926, 5, Oct. 15, 1925, 23, Dec. 15, 1933, 21, July 15, 1928, 20; *Chihuahua Ganadero,* March 1942, 23, March 1940, 30; Circular of the Cámara Nacional de Ganadería de Chihuahua, April 21, 1933, USNARG 84, ACCC, 1933; *El Correo,* April 24, 1930, 1, March 25, 1930, 1; AGN, Obregón-Calles, 101-R2-H-1; AGN, Ortiz Rubio, 137 (1930), 6942.

99. AGN, Obregón-Calles, 101-R2-H1.

100. *El Correo,* April 24, 1930, 1.

101. Cámara Nacional de Ganadería del Estado de Chihuahua to Montes de Oca, Secretario de Hacienda y Crédito Público, Sept. 5, 1927, AGN, Obregón-Calles, 731-G-2.

102. *El Correo,* March 5, 1929, 1.

103. Circular, April 21, 1933, USNARG 84, ACCC, 1933:8.

104. *EMJ* 129 (June 7, 1930): 578; AGN, Ortiz Rubio, 137 (1930), 6942.

105. *El Correo,* Oct. 28, 1925, 1.

106. *El Correo,* Nov. 19, 1927, 1.

107. *El Correo,* April 3, 1930, 1.

108. *El Correo,* March 6, 1930, 1.

109. *El Correo,* June 9, 1928, 4.
110. *El Correo,* May 23, 1929, 1.
111. *El Correo,* April 12, 1930, 1.
112. *POC,* May 7, 1932, 4.
113. *El Correo,* April 10, 1928, 3.
114. *El Correo,* March 25, 1928, 1. Of course, the rehabilitation was helped somewhat by the death of the old guard. General Luis died in 1921; Juan Terrazas, in December 1925; Alberto, in 1926; son-in-law Bernardo Urueta, in September 1931; Creel, in 1931. *El Correo,* Dec. 10, 1925, 1, and Sept. 30, 1931, 1.
115. *El Correo,* Aug. 10, 1929, 1.
116. *El Correo,* Aug. 18, 1931, 1.
117. Luis Vargas Piñera, "El General Terrazas y su familia extraordinaria," *Excelsior,* April 16, 1939.
118. Ramón F. Luján to Obregón, March 3, 1922; Memorandum of R. F. Luján, May 8, 1924; Luján to Ing. Francisco Salido, May 10, 1924; Luján to Obregón, Feb. 20, 1924; Luján to Obregón, March 4, 1924, AGN, Obregón-Calles, 818-S-95.
119. R. F. Luján to President, Jan. 20, 1926, AGN, Obregón-Calles, 241-H-L-34.
120. Ramon F. Luján to Obregón, March 3, 1922; Luján to F. A. Salido, May 10, 1924, R. F. Luján to Obregón, Feb. 20, 1924, AGN, Obregón-Calles, 818-S-95; Lic. Joaquín Ortega, dirección general de bienes nacionales, to Obregón, Dec. 31, 1923, Fernando Brena Alatorre, memorandum on Salaices, May 1, 1921, AGN, Obregón-Calles, 805-L-29. Joaquín Ortega, DirGen de Bienes Nacionales to President, Dec. 31, 1923, AGN, Obregón-Calles, 805-L-29. Luján claimed an investment of 4 million pesos, with an 890,000 pesos mortgage to the Caja.
121. Aparceros de Salaices to President, Sept. 17, 1927, and Jesús Cano, Julián Torres y otros to President, Sept. 19, 1927, AGN, Obregón-Calles, 818-S-95.
122. *POC,* Jan. 6, 1934, 2.
123. *La Nueva Era,* Feb. 9, 1911, 1.
124. The hacienda had 181,114 hectares and was valued at 774,418 pesos. Memorandum, May 2, 1925, AGN, Caja de Préstamos, Box 113.
125. R. Poo S., administrator, Informe, Aug. 11, 1921, AGN, Caja de Préstamos, Box 64.
126. Luis Esther Estrada to private secretary of President, Nov. 10, 1924, AGN, Obregón-Calles, 731-I-7.
127. I. N. Thacker to Calles, March 6, 1928, AGN, Obregón-Calles, 731-I-7.

128. *POC,* Dec. 14, 1929, 6, Nov. 30, 1929, 5–6, Jan. 12, 1929, 9; Chihuahua, *Directorio general de municipios* (Chihuahua, 1927), 365–67; AGN, Obregón-Calles, 202-Ch-48; *Boletín Comercial,* Jan. 15, 1928, 7.

129. *El Correo,* Aug. 13, 1931, 3.

130. *Chihuahua,* July 1933, 30.

131. *Boletín Comercial,* Jan. 15, 1928, 7.

132. *El Correo,* April 24, 1930, 1.

133. AGN, Obregón-Calles, 818-L-95; 818-L-85. *POC,* April 12, 1924, 3. Lic. Manuel L. Luján to Obregón, March 17, 1922, AGN, Obregón-Calles, 809-L-95.

134. "Property in Chihuahua Belonging to Pedro Zuloaga," Nov. 22, 1928, USNARG 84, ACCC, 1928.

135. Testament of Carlos Zuloaga to President Obregón, April 19, 1921; Memo of Guillermo Porras on the Application of the Agrarian Law of Chihuahua to the property of Carlos Zuloaga, AGN, Obregón-Calles, 818-Ch-23.

136. José Calles, auxiliar, procurador de pueblos, to Obregón, Jan. 15, 1924, AGN, Obregón-Calles, 818-Ch-23.

137. *Boletín Comercial,* Dec. 15, 1917, 13.

138. Intestado de Carlos Zuloaga to Obregón, May 7, 1921, AGN, Obregón-Calles, 818-Ch-23.

139. Memo of Guillermo Porras concerning estate of Carlos Zuloaga, Sept. 27, 1922, AGN, Obregón-Calles, 818-Ch-23.

140. *POC,* Oct. 13, 1923, 7. *Boletín Comercial,* July 15, 1923.

141. *POC,* Oct. 4, 1924, 1; Dec. 26, 1925, 2.

142. *El Correo,* March 17, 1926, 1.

143. *POC,* April 7, 1928, 1.

144. *POC,* Aug. 15, 1931, 6.

145. *POC,* Feb. 18, 1928, 7; Feb. 11, 1928, 9; Oct. 5, 1929, 7; Oct. 5, 1929, 6.

146. *POC,* Dec. 21, 1929, 16.

147. *POC,* Oct. 3, 1931, 5.

148. *POC,* Nov. 14, 1931; July 4, 1931, 2–3, 4–7; Jan. 23, 1932, 9; April 30, 1932, 15; Sept. 15, 1934, 4; Aug. 22, 1936, 702; Feb. 8, 1936, 107; Oct. 30, 1937, 875.

149. *POC,* July 25, 1931.

150. *POC,* July 4, 1931, 2–3, 4–7.

151. Ing. Gustavo L. Talamantes, presidente segundo congreso agraria, to Rodríguez, Nov. 22, 1932, AGN, Cárdenas, 552.14/128.

152. Caja de Préstamos to Caja de Préstamos in Chihuahua, May 25,

1932, AGN, Caja de Préstamos, exp. 189, Letterbook, January–June 1932, Letter 468.

153. Nov. 27, 1937, 746; *POC*, July 25, 1936, 609.

154. *POC*, Sept. 16, 1939, 696.

155. *POC*, July 11, 1925, 13.

156. Chihuahua, Secretaría del Gobierno, Sección Estadística, *Chihuahua, 1934*, 79; *Boletín Comercial*, May 15, 1926, 19; *El Correo*, May 24, 1930, 1, Aug. 29, 1930, 1, Aug. 22, 1925, 4, and March 25, 1930, 1; Martín Falomir to Juez Segundo de la Civil, AGN, Obregón-Calles, 818-A-3.

157. Martín Falomir, who had managed some of the Terrazas banking interests, was in exile in El Paso in 1921. Martín Falomir to Obregón, Dec. 27, 1921, AGN, Obregón-Calles, 818-F-9.

158. *POC*, July 16, 1921, 15; Aug. 20, 1921, 16.

159. *POC*, March 5, 1921, 31.

160. *POC*, April 1, 1922, 24.

161. Ornelas list, 1923.

162. Martín Falomir to Juez Segundo de lo Civil, 1922, AGN, Obregón-Calles, 818-A-3.

163. *POC*, Oct. 8, 1927, 16; Feb. 22, 1936, 158; Jan. 20, 1940, 35.

164. Director General del Banco de México to President, April 20, 1926, and Velásquez to Calles, April 28, 1926, AGN, Obregón-Calles, 104-B-53; *Boletín Comercial*, May 15, 1926, 19.

165. Memo to President, May 21, 1929, AGN, Portes Gil, 41336.

166. *El Correo*, March 25, 1930, 1.

167. *El Correo*, Aug. 29, 1930, 1.

168. *POC*, Aug. 4, 1934, 5.

169. *POC*, Jan. 6, 1934, 8; March 9, 1935, 173; March 19, 1938, 211; June 18, 1938, 458; Oct. 23, 1937, 855; March 25, 1939, 316–17.

170. *POC*, June 17, 1922, 8; Dec. 4, 1922, 16; Jan. 31, 1931, 7; May 7, 1938, 243.

171. *POC*, Dec. 4, 1922, 16.

172. *El Correo*, June 9, 1929, 4.

173. *POC*, Jan. 16, 1932, 24.

174. Carlos Grinda to President, March 11, 1919, AGN, Gobernación, Revolución, 274/60.

175. de la Peña, *Chihuahua económica*, 1:183.

176. Gabriel Sáenz to President, May 27, 1929, AGN, Portes Gil, 4/528, 9002.

177. Melchor Carmona, for ejidatarios de la Hacienda de Corral de la Piedra, to Angel Chávez, Jan. 23, 1939; Summary of Joaquín Gardea, repre-

sentative of Comité ejidal de Punto Alegre, to President, June 8, 1935, AGN, Cárdenas, 404.1/7.

178. *El Continental,* Oct. 21, 1929, 1.

179. Rita Murga y socios petition, Sept. 24, 1923, AGN, Obregón-Calles, 818-S-274.

180. *EPT,* April 27, 1923, 14. There were over a million acres involved in the dispute.

181. Eulogio Gallardo, presidente de la comité ejecutivo agrario, to President, April 25, 1939; Gallardo to jefe del departamento agrario, May 23, 1939, AGN, Cárdenas, 404.1/7.

6 Freebooters

1. Knight, *Mexican Revolution,* 2:514.

2. Smith, *Labyrinths of Power,* 102.

3. Knight, *Mexican Revolution,* 2:518.

4. Smith, *Labyrinths of Power,* 102.

5. Roderic A. Camp, "Comparing Political Generations in Mexico, the Last One Hundred Years," paper presented at the Conference of Mexican and North American Historians, San Diego, Calif., October 1990, 6.

6. Knight, *Mexican Revolution,* 2:518–19.

7. Ibid.

8. Smith, *Labyrinths of Power,* 183.

9. Katz, *The Secret War in Mexico,* 11.

10. Camp, *Entrepreneurs and Politics,* 15, 32–33.

11. This is only a tentative conclusion, however. Further research in the municipalities may very well reveal considerably more crossover.

12. Carlos Gallegos Medina to Silvestre Terrazas, Jan. 10, 1913, STP, STC.

13. *La Voz del Obrero* (Hidalgo de Parral), Oct. 15, 1911.

14. *El Correo,* Nov. 27, 1925, 1.

15. Nov. 20, 1922, AGN, Obregón-Calles, 818-Ch-26, and June 13, 1923, AGN, Obregón-Calles, 805-Ch-23.

16. *El Correo,* April 12, 1930, 1.

17. Chávez M., "Hombres de la revolución," (unpublished MS), 315.

18. *La Opinión Pública: Diario Liberal* (Hidalgo de Parral), Oct. 22, 1911; *La Vida Nueva,* Aug. 15, 1915, 4; *POC,* Feb. 22, 1914, 1; *Gazeta Oficial del Gobierno Convencionista Provisional,* March 8, 1915; *La Patria,* Dec. 16, 1913; AGN, Obregón-Calles, 217-Ch-5. Almada, *Diccionario,* 469.

19. The Almeidas included Jesús Antonio, Alberto B., Estebán L., Casí-

miro, Benjamín, Carolina, María, Juan, Dolores, Miguel, and brother-in-law Socorro García.

20. Almada, *Gobernadores,* 559–61; Chávez M., "Hombres de la revolución," 9.

21. *POC,* June 18, 1913, 13.

22. *La Vida Nueva,* June 25, 1915, 1. He hosted a banquet for Luz Corral de Villa.

23. *POC,* April 26, 1919, 9; Jan. 15, 1921, 4; July 16, 1921, 4; and July 22, 1922, 13.

24. *EPMT,* June 29, 1921, 4.

25. Chávez M., *Sesenta años,* 222.

26. *POC,* June 1, 1918, 9.

27. "Review of Commerce and Industry for Quarter Ending Dec. 31, 1925," USNARG 84, ACCC, 1925.

28. "Review of Commerce and Industry for Quarter Ending Mar. 31, 1927," USNARG 84, ACCC, 1927.

29. *El Correo,* July 20, 1929, 4.

30. *EMJ* 120 (July 4, 1925): 27; *EPT,* April 18, 1926, 4. The officers of the Mosqueteros Company included Frank Knotts, Salvador F. Muñoz, Alberto Madero, and Alberto Almeida. *EPT,* May 25, 1924.

31. Roberto López, Jefe del Departamento de Crédito, to the Caja de Préstamos, June 5, 1931, AGN, Caja de Préstamos, Terrazas Latifundio, 160-5. Letterbook, January–June 1932, Letter 0382. These transactions involved at least 56,000 hectares. The family early on recognized the value of the Terrazas properties. Alberto was also involved in a project with Lic. A. B. Valderrama in a company to colonize the Terrazas estate in 1925. *El Correo,* Oct. 29, 1925, 2.

32. Roberto Fierro, *Esta es mi vida.* This answers the question of how the Almeidas, who barely escaped death at the hands of their opponents in 1927, could regain enough influence to acquire such important patronage five years later. It is also possible that the purchase was facilitated by interim governor Eduardo Salido, who was once a partner in a mining claim (*POC,* July 12, 1919, 13). There is also the possibility that Alberto, still highly regarded in Ciudad Juárez, had enough clout to obtain the land.

33. *POC,* March 2, 1940, 151.

34. *POC,* Feb. 24, 1934, 7.

35. J. R. Almeida to unknown, Jan. 20, 1926, AGN, Obregón-Calles, 243-CH-A-1; *POC,* Jan. 11, 1930, 23; *El Correo,* Sept. 4, 1925. Luis Esther Estrada, J. A. and Estebán Almeida, and Juan F. Treviño bought the Chihuahua Lumber Company for 150,000 pesos. Casímiro Almeida purchased Cargill for the same amount.

36. McEnelly, "Review of Commerce and Industry for the Quarter

Ending 30 September 1925," Oct. 19, 1925; McEnelly to SS, May 14, 1924, USNARG 84, Confidential Files, 1922–28.

37. *Chihuahua*, March 1933, 18; AGN, Obregón-Calles, 243-CH-A-1.

38. "Annual Report on Commerce and Industry for 1926," USNARG 84, Confidential Files, 1922–28.

39. Ibid.; McEnelly to SS, April 20, 1927, USNARG 84, ACCC, 1927.

40. G-2, Combat, "Who's Who in Commissioned Personnel," March 27, 1931, no. 3289, USNARG 165, Reel 8.

41. Chávez M., "Hombres de la revolución," 219.

42. Ralph H. Vigil, "Revolution and Confusion: The Peculiar Case of José Inés Salazar," *New Mexico Historical Review* 53:2 (1978): 153.

43. JRB to Hitch, Oct. 24, 1914, USNARG 59, 812.00/13573; Louis F. Post, ASS, to SS, Oct. 27, 1915, 812.00/16655; Solicitor to SS, Nov. 6, 1915, 812.00/16655.

44. Vigil, "Revolution and Confusion," 161–62.

45. *El Continental*, Sept. 14, 1931, 1.

46. *POC*, Nov. 5, 1927, 25.

47. *El Continental*, July 28, 1927, 8.

48. Enclosure to letter of Francisco Castrejón, secretario particular, to Luis I. Rodríguez, secretario particular del presidente, Jan. 23, 1936, AGN, Cárdenas, 544.5/469.

49. Lorenzo Quevedo to Cárdenas, Aug. 20, 1935, AGN, Cárdenas, 444.1/534.

50. USNARG 59, 812.00 Chihuahua/246.

51. Jesús Alanis to Rodríguez, Sept. 13, 1933, AGN, Rodríguez, 525.3/288.

52. Rodríguez to Comisión Liquidador de la Caja de Préstamos, May 25, 1933, AGN, Rodríguez, 329/42.

53. Enclosure to letter of Francisco Castrejón, secretario particular, to Luis I. Rodríguez, PSP, Jan. 23, 1936, AGN, Cárdenas, 544.5/469.

54. Morris B. Parker, *Mules, Mines, and Me in Mexico, 1895–1932*, 159.

55. AGN, Rodríguez, 525.3/288; "Political Conditions in Chihuahua, May 1935," USNARG 59, 812.00 Chihuahua/220; Josephus Daniels to SS, Aug. 23, 1935, USNARG 59, 812.00 Chihuahua/227.

56. Jesús Alanis to Rodríguez, Sept. 13, 1933, AGN, Rodríguez, 525.3/288.

57. Vicente Anguiano, presidente, Partido Socialista del Norte, Oct. 7, 1935, AGN, Cárdenas, 544.5/469.

58. Nabor Balderrama to Lázaro Cárdenas, Dec. 20, 1933, AGN, Rodríguez, 525.3/288.

59. *El Correo,* Aug. 13, 1931, 1. *El Continental,* Dec. 30, 1929, 1; *El Correo,* Aug. 14, 1931, 1.

60. G-2, Gordon Johnston, Military Attaché, "General Mexican Situation," May 7, 1929, USNARG 165, Reel 3.

61. Almada, *Gobernadores,* 571–73.

62. Vicente Fuentes Díaz, *Los partidos políticos en México,* 3d ed., 213; Tzvi Medín, *El minimato presidencial: Historia política del maximato,* 29–38, 77.

63. Thomas McEnelly to Dwight Morrow, March 12, 1928, USNARG 84, ACCJ, 1928:3.

64. Almada, *Gobernadores,* 539–42.

65. *EPMT,* March 14, 1919, 8, and May 27, 1920, 2.

66. *El Correo,* March 25, 1930, 2, and Aug. 28, 1930, 1–2.

67. Document, July 7, 1921, AGN, Obregón-Calles, 818-C-49; *POC,* Nov. 16, 1918, 12, June 1, 1918, 20, Jan. 17, 1920, 17; Almada, *Gobernadores,* 582.

68. *El Correo,* Oct. 9, 1931, 1; *EPT,* June 17, 1972.

69. Valentín Arroyo and others to President, Oct. 1, 1937; Benito Ponce to President, Sept. 20, 1937, AGN, Cárdenas, 544.5/563.

70. Chávez M., *Sesenta años,* 359–60.

71. *El Paso Herald Post,* May 25, 1972. Camp, *Mexican Political Biographies,* 115.

72. Almada, *Diccionario,* 188–89; Almada, *Gobernadores,* 525–31; Chávez M., "Hombres de la revolución," 84–85.

73. Almada, *Gobernadores,* 568–70; Chávez M., "Hombres de la revolución," 47–48; Caraveo, "Memorias."

74. *EPMT,* May 3, 1919, 3.

75. E. Liekens, consular-general of Mexico in El Paso, to President, Aug. 28, 1928, Tsutomu Dyo to Liekens, Aug. 25, 1928, AGN, Obregón-Calles, 707-L-18. This profitable mine was confiscated when Caraveo rebelled. G-2, Military memo, May 18, 1929, USNARG 165, Reel 3; *EMJ* 128 (July 27, 1929): 152.

76. Confidential memo by consul-general in El Paso in re Chihuahua Investment Co. and Marcelo Caraveo, AGN, Portes Gil, 3/604, 7041.

77. Almada, *Gobernadores,* 568–70.

78. Biographical Sketch of Col. Roberto Fierro, April 6, 1932, USNARG 84, ACCC, 1932:6.

79. Chávez M., *Sesenta años,* 119–23; Chávez M., "Hombres de la revolución," 217.

80. Feb. 11, 1918, AGN, Gobernación, 244/47; L. E. Estrada to President, March 18, 1929, AGN, Portes Gil, 2/951, leg. 5, 5367; Agrupaciones Agraristas Guadalupe y San Ignacio to Calles, and Unión Filarmonicos to

Calles, Aug. 30, 1931, APEC, Andrés Ortiz; Politics in Chihuahua, Sept. 1931, USNARG 59, 812.00 Chihuahua/116.

81. G-2, Mexican Politics: Current Legislature, Aug. 21, 1928, USNARG 165, Reel 9; *EPT,* Jan. 10, 1926, 1; *POC,* June 6, 1931, 3, and March 12, 1932, 7.

82. Alejandra Lajous, *Los orígenes del partido único en México,* 28.

83. *POC,* Dec. 15, 1910, 26, and May 21, 1932, 32.

84. USNARG 59, 812.00 Chihuahua/262.

85. *Boletín Comercial,* Oct. 15, 1925, 5; *POC,* Nov. 30, 1929, 16.

86. *El Correo,* June 5, 1930, 1.

87. Antonio Corona to President, May 26, 1930, AGN, Ortiz Rubio 239 (1930), 6601.

88. *El Correo,* Feb. 3, 1929, 4, May 10, 1930, 3, March 4, 1931, 1.

89. *Boletín Comercial,* Oct. 15, 1930, 1–2. When there was a scarcity of cereals in the state in 1918, he and some associates raised $25,000 to purchase seed in order to bring down the cost.

90. *Hoy,* May 3, 1941, 26. Camp, *Mexican Political Biographies,* 259.

91. AGN, Cárdenas, 543.1/18; Jan. 13, 1936, AACC, 621; PRM to PM, June 27, 1939, AACC, 654.

92. Eduardo Hernández Chuzaro to Andrés Mendoza, June 10, 1930, AGN, Ortiz Rubio 8 (1930), 6879. Luis Esther Estrada et al. to President, Sept. 29, 1931, AGN, Ortiz Rubio, 5017A, 1931.

93. Jesús Vargas V., "La historia del agrarismo en Chihuahua: Andrés Mendoza y la Liga de Comunidades Agrarias," *El Heraldo* (Chihuahua), June 2, 1990.

94. Blohm, "Labor Notes from Chihuahua, June 23, 1937," USNARG 59, 1930–39, 812.504/662.

95. *El Correo,* Feb. 15, 1935, 4; PRM to *presidente municipal,* June 27, 1939, AACC 654. June 26, 1936, AACC, 646. *1940,* 39.

96. Smith, *Labyrinths of Power,* 329–40.

97. Alonso Aguilar M., *México: Riqueza y miseria,* 71–72, 68, 55ff., lists the following great fortunes of Chihuahua:

Almeida	Cattle
Bermúdez	Industry and services
Creel	Service and industry
Díaz	Commerce and services
Guerrero	Forest products
González Muzquiz	Forest products
Raynal	Cattle
Villarreal	Commerce
Zaragoza	Cattle

Vallina was ranked as one of the richest men in Mexico.

Aguilar also listed the cattle barons: Quevedo de Villarreal, Hilario Gabilondo, José Díaz, Jeffers, Wallace, Nava, Márquez y Terrazas, Raynal, Mendoza, Schneider, Domínguez y Calderón, Pinoncelly, Laguette, Solís, and Thacker.

98. Unless otherwise noted, the materials on the Vallinas was obtained from José Fuentes Mares, *Don Eloy S. Vallina* (Mexico City: Editorial Jus, 1968). Fuentes Mares, of course, had written a laudatory history of Luis Terrazas some years before. He was a vice president of the Vallina bank when I spoke with him in 1972.

99. *Boletín Financiero y Minero,* June 17, 1925, 1 and 7. Tomás F. Blanco and Rafael Beckmann were other partners.

100. Blocker to SS, Sept. 1, 1932, USNARG 84, ACCJ, 1932. Frederick E. Fransworth, American vice-consul, Ciudad Juárez, to SS, Sept. 21, 1932, USNARG 59, 812.516/495.

101. *POC,* Dec. 21, 1929, 12.

102. Fuentes Mares, *Vallina,* 48.

103. Ibid., 54.

104. *POC,* March 17, 1934, 8. Other officers were Guillermo Rodarte and Hector Raynal. Rafael F. Vallina's companies included: Compañía Mercantil de Inversiones, S.A., Financiadora del Comercio, S.A., and Servicios Técnicos y de Administración, S.A. Rafael headed the Cerveceria de Chihuahua. He was also president of the Compañía Distilladora del Norte, S.A. *1940, 66 (POC,* Feb. 20, 1932, 31). This company evidently leased the brewery from the Terrazas family. *POC,* Feb. 23, 1935, 142. It was also known as the Cía. Arrendatario de Cervecería de Chihuahua.

105. *POC,* Feb. 16, 1935, 122. Dye, "Economic Report for CJ for the Quarter Ending Dec. 31, 1926," USNARG 84, ACCJ, 1927:3; John E. Jones, "Political Conditions in CJ, July 1926," USNARG 84, ACCJ, 1926:3; Dye, "Political Report for CJ, Jan. 1927," USNARG 84, ACCJ, 1927:3. *EPMT,* Nov. 3, 1920, 14. President to Antonio J. Bermúdez, May 17, 1929, AGN, Portes Gil, 3/976, 7450. *El Correo,* Aug. 15, 1935, 3; *El Continental,* Sept. 29, 1929, 7. *El Continental,* Jan. 20, 1937. *POC,* Feb. 16, 1935, 122. *El Correo,* Aug. 15, 1935, 3. John E. Jones, "Political Conditions in Ciudad Juárez, July 1926," Aug. 7, 1926, USNARG 84, ACCJ, 1926:3. *El Continental,* Sept. 29, 1929, 7. *El Continental,* March 2, 1927, 6. Two years earlier, Jesús Antonio Almeida had married Susana Nesbit Becerra, another member of an old elite family like the Lujáns. In both instances numerous guests from old elite families attended.

106. Eduardo Flores G. to Caja de Préstamos, July 7, 1931, AGN, Caja de Préstamos, Latifundio Terrazas, 160-5.

107. Chávez M., *Sesenta años,* 329–33.

108. Ibid., 343–52. His parents were Cléofas Borunda and Aurelia Ortiz de Borunda, both of whom acquired sections of the Terrazas estate. His siblings included Enrique, Roberto, and Aurora.

109. *POC*, Sept. 24, 1938, 763–. In 1938 they sought rulings of *inafectabilidad* from the government. They raised Hereford cattle.

110. Gustavo Segura, Memorandum al Jefe del Departamento Legal, July 18, 1933, AGN, Caja de Préstamos, Latifundio Terrazas, 189-1 y 2.

111. El Procurador de la República to President, March 30, 1922, AGN, Obregón-Calles, 806-T-1; *El Correo,* Jan. 5, 1926, 4.

112. *Chihuahua Ganadero,* Nov. 1939, 17, and March 1940, 30. *POC,* Feb. 18, 1939, 131.

113. Concession of ASARCO, 1924, USNARG 84, ACCJ, 1924; *POC,* July 11, 1925, 11, and April 23, 1932, 4.

114. Louis B. Mazzeo to E. Lohman, Dec. 21, 1933, USNARG 84, ACCC, 1933:8.

115. *POC,* Feb. 13, 1926, 32; Dec. 17, 1931, 16, Dec. 1, 1923, 31, Dec. 13, 1924, 18.

116. *El Correo,* July 11, 1925, has a list of part of the family. See also the Prieto Maíz Collection. Prieto was married to Felicitas Luján de Prieto. *El Correo,* May 25, 1935, 4. Interestingly, Manuel Prieto was the *pro-secretario* of the Junta de Beneficio of Parral in 1915, at the height of the *villista* era. *La Nueva Era,* May 28, 1915, 3.

117. *POC,* Dec. 14, 1929, 11–13. The hacienda had 69,000 hectares. Carrillo started as a cattle agent (*EPT,* Sept. 15, 1923, 3); but by 1929 he was already known as one of the state's largest landowners. In that year he led the fierce landowner resistance to invasions by peasants of Samalayuca. *EPT,* Nov. 1, 1929, 1.

118. *El Correo,* Aug. 1930, 3.

119. *POC,* Feb. 10, 1940, 93, and Feb. 17, 1940, 112. The holdings amounted to at least 50,000 hectares. *POC,* April 4, 1931, 2; Aug. 21, 1926.

120. *POC,* March 17, 1923, 3.

121. Circular of the Cámara Nacional de Ganadera del Estado de Chihuahua, April 21, 1933, USNARG 84, ACCC, 1933:8.

122. *POC,* March 21, 1931, 1; *Chihuahua 1934; POC,* Jan. 23, 1932, 2–4.

123. *POC,* Dec. 4, 1926, 4; Cámara Nacional de Comercio de Chihuahua to President, Dec. 9, 1922, AGN, Obregón-Calles, 805-Ch-14; *EPT,* Dec. 12, 1923, 2, Dec. 14, 1923, 2, and Sept. 20, 1932, 1; *La Patria,* Jan. 2, 1924, 1.

124. AGN, Cárdenas, 432/888.

125. *Boletín Comercial,* 1917–18. He and his brother Ricardo were merchants (Lowenburg and Wisbrun hardware) and local officials. Arturo was

municipal president of Ciudad Chihuahua in 1927 and on the board of the Gran Partido Liberal Progresista in 1928 and 1929. Ricardo was a member of the board of the Junta de Beneficia Privada in Chihuahua in 1920.

126. *EPT,* July 4, 1937, 4. Alvarez, Memorandum, Sept. 3, 1932, USNARG 84, ACCC, 1932:6. He was somewhat older than the others, fifty-two, and was born in the United States.

127. *El Continental,* March 2, 1927, 6.

128. Olga Leticia Moreno, *¿Qué paso en Chihuahua?,* 216.

7   Local Notables

1. Barnett Singer, *Village Notables in Nineteenth-Century France: Priests, Mayors, Schoolmasters,* 1. Stuart Voss has also employed the categorization in his work on Sonora. Diana Balmori et al., *Notable Family Networks in Latin America,* 6–12, 13–51.

2. Singer, *Village Notables,* 39–41; 6, 48.

3. I base these conclusions on research into political officeholders in about two dozen Chihuahuan municipalities. Since I have not researched in the localities themselves, my hypotheses are best used as a framework for future study. A careful look into specific communities will undoubtedly clarify many points.

4. Almada, *Gobernantes,* 89–102; *POC,* Feb. 25, 1930, 7, Jan. 23, 1929, 11, Dec. 21, 1929, 5; Chihuahua, Secretaría del Gobierno, Sección Estadística, *Boletín estadístico del estado de Chihuahua, 1925* (Chihuahua, 1927), 108–9; *Chihuahua, 1934,* 178; Chihuahua, *Directorio general de municipios,* 463–65; Chávez M., "Hombres de la revolución," 226–27; Miguel Angel Giner Rey, *Uruachic: 250 años de historia,* 65–66.

5. Chihuahua, *Directorio general de municipios,* 463; Chihuahua, *Chihuahua, 1934,* 176; Chihuahua, *Boletín estadístico, 1925,* 107–8; *POC,* May 10, 1924, 21; Chávez M., "Hombres de la revolución," 32; Almada, *Gobernantes,* 89–102; H. H. Taft to U.S. Consulate, Chihuahua City, Dec. 3, 1924, USNARG 84, ACCC. Only Alfredo S. Monge and his oldest son, Alfredo, were attacked. Another son, José, stayed and assumed office.

6. *POC,* Nov. 14, 1925, 13; Feb. 24, 1940, 130.

7. *POC,* July 16, 1927, 9.

8. Francisco R. Almada, *Apuntes históricas de la región de Chínipas,* 425–27. They were Porfirio Armendariz (1912, 1913, 1915, 1916), Eduardo Salido (1913, 1914, 1915), Francisco R. Almada (1919–21), Angel Ramos (1919, 1924–25), Alberto Velderrain (1931, 1934–35), and Eduardo Anguis (1931, 1934, 1938–39).

9. They were Rosendo R. Escarcega (1911, 1923), Arnoldo and Castulo de la Rocha (1912, 1914, 1915), Marcos Loya Mascareñas (1916, 1919), and Federico and Bernardo Hasbach (1919, 1921, 1923–24).

10. Francisco R. Almada, *Resumen geográfico del municipio de Jiménez,* 122–23, provides information through 1929. The rest derives from the POC.

11. *El Correo,* March 15, 1903, 2; March 13, 1903, 2.

12. Information on officeholders for the various municipalities discussed below was taken from the POC.

13. There is another possible instance in Namiquipa, involving the Barreras. From 1912 through 1929, Pedro Barrera was municipal president of Namiquipa for eight years. Another Barrera, Prisciliano, had been municipal president in 1898. Anthropologist Daniel Nugent, who lived in Namiquipa for over a year, maintains that these two Barreras were not related. Moreover, it is quite possible that Prisciliano was not an ally of Terrazas, for Miguel Ahumada was governor of Chihuahua at that time.

14. Almada, *Gobernadores,* 580–81.

15. *El Correo,* March 27, 1926, 2.

16. Manuel Mejido, *México Amargo,* 10. L. Escobar and others to President, Jan. 13, 1938, AGN, Cárdenas, 544.5/1090.

17. *El Correo,* Aug. 24, 1935, 1.

18. Angel Rentería to President, June 14, 1938, AGN, Cárdenas, 542.2/843; Jesús R. Martínez to President, July 13, 1940, AGN, Cárdenas, 544.1/7-1.

19. *El Correo,* Nov. 1, 1930, 1; Oct. 13, 1930, 1; Jan. 16, 1930, 1.

20. Ibid., March 24, 1931, 3; Rodrigo M. Quevedo to President, May 15, 1935, AGN, Cárdenas, 559.2/24. Batopilas was adjudged a region "almost beyond the control" of the state government because of the lack of communications.

21. *El Correo,* Sept. 2, 1930, 1.

22. Ibid., Aug. 5, 1935, 3.

23. A. García Toledo to Governor, Oct. 4, 1937, AGN, Cárdenas, 544.5/1010.

24. Circular of Partido Obrero Agrarista, Nov. 1924, AGN, Obregón-Calles, 408-CH-7.

25. *El Correo,* Nov. 28, 1925, 1; Sept. 4, 1925, 2, and Oct. 25, 1925, 1; Oct. 13, 1930, 1.

26. Feliciano E. González to President, July 5, 1935, AGN, Cárdenas, 403/518; Daniel Domínguez to President, Nov. 1, 1940, AGN, Cárdenas, 403/83.

27. Martha Eva Rocha Islas, *Las defensas sociales en Chihuahua,* examines the *defensas* until 1920.

28. Camp, *Entrepreneurs,* 32–33.

29. Ruben Rocha Chávez, *Tres siglos de historia, biografía de una ciudad: Parral* (Parral, 1976), 249–50.

30. *La Nueva Era,* April 27, 1910, 3.

31. Ibid., Dec. 10, 1908, 4.

32. Ruben Rocha, *Gentes conocidos de Parral* (Parral: n.p., n.d.).

33. Oscar J. Martínez, *Border Boom Town: Ciudad Juárez since 1848,* 3–18.

34. Martínez, *Border Boom Town,* 38–56.

35. Unless otherwise noted, my discussion of the liquor trade and gambling in Ciudad Juárez relies on Edward L. Langston, "The Impact of Prohibition on the Mexican–United States Border: The El Paso–Ciudad Juárez Case" (Ph.D. diss., Texas Tech University, 1974), 219–41 and 130–218. See also Martínez, *Border Boom Town,* 57–77.

36. Luis Medina Barrón, Mexican consul, El Paso, to President, July 19, 1930, AGN, Ortiz Rubio, 230 (1930), 8895.

37. "Economic Report: Ciudad Juárez for the Quarter Ending Dec. 31, 1926," USNARG 84, ACCJ, 1927:3.

38. There were two abbreviated, unsuccessful attempts to prohibit or limit the sale of liquor in Chihuahua a decade apart, in 1921 and 1931.

39. Langston, "The Impact of Prohibition," 102.

40. Jacobo Touchet ran casino gambling at the Tivoli for most of the period between 1913 and 1920. Pancho Villa's brother, Hipólito, controlled the city's crap games for a while. The tourist business slowed down from 1916 to 1919 as a consequence of the killing of several U.S. citizens and the Pershing expedition. Knight, *Mexican Revolution,* 2:462; *EPMT,* May 19, 1919, 8.

41. *EPMT,* Feb. 14, 1921, 5; see, for example, *EPT,* July 23, 1923, 1.

42. "Political Conditions in Ciudad Juárez, Nov. 1926," USNARG 84, ACCJ, 1926:3. Also cited in Langston, "The Impact of Prohibition," 151.

43. Blocker to SS, Dec. 19, 1934, USNARG 59, 812.40622/368.

44. Dec. 22, 1922, 8. The newspaper repeated the charge on April 19, 1923, 12.

45. *EPT,* Feb. 17, 1923, p. 1; Dye, "Political Conditions in Ciudad Juárez during November 1928," Dec. 10, 1928, USNARG 84, AACJ, 1928:3. Governor Almeida and his brother Alberto, the municipal president of Juárez, led an antidrug campaign in 1926 that netted a hundred arrests. Dye, "Political and Economic Conditions in Ciudad Juárez during March 1926," April 8, 1926, USNARG 84, ACCJ, 1926:3.

46. Chávez M., *Sesenta años,* ix–xiv, lists all the *presidentes municipales.*
47. Blocker to SS, Aug. 15, 1930, USNARG 84, ACCJ, 1930:4; Rocha Chávez, *Tres siglos,* 249.
48. The city's *ayuntamiento* removed Rodríguez from office after his arrest for involvement in a street brawl, an incident reportedly trumped up by drug dealers in order to prevent an impending police crackdown against them. Modesto Flores, the alternate (*suplente*) municipal president, assumed the post after Rodríguez's ouster. In December, Flores was removed amid charges of misappropriation of public funds. The legislature then came full circle and named Alberto Delgado municipal president. Antonio Corona served as municipal president in 1922. Pedro M. Fierro, a merchant, was elected the municipal president in 1923. *EPMT,* Nov. 8, 1920, 10; Nov. 29, 1920, 10; Dec. 13, 1920, 10; Jan. 1, 1921, 2; Jan. 27, 1921, 10; July 6, 1921, 12; July 12, 1920, 12; Dec. 3, 1921, 8; Dye to SS, Nov. 21, 1922, USNARG 84, ACCJ, 1922:5; *La Patria,* Jan. 3, 1924, 1; *EPT,* Oct. 26, 1923, 8; Nov. 6, 1923, 3; *La Patria,* Jan. 2, 1924, 1.
49. *EPT,* Nov. 16, 1925, 1; Nov. 28, 1925, 1; Dec. 20, 1925, 1; Jan. 20, 1926, 1; *El Correo,* Nov. 19, 1925, 1; Nov. 29, 1925, 1.
50. John E. Jones, vice-consul, "Political and Economic Conditions in Ciudad Juárez, May 1926," June 8, 1926, USNARG 84, ACCJ, 1926:3.
51. *EPT,* Nov. 25, 1926, 1.
52. Dye, "Political Conditions in Ciudad Juárez, April 1929," May 6, 1929, USNARG 84, ACCJ, 1929:4. After federal troops retook the city, Alberto B. Almeida served as provisional mayor until a new administration, headed by Arturo M. Flores, took over.
53. Dye, "Political Conditions in Ciudad Juárez, August 1929," Sept. 6, 1929, USNARG 84, ACCJ, 1929:4; *EPT,* Sept. 9, 1929, 1, and Nov. 18, 1929, 1. In the general election Margarito Herrera ran on the Partido Anti-reelectionista ticket, supporting José Vasconcelos for president.
54. Blocker to SS, Aug. 1, 1930, USNARG 84, ACCJ, 1930:3; *EPT,* Aug. 1 and 2, 1930, 1. Luis Medina Barrón, the Mexican consulate-general in El Paso, described Gustavo Flores as "a vicious, weak man, turned around by the worst elements of the city, protected by drug dealers and extortionists." Barrón to President, July 15, 1930, AGN, Ortiz Rubio, 230 (1930), 8827.
55. Blocker to SS, Aug. 15, 1930, USNARG 84, ACCJ, 1930:4; *EPT,* Aug. 15, 1930, 1, and Nov. 6, 1930, 1.
56. *El Continental,* April 21, 1931, 1; *EPT,* April 21, 1931, 1, April 22, 1931, 1, April 23, 1931, 1, and Nov. 7, 1930, 1.
57. *EPT,* Nov. 8, 1931, 1.
58. *EPT,* Nov. 13, 1931, 1; Nov. 14, 1931, 1; and Nov. 16, 1931, 1.

59. "Political Situation in Ciudad Juárez, Oct. 31, 1935," USNARG 84, ACCJ, 1935:4; Blocker to SS, Oct. 31, 1935, USNARG 84, ACCJ, 1935:7.

60. *EPT*, Dec. 10, 1936, 1; March 6, 1937, 2; March 27, 1937, 1; April 1, 1937, 2.

61. *EPT*, April 8, 1937, 1; Pedro Díaz G., Secretario-General, Frente Unico Obreros y Campesinos de la Frontera, Ciudad Juárez, to president, April 6, 1937, AGN, Cárdenas, 544.5/564.

62. AGN, Cárdenas, 544.5/564, includes an extraordinary "Wanted" poster for José Quevedo for the murders of Posada and Borunda.

63. *EPT*, April 30, 1939, 4.

64. Charles E. Hershberger, "The Death of Borunda, Alcalde of Ciudad Juárez: Chihuahua Politics during the 1930s," 213–14.

65. Chávez M., *Sesenta años*, 3–7, 9–21, 27–30.

66. *POC*, Dec. 14, 1929, 11–13; Chávez M., *Sesenta años*, 69–72, 95–98, 257–68, 269–84, 343–52; William Wallace Mills, *Forty Years in El Paso*, 182–88; Almada, *Gobernadores*, 338–42; Charles W. Kindrick, U.S. consul, Ciudad Juárez, to David J. Hill, assistant secretary of state, Dec. 9, 1898, USNARG 59, Consular Dispatches, Ciudad Juárez, 1850–1906; *Siglo XX* (Ciudad Chihuahua), Aug. 10, 1904, 4; *POC*, Aug. 5, 1882, 3, Feb. 24, 1883, 4.

67. Chávez M., *Sesenta años*, 85–90; 119–23; 129–38.

68. For the takeover, see *EPT*, Aug. 3, 1930, 1.

69. Chávez M., *Sesenta años*, 346.

70. The accusations against the Quevedos are illustrated in AGN, Rodríguez, 525.3/288.

71. Evelyn P. Stevens, "Mexico's PRI: The Institutionalization of Corporatism?" in Malloy, ed., *Authoritarianism and Corporatism in Latin America*, 227–58.

72. James C. Scott, "The Analysis of Corruption in Developing Nations," *Comparative Studies in History and Society* 11 (June 1969): 315–41.

73. Carlos Martínez Assad, Mario Ramírez Rancano, and Ricardo Pozas Horcasitas, *Revolucionarios fueron todos*, 282–340.

74. John Womack, Jr., "The Spoils of the Mexican Revolution," *Foreign Affairs* (1970): 677.

75. Richard R. Fagen and William S. Tuohy, *Politics and Privilege in a Mexican City*, 18–23, provides a good example of this for Jalapa, Veracruz, during the 1960s.

76. Interesting community studies include: Fagen and Tuohy, *Politics and Privilege;* Lawrence S. Graham, *Politics in a Mexican Community;* Henry E. Torres-Trueba, "Factionalism in a Mexican Municipio," *Sociologus* 19

(1962): 134–52; William S. Tuohy, "Centralism and Political Elite Behavior in Mexico," in Thurber and Graham, eds., *Development Administration in Latin America*, 260–80.

77. See, for example, John Walton, *Elites and Economic Development*, 82. William V. D'Antonio and William H. Form, *Influentials in Two Border Cities*, 69–83.

8 Comparative Perspectives

1. Ankerson, "Saturnino Cedillo," 135; Joseph, "Fragile Revolution."
2. Alan Knight, "Peasant and Caudillo in Revolutionary Mexico, 1910–1917," in Brading, ed., *Caudillo and Peasant in the Mexican Revolution*, 34.
3. Ibid., 35.
4. Carlos B. Gil, *Life in Provincial Mexico*, 104.
5. Maria del Carmen Collado, *La burquesía mexicana*, 130–34.
6. Carranza was vengeful against those Porfirians who had opposed him too strenuously. The Braniffs conspired with Huerta and suffered expropriation by the Constitutionalists as a result. Ibid., 152.
7. The discussion of Chiapas from 1920 to 1940 depends entirely on the narrative and analysis of Thomas Benjamin, *A Rich Land, a Poor People: Politics and Society in Modern Chiapas*, 149–94. See especially 150–53.
8. Frans J. Schryer, *Ethnicity and Class Conflict in Rural Mexico*, 12–23.
9. Saragoza, *Monterrey Elite*, 102; 103–6; 109.
10. Ibid., 114.
11. "Political Report: State of Jalisco," Nov. 11, 1936, USNARG 59, 812.00 Jalisco/200.
12. "Political Report of March 1932, Yucatan," USNARG 59, 812.00 Yucatan/5.
13. Rojas, *Aguascalientes*, 122–23.
14. Hector Aguilar Camín, "The Relevant Tradition: Sonoran Leaders in the Revolution," in Brading, ed., *Caudillo and Peasant*, 119.
15. Ibid., 120–23.
16. Ankerson, *Agrarian Warlord*, 134–35; Gruening, *Mexico*, 423.
17. "Monthly Political Report, Torreón," March 31, 1937, USNARG 59, 812.00 Coahuila/275; Nelson R. Park, AC, to SS, May 26, 1937, USNARG 59, 812.00 Coahuila/283.
18. Reuben Clark to SS, May 18, 1931, USNARG 59, 812.00 Guanajuato/5; "Political Report for San Luis Potosí," Aug. 1932, USNARG 59, 812.00 Guanajuato/6.

19. "Political Situation in Monterrey," Jan. 28, 1939, USNARG 59, 812.00 Nuevo León/200.

20. "Monthly Political Report, Nuevo Laredo," Dec. 31, 1938, USNARG 59, 812.00 Tamaulipas/383.

21. Ankerson, *Saturnino Cedillo*, 134.

22. Nelson R. Clark, "The Ejidal System in the Laguna," Dec. 26, 1937, USNARG 59, 812.52/2316.

23. Joseph, *Revolution from Without*, 292.

24. Tobler, "Las paradojas del ejército," 51.

25. Tobler, "La burguesía revolucionaria," 215.

26. Benjamin, *A Rich Land, a Poor People*, 195.

27. Balmori, *Notables*, 127.

28. Warman, *We Come to Object*, 138.

29. Hamilton, *The Limits of State Autonomy*, 26–27.

30. Ibid., 27.

31. Ibid., 68.

32. Ibid., 74–75, 76.

33. Heather Fowler Salamini, "Revolutionary Caudillos in the 1920s: Francisco Múgica and Adalberto Tejeda," in Brading, ed., *Caudillo and Peasant*, 170–71.

34. Ibid., 176–79.

35. Ibid., 182–89.

36. Heather Fowler Salamini, "Tamaulipas: Land Reform and the State," in Benjamin and Wasserman, eds., *Provinces of the Revolution*, 185.

37. Ibid., 186.

38. Ibid., 211; Benjamin, "Laboratories of the New State," 85–86.

39. Benjamin, "Laboratories of the New State," 72.

40. J. Reuben Clark to SS, Aug. 17, 1931, USNARG 59, 812.00 Colima/48; C. E. Macy, AC, Tampico, to SS, Oct. 2, 1931, USNARG 59, 812.00 Tamaulipas/44.

41. Warman, *We Come to Object*, 136.

42. "Political Report, Tampico, January 1935," USNARG 59, 812.00 Tamaulipas/175; "Political Report, Tampico, March 1930," 812.00 Tamaulipas/183. "Political Report, Tampico, May 1935," USNARG 59, 812.00 Tamaulipas/195.

43. "Review of the Political Situation in San Luis Potosí," Jan. 31, 1931, USNARG 59, 812.00 San Luis Potosí/28.

44. Ankerson, *Agrarian Warlord*, 136; "Review of the Political Situation in San Luis Potosí," Jan. 31, 1931, USNARG 59, 812.00 San Luis Potosí/28; Gruening, *Mexico*, 443.

45. E. W. Eaton, Mazatlán, to SS, Aug. 10, 1931, USNARG 59, 812.00

Nayarit/10. Reportedly, the governor was related to Portes Gil, to whom he paid 5,000 pesos a month.

46. "Political Situation in Northern Sonora," Aug. 27, 1930, USNARG 59, 812.00 Sonora/1040; Altoffer to SS, March 10, 1931, 812.00 Sonora/1056; Altoffer to SS, April 30, 1931, 812.00 Sonora/1067. Altoffer reported that crucial positions in Sonora were occupied by relatives and friends of Calles.

47. Warman, *We Come to Object*, 181–86; Gruening, *Mexico*, 153.

48. Ellis Bonnet, AC, Durango, to SS, Feb. 14, 1931, USNARG 59, 812.52/1687; Gruening, *Mexico*, 423–25.

49. "Political Developments in Durango," March 26, 1930, USNARG 59, 812.00 Durango/33; "Political Situation in Durango," April 4, 1930, USNARG 59, 812.00 Durango/35.

50. "Political Situation in Durango," Aug. 8, 1930, 812.00 Durango/37.

51. "Political Situation in Durango," Sept. 17, 1930, USNARG 59, 812.00 Durnago/41.

52. Ellis A. Bonnet, AC, Durango, to SS, June 28, 1932, USNARG 59, 812.00 Durango/84; "Political Situation in Durango," Aug. 27, 1932, 812.00 Durnago/92 and June 30, 1934, 812.00 Durango/120.

53. E. W. Eaton, AVC, to SS, Dec. 31, 1934, USNARG 59, 812.00 Durango/130.

54. E. W. Eaton to SS, Dec. 17, 1935, USNARG 59, 812.00 Durango/176. "Resume of Conditions in Mexico, August 1936," USNARG 59, 812.00/30409.

55. Salamini, "Tamaulipas," 193–94.

56. The narrative and interpretation of Portes Gil's career in Tamaulipas derives from Salamini, "Tamaulipas."

57. Salamini, "Tamaulipas," 202.

58. Gruening, *Mexico*, 442.

59. USNARG 59, 812.00 Jalisco/200; George H. Winters to SS, May 6, 1938, 812.00 Jalisco/208; James B. Riddle to SS, 812.00 Jalisco/218.

60. Henry A. Balch, AC, Monterrey, to SS, March 19, 1930, USNARG 59, 812.00 Nuevo León/4; Edward I. Nathan to SS, July 29, 1931, 812.00 Nuevo León/15; Nathan to SS, Dec. 8, 1932, 812.00 Nuevo León/38; Nathan to SS, Oct. 20, 1933, 812.00 Nuevo León/50. The PNR was known as the Social Democratic Party.

61. "Political, Religious, and Economic Situation in Nuevo León," Feb. 28, 1935, USNARG 59, 812.00 Nuevo León/93, and May 31, 1935, 812.00 Nuevo León/104; Nathan to SS, Nov. 18, 1935, 812.00 Nuevo León/120.

62. *EPT*, Oct. 16, 1938, 1.

63. *EPT*, June 26, 1938, 2.

64. "Political Report, Guaymas, August 1936," USNARG 59, 812.00 Sonora/1332.

65. A. F. Yepis, American vice-consul, Guaymas, to SS, Dec. 12, 1936, USNARG 59, 812.00 Sonora/1367.

66. The narrative and interpretation of politics in Chiapas relies on Benjamin, *A Rich Land, a Poor People,* 149–95.

67. Ibid., 154.

68. Ibid., 161–64.

69. The narrative and analysis of San Luis Potosí relies on Ankerson, *Agrarian Warlord,* 92-192, unless otherwise noted.

70. Ibid., 97.

71. Ibid., 123.

72. Ibid., 111–13.

73. Ibid., 118–19.

74. Ibid., 183.

75. Ibid., 129.

76. See Voss, "Nationalizing the Revolution," 287–95.

77. Ankerson, *Agrarian Warlord,* 132–33; Salamini, "Revolutionary Caudillos in the 1920s."

78. Ankerson, *Agrarian Warlord,* 133, 135.

79. For the narrative and analysis for Puebla, I depend on Wil Pansters, *Politics and Power in Puebla: A Political History of a Mexican State, 1937–1987,* 47–63. See also Gruening, *Mexico,* 468–69.

80. Pansters, *Politics and Power,* passim.

81. The analysis and narrative on Guerrero relies on Ian Jacobs, *Ranchero Revolt: The Mexican Revolution in Guerrero,* 110–37.

82. The battle followed a bullfight. Seven were killed, seventeen wounded (ibid., 133).

83. Gruening, *Mexico,* 399–403.

84. Ibid., 413–17.

85. Ibid., 452–60.

86. *El Continental,* Feb. 13, 1927, 1.

87. "Monthly Political Report, Torreón," Jan. 30, 1937, USNARG 59, 812.00 Coahuila/268.

88. Nathan to SS, Dec. 17, 1935, USNARG 59, 812.00 Nuevo León/122; Nathan to SS, Dec. 18, 1935, 812.00 Nuevo León/123.

89. "Monthly Political Report, Nuevo Laredo," Aug. 1, 1935, USNARG 59, 812.00 Tamaulipas/214.

90. "Political, Economic, and Religious Events in Veracruz, June 1936," USNARG 59, 812.00 Veracruz/89, and ". . . June 1937," 812.00 Veracruz/106; "Political Report, October 1937," 812.00 Veracruz/110.

91. Garza was Chief of the Federal Office of Hacienda. "Political Situation in Nuevo Laredo," Dec. 11, 1930, USNARG 59, 812.00 Tamaulipas/18.

92. "Political Despatch, July 1931," USNARG 59, 812.00 Tamaulipas/36.

93. "Political Report, Matamoros, July 1933," USNARG 59, 812.00 Tamaulipas/116; "Political Report, Tampico, July 1933," USNARG 59, 812.00 Tamaulipas/118; Altoffer, AC, Nogales, to SS, March 10, 1931, USNARG 59, 812.00 Sonora/1056.

94. John E. Holler, Matamoros, to SS, Oct. 8, 1931, USNARG 812.00 Tamaulipas/45.

95. Wormoth to SS, Feb. 18, 1938, USNARG 59, 812.00 Tamaulipas/339; Wormoth to SS, March 29, 1938, 812.00 Tamaulipas/340.

96. Lewis V. Boyle, AC, to SS, June 14, 1939, USNARG 59, 812.00 Sonora/1498.

97. "Resume of Conditions in Mexico, July 1936," USNARG 59, 812.00/30394.

98. *EPT,* May 2, 1937, 1.

99. There are a number of other comparative issues: the regional nature of both countries' politics and economy; the successive stages of the revolution that each arguably experience—1911, 1920, 1934, in the Mexican case, and 1789, 1830, 1848, in France; the role of the peasantry; and the consolidation of the state.

100. Roger Price, *A Social History of Nineteenth-Century France,* 96.

101. Higgs, *Nobles,* 51–52.

102. Hampson, *A Social History,* 252.

103. Price, *A Social History,* 99.

104. Higgs, *Nobles,* 52.

105. Ibid.

106. Ibid., 53, 217, 223.

107. Ibid., 53–54.

108. Hampson, *A Social History,* 250–51.

109. Higgs, *Nobles,* 3, 6–7, 41.

110. Ibid., 135.

111. Price, *A Social History,* 108; 104, 113–15; 106; 107.

112. Gibson, "The French Nobility," 11.

113. Price, *A Social History,* 103; Higgs, *Nobles,* 132.

114. Price, *A Social History,* 108, 110.

115. Higgs, *Nobles,* 15; 124.

116. Price, *A Social History,* 103.

117. See Enrique Semo, *Historia mexicana: Economía y luchas de clases*

(Mexico City, 1978), 299, as cited in Knight, *Mexican Revolution,* for an explanation of the successive stages hypothesis.

118. Hansen, *The Politics of Mexican Development,* passim.
119. Joseph, *Revolution from Without,* 298.
120. Ibid., 292–94.

Bibliography

Primary Sources

Archives, Collections, Papers

Austin, Texas
  University of Texas
    Nettie Lee Benson Collection
      Archivo del Ferrocarril de Noroeste de México
      William F. Buckley Collection
      Thomas Wentworth Peirce Papers (Corralitos)
      Lázaro de la Garza Archive
Berkeley, California
  Bancroft Library
    Silvestre Terrazas Collection
      Correspondence and Papers
El Paso, Texas
  University of Texas at El Paso
    Archivo del Ayuntamiento de Ciudad Chihuahua
    Archivo del Municipio de Ciudad Juárez
    John H. McNeely Collection
      Benton Collection
      James Hyslop Collection
      Mexican North Western Railway Papers
    Max Weber Collection
    Francisco R. Almada Collection
Mexico City
  Archivo General de la Nación
    Ramo Presidentes
      Obregón-Calles
      Portes Gil
      Rodríguez
      Cárdenas
    Secretario de Trabajo
    Gobernación
      Revolución
    Caja de Préstamos para Obras de Irrigación y Fomento de la Agri-
      cultura

Fideicomiso Archivos Plutarco Elías Calles y Fernando Torreblanca
  Archivo de Plutarco Elías Calles
Condumex
  Venustiano Carranza Telegramas
  Venustiano Carranza Manuscritos
Princeton, New Jersey
  Princeton University
  Prieto Maíz Papers
Tucson, Arizona
  Arizona Historical Society
  C. L. Sonnichsen Collection
  Robert E. Torrance Collection
Washington, D.C.
  National Archives
    Record Group 59, Department of State, Decimal Files, Internal Affairs
      of Mexico, 1910–29
    Record Group 59, Department of State, Decimal Files, Internal Affairs
      of Mexico, 1930–39
    Record Group 84, Records of the American Consular Post in Ciudad
      Juárez, Mexico, 1918–35
    Record Group 84, Records of the American Consular Post in Chi-
      huahua City, Mexico, 1918–35
    Record Group 165, U.S. Military Intelligence Reports: Mexico, 1919–
      41

Newspapers and Periodicals

Boletín Comercial, 1918–20
Chihuahua, 1933
El Clarín, 1912
El Continental (El Paso), 1927, 1931, 1934, 1936–37
El Correo de Chihuahua (Ciudad Chihuahua), 1925–29, 1931–35
El Correo de Parral, 1928–29
El Diario (Ciudad Chihuahua), 1925
El Eco de Pueblo, 1913
Engineering and Mining Journal, 1910–45
El Fantasma (Ciudad Chihuahua), 1913
El Heraldo (Ciudad Chihuahua), 1938–40
Hoy, 1941
La Opinión Pública: Diario Liberal (Hidalgo de Parral), 1911
El Padre Padilla (Ciudad Chihuahua), 1912

El Paso Morning Times/El Paso Times, 1910–40
La Patria (El Paso), 1919–25
El Periódico Oficial del Estado de Chihuahua, 1910–40
La Voz del Obrero (Hidalgo de Parral), 1911
La Voz del Pueblo (Hidalgo de Parral), 1911
La Voz de Parral, 1929

Government Documents

Chihuahua. Gobernador. *Informe que el C. Gobernador Militar del estado Fidel Avila rinde al pueblo Chihuahuense, comprendiendo los tabajos efectuosas hasta el día 1 de abril del corrient año, 1915.* Chihuahua: Imprenta del Gobierno, 1915.

———. *Informe del Gobernador Provisional Gral. Arnulfo Gómez, 1918.* Chihuahua: n.p., 1918.

———. *Informe de Gobernador Andrés Ortiz que rinde al presidente de la República Mexicana por 15 de noviembre de 1918 a 29 de febrero de 1920.* Chihuahua: n.p., 1920.

———. *Informe del Gobernador Provisional Profesor Abel S. Rodríguez, 4 de octubre de 1920.* Chihuahua: n.p., 1920.

———. *Informe del Gobernador Constitucional Jesús Antonio Almeida al Congreso del Estado, 1924–1925.* Chihuahua: n.p., n.d.

———. *Informe del Gobernador Provisional Francisco L. Treviño de 30 de septiembre de 1916.* Chihuahua: n.p., 1916.

———. *Informe del Gobernador Constitucional Ing. Gustavo L. Talamantes al Congreso del Estado, 1938.* Chihuahua: Talleres del Gobierno, 1938.

———. *Informe del Gobernador Constitucional Ing. Gustavo L. Talamantis al Congreso del Estado, 1939.* Chihuahua: Talleres del Gobierno, 1939.

———. *Informe del Gobernador Constitucional Ing. Gustavo L. Talamantes al Congreso del Estado, 1940.* Chihuahua: Talleres del Gobierno, 1940.

Chihuahua. Secretaría de Gobierno. Sección de Estadística. *Boletín estadística del estado de Chihuahua (años 1910 a 1921).* Chihuahua: Imprenta del Gobierno, 1922.

Chihuahua. Secretaría General de Gobierno. Sección de Estadística. *Boletín estadística del estado de Chihuahua, 1923–1924.* Chihuahua: Imprenta del Gobierno, 1926.

———. *Boletín estadístico del Estado de Chihuahua, 1925.* Chihuahua: Imprenta del Gobierno, 1927.

Mexico City. Comité Directivo para la Investigación de los Recursos Minerales de México. *La industria minera en el estado de Chihuahua.* Boletín No. 7. Mexico City, 1946.

Mexico. Departamento Agrario. Oficina de Planeación, Programa y Divulgación. *Memoria, 1940–1941*. Mexico City: n.p., n.d.

Mexico. Departamento Agrario. Oficina de Planeación, Programa y Divulgación. *Memoria, 1941–1942*. Mexico City: n.p., n.d.

Mexico. Departamento de Estadística Nacional. Dirección de Estadística Económica. *Aspectos estadísticos de un quinquenio, 1921–1925*. Mexico City: Imprenta Mundial, 1927.

Mexico. Secretaría de Industria y Comercio. Departamento de Minas. *Anuario estadistica minera*, años de 1922–23, 1925–27, 1929–33. Mexico City: Talleres Graficos de la Nacíon, 1924–35.

Mexico. *Boletín Minero* 3 (enero–junio 1917). Mexico City, 1917.

Compendiums and Reports

Irigoyen, Ulises. *Chihuahua en cifras*. Chihuahua: n.p., 1943.

de la Peña, Moíses T. *Chihuahua ecónomico*. 3 vols. Chihuahua: Gobierno de Chihuahua, 1958.

Ponce de León; José María; and Gómez, Manuel A. *Año de 1918: Primer Almanaque Chihuahuense*. Chihuahua, n.d.

1936: Ultimo año de gobierno del General Rodrigo M. Quevedo. Mexico City, 1937.

Memoirs

Caraveo, Marcelo. "Memorias del General Marcelo Caraveo." Unpublished MS. Chihuahua, 1931.

Fierro Villalobos, Roberto. *Esta es mi vida*. Mexico City: Talleres Gráficos de la Nación, 1964.

León, Luis L. *Crónica del poder: En los recuerdos de un político en el México revolucionario*. Mexico City: Fondo de Cultura Económica, 1987.

Mills, William Wallace. *Forty Years at El Paso*. Intro. and Notes by Rex W. Strickland. El Paso: Carl Hertzog, 1962.

O'Shaugnessy, Edith. *A Diplomat's Wife in Mexico*. New York: Harper and Brothers, 1916.

Parker, Morris B. *Mules, Mines, and Me in Mexico, 1895–1932*. Ed. James M. Day. Tucson: University of Arizona Press, 1979.

Shepherd, Grant. *The Silver Magnet: Fifty Years in a Mexican Silver Mine*. New York: Dutton, 1938.

Terrazas, Silvestre. *El verdadero Pancho Villa*. Chihuahua: Talleres Gráficos del Gobierno del Estado, 1984.

Secondary Sources

Books

Aboites Aguilar, Luis, comp. *Agua y tierra en la región del conchos: San Pedro, Chihuahua, 1720–1938*. Mexico City: Cuadernos de Casa Chata no. 131. Mexico City: Centro de Investigaciones y Estudios Superiores en Antropología Social, 1986.

———. *La irrigación revolucionaria*. Mexico City: SEP-CIESAS, 1987.

Aguilar Camín, Hector. *La frontera nomada: Sonora y la Revolución Mexicana*. Mexico City: Siglo XXI, 1977.

Aguilar M., Alonso y Carmona, Fernando. *México: Riqueza y miseria*. 9th ed. Mexico City: Editorial Nuestro Tiempo, 1976.

Almada, Francisco R. *Apuntes históricos de la región de Chínipas*. Chihuahua: n.p., 1937.

———. *Apuntes históricos del municipio de Madera*. Chihuahua: n.p., 1946.

———. *Diccionario de historia, geografía, y biografía chihuahuense*. 2d ed. Chihuahua: Universidad de Chihuahua, Departmento de Investigaciones Sociales, Sección de Historia, n.d.

———. *Geografía del estado de Chihuahua*. Chihuahua: n.p., n.d.

———. *Gobernadores del estado de Chihuahua*. México: Centro Librero La Prensa, 1980.

———. *Gobernantes de Chihuahua*. Chihuahua: Talleres Gráficos de Gobierno del Estado, 1929.

———. *Resumen geográfico del municipio de Jiménez*. Ciudad Juárez: Editorial El Labrador, n.d.

———. *La revolución en el estado de Chihuahua*. 2 vols. Chihuahua: Biblioteca del Instituto Nacional de Estudios Históricos de la Revolución Mexicana, 1964.

———. *Vida, proceso y muerte de Abraham González*. Mexico City: Biblioteca del Instituto Nacional de Estudios Históricos de la Revolución Mexicana, 1967.

Anguiano, Arturo. *El estado y la política obrera del cardenismo*. Mexico City: Era, 1984.

Ankerson, Dudley. *Agrarian Warlord: Saturnino Cedillo and the Mexican Revolution in San Luis Potosí*. DeKalb, Ill.: Northern Illinois University Press, 1984.

Ashby, Joe C. *Organized Labor and the Mexican Revolution under Lázaro Cárdenas.* Chapel Hill: University of North Carolina Press, 1967.

Balmori, Diana; Voss, Stuart F.; and Wortman, Miles. *Notable Family Networks in Latin America.* Chicago: University of Chicago Press, 1984.

Bartra, Roger. *Campesinado y poder político en México.* Mexico City: Era, 1982.

Beezley, William H. *Insurgent Governor: Abraham González and the Mexican Revolution in Chihuahua.* Lincoln: University of Nebraska Press, 1973.

Benjamin, Thomas. *A Rich Land, a Poor People: Politics and Society in Modern Chiapas.* Albuquerque: University of New Mexico Press, 1989.

Benjamin, Thomas, and Wasserman, Mark, eds. *Provinces of the Revolution: Essays on Regional Mexican History, 1910–1929.* Albuquerque: University of New Mexico Press, 1990.

Bethell, Leslie, ed. *The Cambridge History of Latin America, 1870–1930.* Vol. 5. Cambridge: Cambridge University Press, 1986.

Brading, David A., ed. *Caudillo and Peasant in the Mexican Revolution.* Cambridge: Cambridge University Press, 1980.

Brand, Donald D. *Quiroga: A Mexican Municipio.* Washington, D.C.: Smithsonian Institution, 1951.

Camp, Roderic A. *Entrepreneurs and Politics in Twentieth-Century Mexico.* New York: Oxford University Press, 1989.

———. *Mexican Political Biographies, 1935–1975.* Tucson: University of Arizona Press, 1976.

———. *Mexico's Leaders: Their Education and Recruitment.* Tucson: University of Arizona Press, 1980.

Campbell, Hugh. *La derecha radical en México, 1929–1949.* Mexico City: SepSetentas, 1976.

Carr, Barry. *El movimiento obrero y la política en México, 1910–1929.* 2 vols. Mexico City: SepSetentas, 1976.

Ceceña, José Luis. *México en la orbita imperial.* 7th ed. Mexico City: Ediciones El Caballito, 1976.

Chávez M., Armando B. *Historia de Ciudad Juárez, Chihuahua.*

———. *Sesenta años de gobierno municipal: Jefes políticos del Distrito Bravos y presidentes municipales del municipio de Juárez.* Mexico City: n.p., 1959.

Clark, Marjorie Ruth. *Organized Labor in Mexico.* New York: Russell and Russell, 1934.

Collado, Maria del Carmen. *La burguesía mexicana: El emporio Braniff y su participación política, 1865–1920.* Mexico City: Siglo XXI, 1987.

Conquest, Robert. *Harvest of Sorrow: Soviet Collectivization and the Terror-Famine.* New York: Oxford University Press, 1986.

247   *Bibliography*

Contreras, Ariel Jose. *México 1940: Industrialización y crisis política.* Mexico City: Siglo XXI, 1977.

Contreras Orozco, Javier. *Chihuahua: Trampa del sistema.* Mexico City: Edamex, 1987.

Cordova, Arnaldo. *La clase obrera en la historia de México: En una época de crisis (1928–1934).* Mexico City: Siglo XXI, 1989.

Couturier, Edith B. *La hacienda de Hueyapán, 1550–1936.* Mexico City: Sep-Setentas, 1976.

Creel Cobián, Alejandro. *Enrique C. Creel: Apuntes para su biografía.* Mexico City: n.p., 1974.

Creel de Muller, Lulu. *El conquistador del desierto.* Chihuahua: Imprenta Muller, 1982.

Cumberland, Charles C. *The Mexican Revolution: The Constitutionalist Years.* Austin: University of Texas Press, 1972.

D'Antonio, William V., and Form, William H. *Influentials in Two Border Cities.* South Bend, Ind.: University of Notre Dame Press, 1965.

Fagen, Richard R., and Tuohy, William S. *Politics and Privilege in a Mexican City.* Stanford, Calif.: Stanford University Press, 1972.

Falcon, Romana. *Agrarismo en Veracruz: La etapa radical, 1928–1935.* Mexico City: El Colegio de México, 1977.

—. *Revolución y caciquismo: San Luis Potosí, 1910–1938.* Mexico City: El Colegio de México, 1984.

Friedrich, Paul. *Agrarian Revolt in a Mexican Village.* Englewood Cliffs, N.J.: Prentice-Hall, 1970.

—. *The Princes of Naranja.* Austin: University of Texas Press, 1986.

Fuentes Díaz, Vicente. *Los partidos políticos en México.* 3d ed. Mexico City: Editorial Altiplano, 1972.

Fuentes Mares, José. *Don Eloy S. Vallina.* Mexico City: Editorial Jus, 1968.

—. *Y México se refugió en el desierto: Luis Terrazas, historia y destino.* Mexico City: Editorial Jus, 1954.

Gil, Carlos B. *Life in Provincial Mexico: National and Regional History Seen from Mascota, Jalisco, 1867–1972.* Los Angeles: UCLA, 1983.

Gilly, Adolfo. *The Mexican Revolution.* London: Verso, 1983.

Giner Rey, Miguel Angel. *Uruachic: 250 años de historia.* Chihuahua: Centro Librero La Prensa, 1986.

Gómez Serrano, Jesús. *Ojocaliente: Una hacienda devorada por la urbe.* Aguascalientes: Centro de Investigaciónes Regionales, 1983.

González, Hugo Pedro. *Portesgilismo y Alemanismo en Tamaulipas.* Ciudad Victoria: Universidad Autonoma de Tamaulipas, 1983.

González, Luis. *Historia de la Revolución Mexicana, 1934–1940: Los artifices del cardenismo.* Mexico City: El Colegio de México, 1979.

──────. *Historia de la Revolución Mexicana, 1934–1940: Los dias del presidente Cárdenas*. Mexico City: El Colegio de Mexico City, 1981.

González Casanova, Pablo. *La clase obrera en la historia de México: En el primer gobierno constitucional (1917–1920)*. Mexico City: Siglo XXI, 1987.

Graham, Lawrence S. *Mexican State Government: A Prefectural System in Action*. Austin: Institute of Public Affairs, 1971.

──────. *Politics in a Mexican Community*. Gainesville: University of Florida Press, 1968.

Gruening, Ernest. *Mexico and Its Heritage*. New York: The Century Company, 1928.

Guardarrama, Rocio. *Los síndicatos y la política en México: La CROM, 1918–1928*. Mexico City: Era, 1981.

Guerra, François-Xavier. *México: El antiguo régimen a la Revolución*. 2 vols. Mexico City: Fondo de Cultura Económica, 1988.

Hall, Linda. *Alvaro Obregón: Power and Revolution in Mexico, 1911–1920*. College Station: Texas A&M Press, 1981.

Hamilton, Nora. *The Limits of State Autonomy: Post-Revolutionary Mexico*. Princeton, N.J.: Princeton University Press, 1982.

Hampson, Norman. *A Social History of the French Revolution*. Toronto: University of Toronto Press, 1963.

Hansen, Roger D. *The Politics of Mexican Development*. Baltimore: Johns Hopkins University Press, 1971.

Hart, John Mason. *Revolutionary Mexico: The Coming and Process of the Mexican Revolution*. Berkeley and Los Angeles: University of California Press, 1987.

Hernández Chávez, Alicia. *Historia de la Revolución Mexicana, 1934–1940: La mecánica cardenista*. Mexico City: El Colegio de Mexico City, 1979.

Higgs, David. *Nobles in Nineteenth-Century France*. Baltimore: Johns Hopkins University Press, 1987.

Jacobs, Ian. *Ranchero Revolt: The Mexican Revolution in Guerrero*. Austin: University of Texas Press, 1982.

Joseph, Gilbert M. *Revolution from Without: Yucatán, Mexico, and the United States, 1880–1924*. Durham: Duke University Press, 1988.

Katz, Friedrich, ed. *Riot, Rebellion, and Revolution: Rural Social Conflict in Mexico*. Princeton, N.J.: Princeton University Press, 1988.

──────. *The Secret War in Mexico: Europe, the United States, and the Mexican Revolution*. Chicago: University of Chicago Press, 1981.

Kirshner, Alan M. *Tomás Garrido Canabal y el movimiento de las Camisas Rojas*. Mexico City: SepSetentas, 1976.

Knight, Alan. *The Mexican Revolution*. 2 vols. Cambridge: Cambridge University Press, 1986.

Krauze, Enrique. *La Historia de la Revolución Mexicana, 1924–1928: La recon-strucción económica*. Mexico City: El Colegio de México, 1977.

LaFrance, David G. *The Mexican Revolution in Puebla, 1908–1913*. Wilmington, Del.: Scholarly Resources, 1989.

Lajous, Alejandra. *Los origenes del partido único en México*. Mexico City: UNAM, 1981.

Lartigue, François. *Indios y bosques: Políticas forestals y comunales en la Sierra Tarahumara*. Mexico City: Ediciones de Casa Chata 19, Centro de Investigaciones Superiores en Antropología Social, 1983.

Leal, Juan Felipe. *La burguesía y el estado mexicano*. Mexico City: Ediciones El Caballito, 1972.

Leal, Juan Felipe, and Villaseñor, José. *La clase obrera en la historia de México: En la Revolución, 1910–1917*. Mexico City: Siglo XXI, 1988.

Lefevre, Georges. *The Thermidorian and the Directory: Two Phases of the French Revolution*. New York: Random House, 1964.

Leon, Samuel, and Marvan, Ignacio. *La clase obrera en la historia de México: El cardenismo (1934–1940)*. Mexico City: Siglo XXI, 1985.

Lerner, Victoria. *Historia de la Revolución Mexicana, 1934–1940: La educación socialista*. Mexico City: El Colegio de México, 1979.

Loya Díaz, Rafael. *La crisis Obregón-Calles y el estado en México*. Mexico City: Siglo XXI, 1980.

Machado, Manuel A., Jr. *The North Mexican Cattle Industry, 1910–1975: Ideology, Conflict, and Change*. College Station: Texas A&M Press, 1981.

Martínez, Oscar J. *Border Boom Town: Ciudad Juárez since 1848*. Austin: University of Texas Press, 1978.

Martínez Assad, Carlos; Ramírez Rancano, Mario; and Pozas Horcasitas, Ricardo. *Revolucionarios fueron todos*. Mexico City: Fondo de Cultura Económica, 1982.

Martínez Saldana, Tomás, and Gandara Mendoza, Leticia. *Política y sociedad en México: El caso de los Altos de Jalisco*. Mexico City: SEP-INAH, 1976.

Matute, Alvaro. *Historia de la Revolución Mexicana, 1917–1924: La carrera del caudillo*. Mexico City: El Colegio de México, 1980.

Mayer, Arno J. *The Persistence of the Old Regime: Europe to the Great War*. New York: Pantheon, 1981.

Medín, Tzvi. *Ideología y praxis política de Lázaro Cárdenas*. Mexico City: Siglo XXI, 1976.

————. *El minimato presidencial: Historia política del maximato*. Mexico City: Ediciones Era, 1990.

Mejido, Manuel. *México amargo*. 3d ed. Mexico City: Siglo XXI, 1976.

Merriman, John M. *The Red City: Limoges and the French Nineteenth Century*. New York: Oxford University Press, 1985.

Meyer, Jean. *The Cristero Rebellion*. New York: Cambridge University Press, 1976.

———. *La cristiada*. 3 vols. Mexico City: Siglo XXI, 1973–74.

———. *Historia de la Revolución Mexicana, Periódo 1924–1928: Estado y sociedad con Calles*. Mexico City: El Colegio de México, 1977.

Meyer, Lorenzo. *Historia de la Revolución Mexicana, 1928–1934: El conflicto social y los gobiernos del maximato*. Mexico City: El Colegio de México, 1978.

———. *Historia de la Revolución Mexicana, 1928–1934: Los inicios de la institucionalización. La politica del maximato*. Mexico City: El Colegio de México, 1978.

Meyer, Michael C. *Mexican Rebel: Pascual Orozco and the Mexican Revolution, 1910–1915*. Lincoln: University of Nebraska Press, 1967.

Moreno, Olga Leticia. *¿Qué paso en Chihuahua?* Mexico City: Edamex, 1986.

Nagle, John D. *Systems and Succession: The Social Bases of Elite Political Recruitment*. Austin: University of Texas Press, 1977.

Nugent, Daniel, ed. *Rural Revolt in Mexico and U.S. Intervention*. San Diego, Calif.: Center for U.S.-Mexican Studies, 1988.

Palomares Peña, Noe G. *Proprietarios Norteamericanos y reforma agraria en Chihuahua, 1917–1942*. Chihuahua: Universidad Autonoma de Ciudad Juárez, 1992.

Pansters, Wil. *Politics and Power in Puebla: The Political History of a Mexican State, 1937–1987*. Amsterdam: CEDLA, 1990.

Paoli, Francisco J., and Montalvo, Enrique. *El socialismo olvidado de Yucatán*. Mexico City: Siglo XXI, 1977.

Perry, Geraint. *Political Elites*. New York: Praeger, 1969.

Price, Roger. *An Economic History of Modern France, 1730–1914*. London: Macmillan, 1981.

———. *A Social History of Nineteenth-Century France*. New York: Holmes and Meier, 1987.

Putnam, Robert D. *The Comparative Study of Political Elites*. Englewood Cliffs, N.J.: Prentice-Hall, 1976.

Rivera Castro, José. *La clase obrera en la historia de México: El la presidencia de Plutarco Elías Calles (1924–1928)*. Mexico City: Siglo XXI, 1987.

Rocha Chávez, Ruben. *Tres siglos de historia, biografía de una ciudad: Parral*. Parral: Talleres Gráficos del Estado de Chihuahua, 1976.

Rocha Islas, Martha Eva. *Las defensas sociales en Chihuahua*. Mexico City: INAH, Colección Divulgación, 1988.

Rojas, Beatriz. *La destrucción de la hacienda en Aguascalientes 1910–1931*. Zamora: El Colegio de Michoacán, 1981.

Ronfeldt, David. *Atencingo: The Politics of Agrarian Struggle in a Mexican Ejido.* Stanford, Calif.: Stanford University Press, 1973.

Ruiz, Ramon E. *The Great Rebellion: Mexico, 1905–1924.* New York: Norton, 1980.

———. *Labor and the Ambivalent Revolutionaries: Mexico, 1911–1923.* Baltimore: Johns Hopkins University Press, 1976.

Saboul, Albert. *The French Revolution, 1787–1799: From the Storming of the Bastille to Napoleon.* Trans. Alan Forrest and Colin Jones. New York: Vintage, 1975.

Salamini, Heather Fowler. *Agrarian Radicalism in Veracruz, 1920–38.* Lincoln: University of Nebraska Press, 1971.

Santos Valdes, José. *Madera: Razón de un martiriologio.* Mexico City: Imprenta Laura, 1968.

Saragoza, Alex M. *The Monterrey Elite and the Mexican State, 1880–1940.* Austin: University of Texas Press, 1988.

Saucedo Montemayor, Pedro. *Historia de la ganadería en México.* Mexico City: UNAM, 1984.

Schryer, Frans J. *Ethnicity and Class Conflict in Rural Mexico.* Princeton, N.J.: Princeton University Press, 1990.

———. *The Rancheros of Pisaflores: The History of a Peasant Bourgeoisie in Mexico.* Toronto: University of Toronto Press, 1980.

Sepúlveda Otaiza, Ximena. *La revolución en Bachíniva.* Mexico City: INAH, Departamento de Etnología y Antropología Social, 1975.

Simpson, Eyler N. *The Ejido: Mexico's Way Out.* Chapel Hill: University of North Carolina Press, 1937.

Singer, Barnett. *Village Notables in Nineteenth-Century France: Priests, Mayors, Schoolmasters.* Albany: State University of New York Press, 1983.

Skirius, John. *José Vasconcelos y la cruzada de 1929.* Mexico City: Siglo XXI, 1978.

Smith, Peter H. *Labyrinths of Power: Political Recruitment in Twentieth-Century Mexico.* Princeton, N.J.: Princeton University Press, 1979.

Spring, David, ed. *European Landed Elite in the Nineteenth Century.* Baltimore: Johns Hopkins University Press, 1977.

Tamayo, Jaime. *La clase obrera en la historia de México: En el interinato de Adolfo de la Huerta y el gobierno de Alvaro Obregón (1920–1924).* Mexico City: Siglo XXI, 1987.

Tamayo, Jaime, and Romero, Laura. *La rebelión estradista y el movimiento campesino, 1923–1924.* Mexico City: Centro de Estudios Históricos del Agrarismo en México, 1983.

Tannenbaum, Frank. *The Mexican Agrarian Revolution.* New York: Archon Books, 1968.

Ugalde, Antonio. *Power and Conflict in a Mexican Community.* Albuquerque: University of New Mexico Press, 1970.

Ulloa, Berta. *Historia de la Revolución Mexicana, 1914–1917: La constitución de 1917.* Mexico City: El Colegio de México, 1983.

———. *Historia de la Revolución Mexicana, 1914–1917: La encrucijada de 1915.* Mexico City: El Colegio de México, 1979.

———. *Historia de la Revolución Mexicana, 1914–1917: La revolución escindida.* Mexico City: El Colegio de México, 1979.

Walton, John. *Elites and Economic Development: Comparative Studies on the Political Economy of Latin American Cities.* Austin: University of Texas Press, 1977.

Warman, Arturo. *We Come to Object: The Peasants of Morelos and the National State.* Trans. Steven Ault. Baltimore: Johns Hopkins University Press, 1980.

Wasserman, Mark. *Capitalists, Caciques, and Revolution: The Native Elite and Foreign Enterprise in Chihuahua, Mexico, 1854–1911.* Chapel Hill: University of North Carolina Press, 1984.

Wolfskill, George, and Richmond, Douglas W., eds. *Essays on the Mexican Revolution: Revisionist Views of the Leaders.* Austin: University of Texas Press, 1979.

Womack, John, Jr. *Zapata and the Mexican Revolution.* New York: Knopf, 1968.

Articles and Chapters in Books

Aboites, Luis. "Agricultura de riego en el norte de México: Las peculiaridades de Chihuahua, 1920–1940." In *Actas del Primer Congreso de Historia Regional Comparada.* Ciudad Juárez: Universidad Autonoma de Ciudad Juárez, 1990.

———. "De Almeida a Quevedo: Lucha política en Chihuahua, 1927–1932." *Actas del Segundo Congreso de Historia Regional Comparada.* Ciudad Juárez: Universidad Autonoma de Ciudad Juárez, 1991. Pp. 435–49.

Aguilar Camín, Hector. "The Relevant Tradition: Sonoran Leaders in the Revolution." In Brading, ed., *Caudillo and Peasant in the Mexican Revolution.*

Alonso, Ana Maria. "U.S. Military Intervention, Revolutionary Mobilization, and Popular Ideology in Chihuahuan Sierra, 1916–1917." In Nugent, ed., *Rural Revolt in Mexico and U.S. Intervention.*

Ankerson, Dudley. "Saturnino Cedillo: A Traditional Caudillo in San Luis Potosí." In Brading, ed., *Caudillo and Peasant in the Mexican Revolution.*

Baily, David C. "Revisionism and the Recent Historiography of the Mexican Revolution." *Hispanic American Historical Review* 58 (February 1978): 62–78.

Beck, Thomas. "The French Revolution and the Nobility: A Reconsideration." *Journal of Social History* 15:2 (Winter 1981): 219–34.

Becker, Marjorie. "Black and White and Color: *Cardenismo* and the Search for a *Campesino* Ideology." *Comparative Studies in Society and History* 29:3 (July 1987): 453–65.

Beezley, William H. "Madero: The Unknown President and His Failure to Organize Rural Mexico." In Wolfskill and Richmond, eds., *Essays on the Mexican Revolution.*

———. "The Mexican Revolution: A Review." *Latin American Research Review* 13:2 (1978): 299–306.

———. "State Reform during the Provisional Presidency: Chihuahua, 1911." *Hispanic American Historical Review* 50 (August 1970): 524–38.

Benjamin, Thomas. "Laboratories of the New State, 1920–1929: Regional Social Reform and Experiments in Mass Politics." In Benjamin and Wasserman, eds., *Provinces of the Revolution.*

———. "The Leviathan on the Zócalo: Recent Historiography of the Postrevolutionary Mexican State." *Latin American Research Review* 20:3 (1985): 195–217.

———. "Revolución interrumpida—Chiapas y el interinato presidencial—1911." *Historia Mexicana* 30:1 (July–September 1980): 79–98.

———. "El trabajo en las monterias de Chiapas y Tabasco." *Historia Mexicana* 30:4 (April–June 1981): 506–29.

Bermejo, Guillermo, and Espejel L., Laura. "Conflicto por el poder y contradicciónes de clase: El caso de Michoacán, 1920–1926." *Boletín del Centro de Estudios de la Revolutión Mexicana "Lázaro Cárdenas"* (May 1982): 23–31.

Buve, Raymond Th. J. "Patronaje en las zonas rurales de México." *Boletín de Estudios Latinoamericanos* 13 (December 1974): 3–15.

———. "Peasant Movements, Caudillos, and Land Reform during the Revolution (1910–1917) in Tlaxcala, Mexico." *Boletín de Estudios Latinoamericanos* 18 (June 1976): 112–52.

———. "State Governors and Peasant Mobilization in Tlaxcala." In Brading, ed., *Caudillo and Peasant in the Mexican Revolution.*

———. "Tlaxcala: Consolidating a Cacicazgo." In Benjamin and Wasserman, eds., *Provinces of the Revolution.*

Camp, Roderic A. "La campana presidencial de 1929 y el liderazgo político en México." *Historia Mexicana* 27:2 (1977): 231–59.

———. "Family Relationships in Mexican Politics: A Preliminary View." *Journal of Politics* 44 (1982): 848–62.

———. "El sistema mexicano y las decisiones sobre el personal político." *Foro Internacional* 17:1 (1976): 51–83.

Falcón, Romana. "San Luis Potosí: Confiscated Estates—Revolutionary Conquest or Spoils?" In Benjamin and Wasserman, eds., *Provinces of the Revolution.*

Forster, Robert. "The Survival of the Nobility during the French Revolution." *Past and Present* 37 (1967): 71–86.

García, Alma M. "Recent Studies in Nineteenth- and Early Twentieth-Century Regional Mexican History." *Latin American Research Review* 22:2 (1987): 255–66.

Gibson, Ralph. "The French Nobility in the Nineteenth Century." In J. Howarth and P. G. Cerny, eds., *Elites in France.* New York: St. Martin's Press, 1982. Pp. 5–45.

Gilderhus, Mark T. "Many Mexicos: Tradition and Innovation in Recent Historiography." *Latin American Research Review* 22:1 (1987): 204–13.

González Herrera, "La política Chihuahuense de los años veinte: El gobierno de Ignacio C. Enríquez, 1920–1923." *Noesis* 2 (July 1990): 89–113.

González Navarro, Moises. "El maderismo y la revolución agraria." *Historia Mexicana* 37:1 (1987): 5–27.

Hall, Linda. "Alvaro Obregón and the Politics of Mexican Land Reform, 1920–1924," *Hispanic American Historical Review* 60:2 (May 1980): 213–38.

Hart, John M. "The Dynamics of the Mexican Revolution: Historiographical Perspectives." *Latin American Research Review* 19:3 (1984): 223–31.

Hayner, Norman S. "Differential Social Change in a Mexican Town," *Social Forces* 26:4 (May 1948): 381–90.

Hernández Chávez, Alicia. "Militares y negocios en la Revolución Mexicana." *Historia Mexicana* 34:2 (October–December 1984): 181–212.

Hershberger, Charles E. "The Death of Borunda, Alcalde of Ciudad Juárez: Chihuahuan Politics during the 1930s." *Arizona and the West* 8 (August 1966): 207–24.

Higgs, D. "Politics and Landownership among the French Nobility after the Revolution." *European Studies Review* 1:2 (April 1971): 102–22.

Jacobs, Ian. "Rancheros of Guerrero: The Figueroa Brothers and the Revolution." In Brading, ed., *Caudillo and Peasant in the Mexican Revolution.*

Joseph, Gilbert M. "Caciquismo and the Revolution: Carrillo Puerto in Yucatán." In Brading, ed., *Caudillo and Peasant in the Mexican Revolution.*

———. "The Fragile Revolution: Cacique Politics and the Revolutionary Process in Yucatán." *Latin American Research Review* 15:1 (1980): 41–64.

Juanico, Diana. "Partidos, facciones políticas, y elecciones: Tlaxcala en 1924." *Historia Mexicana* 37:1 (July–September 1987): 75–100.

Katz, Friedrich. "Agrarian Changes in Northern Mexico in the Period of Villista Rule, 1913–1915." In James W. Wilkie, Michael Meyer, and Edna Monzón de Wilkie, eds., *Contemporary Mexico: Papers of the Fourth International Congress of Mexican History.* Berkeley and Los Angeles: University of California Press, 1976.

———. "Mexico: Restored Republic and Porfiriato, 1867–1910." In Bethell, ed., *The Cambridge History of Latin America, 1870–1930.*

———. "Pancho Villa, Peasant Movements, and Agrarian Reform in Northern Mexico." In Brading, ed., *Caudillo and Peasant in the Mexican Revolution.*

———. "Pancho Villa: Reform Governor of Chihuahua." In Wolfskill and Richmond, eds., *Essays on the Mexican Revolution.*

———. "Peasants in the Mexican Revolution." In Joseph Spielburg and Scott Whiteford, eds., *Forging Nations: A Comparative View of Rural Ferment and Revolt.* East Lansing: Michigan State University Press, 1976.

Klapp, Orrin E., and Padgett, L. Vincent. "Power Structure and Decision-making in a Mexican Border City." *American Journal of Sociology* 65:4 (December 1960): 400–406.

Knight, Alan. "Interpreting the Revolution." *Texas Papers on Mexico.* Austin: Institute of Latin American Studies, n.d.

———. "Land and Society in Revolutionary Mexico: The Destruction of the Great Haciendas." *Mexican Studies/Estudios Mexicanos* 7:1 (Winter 1991): 73–104.

———. "The Mexican Revolution." *History Today* 30 (May 1980): 28–34.

———. "The Mexican Revolution: Bourgeois? Nationalist? Or Just a 'Great Rebellion'?" *Bulletin of Latin American Research* 4:2 (1985): 1–37.

———. "Peasant and Caudillo in Revolutionary Mexico, 1910–1917." In Brading, ed., *Caudillo and Peasant in the Mexican Revolution.*

———. "The Political Economy of Revolutionary Mexico, 1900–1940." In Christopher Abel and Colin M. Lewis, eds., *Latin America, Economic Imperialism and the State: The Political Economy of the External Connection from Independence to the Present.* London: Athlone Press, 1985. Pp. 288–317.

Lerner, Victoria. "Los fundamentos socioeconomicos del cacicazgo en el

México postrevolucionario—el caso de Saturnino Cedillo." *Historia Mexicana* 29:3 (January–March 1980): 375–446.

———. "La suerte de las haciendas: Decadencia y cambio de proprietarios (1910–1920)." *Historia Mexicana* 36:4 (April–June 1987): 661–98.

———. "Las zozobras de los hacendados de algunos municipios del oriente de San Luis Potosí (1910–1920)." *Historia Mexicana* 36:2 (October–December 1986): 323–62.

Machado, Manuel A., Jr. "Aftosa and the Mexican-American Sanitary Commission of 1928." *Agricultural History* 39 (October 1965): 240–45.

———. "An Industry in Limbo: The Mexican Cattle Industry, 1920–1934." *Agricultural History* 50:4 (October 1976): 615–25.

———. "The Mexican Revolution and the Destruction of the North Mexican Cattle Industry." *Southwestern Historical Quarterly* (July 1975): 1–20.

Meyer, Jean. "Mexico: Revolution and Reconstruction in the 1920s." In Bethell, ed., *The Cambridge History of Latin America, 1870–1930.*

Meyer, Michael C. "Perspectives on Mexican Revolutionary Historiography." *New Mexico Historical Review* 44:4 (1969): 167–80.

Nugent, Daniel. "Paradojas en el desarrollo de la 'cuestión agraria' en Chihuahua, 1885–1935." In *Actas del primer Congreso de Historia Regional Comparada.* Ciudad Juárez: Universidad Autonoma de Ciudad Juárez, 1989.

Palacios, Guillermo. "México en los años treinta." In *America en los años treinta.* Mexico City: UNAM, 1977.

Purcell, John F. H., and Purcell, Susan Kaufman. "Mexican Business and Public Policy." In James Malloy, ed., *Authoritarianism and Corporatism in Latin America.* Pittsburgh, Pa.: University of Pittsburgh Press, 1977.

Rabinowitz, Francine F. "Sound and Fury Signifying Nothing? A Review of Community Power Research in Latin America." *Urban Affairs Quarterly* 3 (March 1968): 111–22.

Richmond, Douglas W. "Factional Political Strife in Coahuila, 1910–1920." *Hispanic American Historical Review* 60 (February 1980): 49–68.

Rivera Castro, José. "Política agraria, organizaciones, luchas y resistencias campesinas entre 1920 y 1928." In Enrique Montalvo, ed., *Historia de la cuestión agraria mexicana: Modernizacion, lucha agraria y poder político, 1920–1934.* Vol. 4. Mexico City: Siglo XXI, 1988.

Salamini, Heather Fowler. "Revolutionary Caudillos in the 1920s: Francisco Múgica and Adalberto Tejeda." In Brading, ed., *Caudillo and Peasant in the Mexican Revolution.*

———. "Tamaulipas: Land Reform and the State." In Benjamin and Wasserman, eds., *Provinces of the Revolution.*

Scott, James C. "The Analysis of Corruption in Developing Nations." *Comparative Studies in Society and History* 11 (June 1969): 315–41.

Smith, Michael S. "Thoughts on the Evolution of the French Capitalist Community in the XIXth Century." *The Journal of European Economic History* 7:1 (Spring 1978): 139–44.

Stevens, Evelyn P. "Mexico's PRI: The Institutionalization of Corporatism?" In Malloy, ed., *Authoritarianism and Corporatism in Latin America*, 227–58.

Tardanico, Richard. "Revolutionary Nationalism and State Building in Mexico, 1917–1924." *Politics and Society* 10:1 (1980): 59–86.

———. "State, Dependency, and Nationalism: Revolutionary Mexico, 1924–1928." *Comparative Studies in Society and History* 24:3 (July 1982): 400–423.

Tobler, Hans Werner. "La burguesía revolucionaria en México: Su origen y su papel, 1915–1935." *Historia Mexicana* 34 (October–December 1984): 213–37.

———. "Las paradojas del ejército revolucionario: Su papel social en la reforma agraria mexicana." *Historia Mexicana* 21:1 (July–September 1971): 38–79.

———. "Peasants and the Shaping of the Revolutionary State, 1910–1940." In Katz, ed., *Riot, Rebellion, and Revolution: Rural Social Conflict in Mexico*.

Torres-Trueba, Henry E. "Factionalism in a Mexican Municipio." *Sociologus* 19 (1962): 134–52.

Tuohy, William S. "Centralism and Political Elite Behavior in Mexico." In Clarence E. Thurber and Lawrence S. Graham, eds., *Development Administration in Latin America*. Durham, N.C.: Duke University Press, 1973.

Vanderwood, Paul J. "Building Blocks But Yet No Building: Regional History and the Mexican Revolution." *Mexican Studies/Estudios Mexicanos* 5:2 (Summer 1987): 421–32.

Vigil, Ralph H. "Revolution and Confusion: The Peculiar Case of José Inés Salazar." *New Mexico Historical Review* 53:2 (1978): 145–70.

Voss, Stuart F. "Nationalizing the Revolution: Culmination and Circumstance." In Benjamin and Wasserman, eds., *Provinces of the Revolution*.

Wasserman, Mark. "Strategies for Survival of the Porfirian Elite in Revolutionary Mexico: Chihuahua during the 1920s." *Hispanic American Historical Review* 67:1 (February 1987): 87–108.

Weston, Charles H., Jr. "The Political Legacy of Lázaro Cárdenas." *The Americas* 39:3 (January 1983): 383–405.

Womack, John, Jr. "The Mexican Economy during the Revolution, 1910–

1920: Historiography and Analysis." *Marxist Perspectives* (Winter 1978): 80–123.

———. "The Mexican Revolution." In Bethell, ed., *The Cambridge History of Latin America, 1870–1930.*

Yaney, George L. "Agricultural Administration in Russia from the Stolypin Land Reform to Forced Collectivization: An Interpretive Study." In James R. Millar, ed., *The Soviet Rural Community.* Urbana: University of Illinois Press, 1971.

Zeldin, Theodore. "France." In Spring, ed., *European Landed Elites in the Nineteenth Century.*

Unpublished Materials

Brown, James C. "Consolidation of the Mexican Revolution under Calles, 1924–1928: Politics, Modernization, and the Roots of the Revolutionary National Party." Ph.D. diss., University of New Mexico, 1979.

Brush, David A. "The de la Huerta Rebellion in Mexico, 1923–1924." Ph.D. diss., Syracuse University, 1975.

Buford, Nick. "A Biography of Luis Morones: Mexican Labor and Political Leader." Ph.D. diss., Louisiana State University, 1971.

Camp, Roderic A. "Comparing Political Generations in Mexico, the Last One Hundred Years." Paper presented at the Conference of Mexican and North American Historians, San Diego, Calif., October 1990.

Chávez M., Armando B. "Hombres de la revolución en Chihuahua." Unpublished MS. Chihuahua, n.d.

Langston, Edward L. "The Impact of Prohibition on the Mexican–United States Border: The El Paso–Ciudad Juárez Case." Ph.D. diss., Texas Tech University, 1974.

Manahan, R. F. "Historical Sketch of the Mining Operations of the American Smelting and Refining Company in Mexico." Unpublished MS. 1948.

Oñate Villarreal, Abdiel. "Banca y agricultura en México: La Caja de Préstamos para Obras de Irrigación y Fomento de la Agricultura, 1908–1926." Ph.D. diss., El Colegio de México, 1984.

Proffitt, Thurber D. "The Symbiotic Frontier: The Emergence of Tijuana since 1769." Ph.D. diss., UCLA, 1988.

Salamini, Heather Fowler. "Caciquismo and the Mexican Revolution: The Case of Manuel Palaez." Paper presented at the Sixth Conference of Mexican and United States Historians, Chicago, September 1980.

Index

Public works. *See also* Patronage
Puebla (state), 163–64

Quevedo, Guillermo, 61
Quevedo, Jesús, 58, 101, 136
Quevedo, José, 61, 101
Quevedo, Lorenzo, 101
Quevedo, Rodrigo, 34, 40, 46, 52,
 54, 61, 66, 96, 100–101, 120,
 140, 163; governorship, 56–60;
 opposition to, 59–60
Quevedo family, 13, 43, 63, 67, 98,
 100–103, 117, 118, 130, 140, 141,
 207 n. 48; criminal activity, 101–
 102; gambling, 133; use of public
 position, 101
Quiroz Reyes, Dr. Daniel, 136

Rabago, Antonio, 15
Rabasa, Isidro, 152
Ramirez family, 124. *See* Coyame
Rascon family, 23, 47, 122–23
Raynal family, 114
Regionalism, 6
Revolutionary change, 1–2
Revolutionary leaders, casualty
 rate, 25
Rodríguez, Abelardo, 6, 71, 143
Rodríguez, Francisco G., 134
Rodríguez, Nicolás, 197 n. 11
Rodríguez Triana, Pedro, 149
Rosales, 125
Rosales, Juan B., 97
Russek, David, 114–115
Russek, Marcos, 89
Russek family, 43

Saenz, Aaron, 108, 158–59
Salido, Eduardo, 125
Samaniego, Dr. Mariano, 138
Samaniego family, 47, 90, 138
San Andrés, 86, 108, 126
San Carlos, 86
San Luis Potosí, 149, 155
San Pedro, Coahuila, 165

Sánchez, Guadalupe, 70, 72, 154,
 155
Serrano movement, 146
Sisniega, Carlos, 79, 80, 112
Sisniega, Federico, Jr., 38–39, 78,
 79
Sonora, 156, 159
Staple crops, 175; prices, 176
State, revolutionary, 152–53
Strikes, 39, 210 n. 76

Talamantes, Gustavo L., 66, 95, 96,
 105, 107, 120, 129, 140, 168, 209
 n. 74, 211 n. 85; governorship,
 61–66; split with Quevedos, 129,
 136, 137
Talamantes, Narciso, 64, 65
Talavera, Reinaldo, 36–37, 96, 103,
 129
Tamaulipas, 155, 156, 157–58,
 166
Taxes, land, 42
Tejeda, Adalberto, 39, 45, 154,
 155, 167
Temósachic, 126
Terrazas, Luis, 22, 25–26, 28, 76,
 77, 83, 137, 172, 193 n. 70
Terrazas, Silvestre, 15
Terrazas de Sisniega, Amanda, 77
Terrazas-Creel family, 9–10, 14, 38,
 73, 74–83, 88, 94, 111, 144, 146,
 147; banks, 27–28, 80, 150, 151,
 173; expropriation of property by
 Villa, 21–22, 27; industrial interests, 80–81; landholdings, 75–78;
 social activities, 82; strategies,
 25–29; taxes, 81; women, 82. *See
 also* Banco Minero de Chihuahua;
 Pascual Orozco, Jr.
Terrazas estate, 38, 43, 53, 86, 99,
 102, 104, 112, 117, 141, 150;
 sale to McQuatters, 35, 45, 76–
 77, 79
Torreón, 165
Treviño, Francisco L., 17

About the Author

Mark Wasserman is Associate Professor of
History at Rutgers University. He is the author
of *Capitalists, Caciques, and Revolution: The Native Elite
and Foreign Enterprise in Chihuahua, Mexico, 1854–1911;*
with B. Keen, *A History of Latin America;* and, with
T. Benjamin, *Provinces of the Revolution: Essays
on Regional Mexican History.*

Library of Congress Cataloging-in-Publication Data

Wasserman, Mark, 1946–
Persistent oligarchs : elites and politics in Chihuahua, Mexico,
1910–1940 / Mark Wasserman.
p.   cm.
Includes bibliographical references (p.   ) and index.
ISBN 0–8223–1329–4 (cl : acid-free paper) ISBN 0–8223–1345–6 (pa)
1. Elite (Social sciences)—Mexico—Chihuahua (State)—
History—20th century. 2. Chihuahua (Mexico : State)—Politics and
government. 3. Mexico—Politics and government—1910–1946.
I. Title.
HN120.C46W39   1993
305.5'2'097216—dc20